"This book is a great investment. In fact, it is **the** handbook for selling in the twenty-first century! Chock-full of stuff you need now and in the future: The list of ten ways to make your presentation irresistible is pure gold; the "send it back" strategy is one of the most clever sales moves around; and the section on communication styles is the funniest thing I've ever read on human psychology in the sales arena. Of course, in true guerrilla styles, it's right on target."

—**David Garfinkel**
Author, *How To Write Letters That Make Your Phone Ring*

"I hang up on telemarketers, but I'd wind up talking to anyone using these techniques. The most comprehensive book on sales skills I've ever read. The techniques aren't restricted to telemarketing, but they are applicable for anyone in sales."

—**Alan Weiss, Ph.D.**
President, Summit Consulting Group
Author, *Million Dollar Consulting*

"Another great guerrilla book filled with powerful and practical suggestions for getting the sale. I highly recommend it."

—**Jack Canfield**
ken Soup for the Soul at Work

"The case ᴅᴏ974068 ated ideas work. I find that these ideas American and the European business community. It clearly supplies hands-on tools for us who need to get the job done on a daily basis. The techniques described in Chapter 20 recently landed us a $183,000 account. We most likely wouldn't have seen the signature on the contract if we had used the classic sales approach."

—**Martien Eerhart**
President, Global Gateway LLC

"When most of us learned to use the telephone, it was before the days of voice mail, Internet communications, and wireless technology. The skills we learned back then are inadequate for today's marketplace. *Guerrilla TeleSelling* brings you up to date by showing you how to think and act by the hyperconnect business world in which we currently live. Things are changing rapidly and unless you constantly change using guerrilla thinking, you'll be left behind."

—**Jim Cathcart, CSP**
Author, *Relationship Selling* and *The Acorn Principle*

the reader gets a list of '27 Ways to Get Dialing.' For *anyone* who has ever attempted TeleSelling, they know how difficult it can be to make those calls. This list, and the many others that the book contains, will be invaluable in overcoming the reluctance and fear that keep so many salespeople from being successful."

—James A. DeSena, CSP
Publisher, *Sales Leaders Briefing*™

"We all know the world of selling has changed to the point that many of us will throw up our hands. If you and I decide to stay the course, we'll need bright, accurate, and exciting inputs to keep us current and keep us moving and competing successfully. Here it is: *Guerrilla Tele-Selling* . . . by researchers who have dug deep and produced a 'must-read, must-study' guide!"

—Nick Carter
Vice President, Communications Research,
Nightengale-Conant Corporation

"The guerrillas have done it again! Another great book full of sage advice that would take 50 years to acquire on your own. Read it and reap—the benefits of TeleSelling success."

—Mark Sanborn, CSP, CPAE
Author, *Teambuilt: Making Teamwork*

"Fantastic! If you don't get at least ten great, money-making ideas from reading *Guerrilla TeleSelling* that will help you sell your way into the twenty-first century, then read it again."

—Art Fettig, CSP
Author, *The Platinum Rule* and *Selling Lucky*

"TeleSelling can be an effective way to close new business. In today's business climate, you need to know how. *Guerrilla TeleSelling* is the fastest, most effective way to learn the weapons and tactics you need to succeed."

—Patricia Fripp, CPAE
Past President National Speakers Association
Author, *Get What You Want*

"Practical, common sense, but sometimes little used ideas. In the future, our TelePresence will be more important than ever. This book is packed with usable ideas. Once through the book, I had dozens of ideas—no telling how many more I'll get with future study."

—Dennis E. Mannering, CSP
Professional Speaker, Sales Trainer

"Open this book to any page and go to work. If you use 10 percent of it 10 percent of the time, you'll achieve results never imagined. What if you use even more?"

—W. Mitchell, CPS, CSP, CPAE
Author, *It's Not What Happens to You, It's What You Do About It* and
PBS TV Host *Finding Common Ground*

"TeleSelling requires its own set of communication rules, tactics, and timetables. Now I know how those super-salespeople always find a way to get through to me! This book provides *A* to *Z* guidelines to keep the whole process on target. No time to train new sales staff? Then provide this book to your team, and let them train themselves in a matter of hours."

—Dianna Booher
Author of *Communicate with Confidence*
and *Get Ahead, Stay Ahead*

"I can't think of a more relevant book for selling in the accelerated world of the twenty-first century. The telephone was, is, and always will be the most valuable tool in selling."

—David A. Rich, CSP
Author, *The Question to Everyone's Answer:
How to Stay Motivated on a Daily Basis!*

"I would be hard-pressed to find a telemarketing book that is as chock-full of useful ideas and strategies as this one. It covers everything from in which ear to wear your single earpiece set to the big picture and just about everything in between. Which is just what I would expect from the latest selection in the best-selling *Guerrilla Marketing* series. Because, as we know, we guerrillas leave no stone unturned!"

—Donald Purdy
President, Purdy & Associates, Program Director,
American Marketing Association

"Finally, a book that makes it clear that *TeleSelling* is not only an essential part of a successful, small-business program, yet it can be done calmly, professionally, and deliver the results of other parts of your marketing campaign. Levinson, Wilson, and Smith have combined clear thinking, practical advice, and clever ideas into a highly readable and useful book. I'm putting their ideas to work immediately."

—Patrick M. D'Acre
CyberEntrepreneur, Developer of "Conversations with an Expert"
On-Line Interview Program

Guerrilla TeleSelling

NEW UNCONVENTIONAL WEAPONS AND TACTICS
TO SELL WHEN YOU CAN'T
BE THERE IN PERSON

JAY CONRAD LEVINSON

MARK S. A. SMITH

ORVEL RAY WILSON, CSP

John Wiley & Sons, Inc.

New York ➤ Chichester ➤ Weinheim ➤ Brisbane ➤ Singapore ➤ Toronto

Copyright © 1998 by Jay Conrad Levinson, Mark S. A. Smith, and Orvel Ray Wilson, CSP. All rights reserved.
Published by John Wiley & Sons, Inc.
Published simultaneously in Canada.

This publication is designed to provide accurate and authoritative information in regard to the subject matter covered. It is sold with the understanding that the publisher is not engaged in rendering professional services. If professional advice or other expert assistance is required, the services of a competent professional person should be sought.

Library of Congress Cataloging-in-Publication Data:

Levinson, Jay Conrad.
    Guerrilla teleselling : new unconventional weapons and tactics to sell when you can't be there in person / Jay Conrad Levinson, Mark S. A. Smith, Orvel Ray Wilson.
        p.   cm.
    Includes index.
    ISBN 0-471-24279-9 (pbk. : alk. paper)
    1. Telephone selling.   I. Smith, Mark S. A.   II. Wilson, Orvel Ray.   III. Title.
    HF5438.3.L48   1998
    658.85—dc21   98-21027
                                                                         CIP

Printed in the United States of America.
10 9 8 7 6 5 4 3 2 1

Dedicated to the late Og Mandino,
who changed forever the way the world sells.

Preface

There is no one right way to approach your customers. What works for one person may not work for another, and practices that are considered acceptable in real estate may be inappropriate for selling industrial chemicals. What works for you works for you.

In our seminars all around the world, we've talked to tens of thousands of salespeople, working in thousands of different companies, representing hundreds of industries. We've collected their favorite tactics, ideas, and war stories, and we've compiled them here for you. But, you must choose what will work for you.

Guerrillas will deploy as many of these weapons and tactics as possible. Our job is to make you *think* about how you sell and help you discover ways to *improve*. You may disagree with our advice, but either way, we've made you think. If you think your way is better, you're probably right.

■ BEWARE OF THE OUTRAGEOUS

You may judge some of our suggestions as outrageous, inappropriate, or even offensive. We will offer you this agreement: we will accept the risk of being controversial if you'll accept the responsibility for selecting what's appropriate for your personality, your industry, and your customers.

■ KNOW SELLING FIRST

This book isn't designed to teach you how to sell. There are many great books and courses on sales.[1] This book is designed to take your sales knowledge and tune it for TeleSelling, making your presence felt when you can't be there in person.

---

[1] This includes the predecessor of this book: *Guerrilla Selling: Unconventional Weapons and Tactics to Close More Sales,* by Jay Conrad Levinson, Bill Gallagher, and Orvel Ray Wilson. New York: Houghton Mifflin, 1992.

Acknowledgments

For all of the editors of publications, magazines, newsletters, and trade journals who ask us to write articles; the fodder for every book we write.

A special thanks to Mike Hamilton, our editor at John Wiley & Sons. He keeps going to bat for us and keeps hitting home runs.

To Mike Larsen and Elizabeth Pomada, our literary agents, who are so fond of saying, "There's a book in that!"

To our colleagues in the National Speakers Association, who keep cheering us on and on and on.

To our wives and families, who put up with us being gone on tour for months at a stretch while we travel the globe collecting all these ideas.

Contents

Introduction   1

The Real Enemies Are Time and Distance   2
The Future Is TeleSelling   2
Creating a TelePresence   3
Who Will Get the Most from *Guerrilla TeleSelling?*   4

PART I: GETTING READY FOR BUSINESS

Chapter 1:   Why TeleSelling?   9

The Consumer Backlash   9
Know the Law   10
You Must Become a Guerrilla   12

**Chapter 2:   What Makes Guerrilla TeleSelling
              Unique?**   14

What's a Guerrilla?   14
Setting Yourself Up to Win   15
TeleSelling Is a Unique Environment   17
Five Reasons Why the Skills That Usually Make
   Salespeople Great Will Kill Them over the Phone   18
The 17 Things That Drive Buyers Nuts and How
   to Avoid Them   19

Chapter 3:   Setting Goals and Objectives   24

11 Telephone Sales Strategies   24
TeleSelling   25
What Are You Willing to Spend?   25
How Many People Should Staff Your Call Center?   26
11 Ways to Get Your Customers to Buy More
  from You   27

Chapter 4:   How to Stay Motivated   32

The Most Common Cause of Failure   32
The Biggest Weakness of Salespeople   32
What Holds People Back from Success   33
27 Ways to Get Dialing   35
Guerrilla Incentives   39

Chapter 5:   Preparing Your TeleSelling Workspace 45

Elements of the TeleSelling Workspace   45
Biological Factors   47
Build a Training Resource Center   48

Chapter 6:   Controlling Interruptions   51

Standing Morning Meetings   51
Sacred Hour   51
Close the Door   52
Face the Wall   52
Clinic Time   52
By Appointment Only   52
Interruption Log   52
Blurting   52
Bio Breaks   53

Chapter 7: Managing Pressure and Stress — 54

Music — 54
Moisture — 54
Movement — 54
Massage — 55
Meditation — 55
Menu — 55
Mirth — 55

Chapter 8: Your TeleSelling Voice — 56

How to Talk All Day and Still Sound Great — 56
Keep Your Voice Healthy — 60
How to Warm Up Your Voice — 61
Warm Up Your Body — 62
Be Understood — 63

Chapter 9: Greeting Inbound Calls — 65

Company and Name — 65
Never the Same Way Twice — 66
Tone and Attitude — 66
Handling Handoffs — 67
Ask Permission — 67
International Callers — 67

Chapter 10: Increase Your Caller's Satisfaction — 69

Evaluating Your Salespeople — 72
Putting the Customer in Control — 76
Are You Being Politically Correct? — 77
The Communication Gap between Men and
  Women — 79

Chapter 11: Developing an Effective Script   80

Developing Scripted Presentations   80
Keep Testing   82
The Right Words Work   82
Rules of Power Talking   83
The Ten Magic Words   86
Avoid Superlatives   88
Use Evocative Language   89
Keep Customers Motivated   89
Your Call Guide   89

Chapter 12: Lead Management Systems   91

Computer-Based Systems   91
Are Computers Worth the Money?   91
Dual Systems   92
Daily Planner   93
Index Cards   93
Binders   94

Chapter 13: Whom to Call?   95

Who's Involved in the Decision   95
How to Find Lists of New Prospects   98
Using a Database to Sell   99
Qualify and Test Lists   100
Precall Letters   100

PART II: GUERRILLA TACTICS THAT GET THE BUSINESS

Chapter 14: Opening Moves   103

Precall Sales Meeting   103
Daily Debriefs   103
How to Organize Your Telephoning for
  Appointments   103

Make 1,000 Extra Calls a Year 104
Call a Customer First 105
The Golden Selling Hour 105
Call Early 105
Call Late 105
The Best Time to Reach Your Prospects 106
Snappy Answers to Stupid Questions 107
How to Get Unlisted Addresses 108
Guerrilla Cold Calls 108
Your First Contact 110
I'm Buying! 112
Dealing with Gatekeepers 113
Finding the Decision Maker 115
Follow-up Calls 116
Maintaining Rapport 118
Controlling Attention 118
Becoming a Better Listener 119
Take Notes 120
How to Handle Sensitive Subjects 121

Chapter 15: Getting through Voice Mail   123
Creating Effective Voice Mail Messages 123
Using Voice Mail to Sell 128
Getting Your Call Returned 130

Chapter 16: Questioning and Qualifying   136
Find a Real Need 136
Prospecting, Guerrilla Style 138
Getting Them to Keep the Appointment 140

Chapter 17: The 37 Magic Selling Questions   142
Questioning Skills 142

Chapter 18: Presenting Your Proposal — 147

Expedite Everything — 147
How Guerrillas Influence Prospects and Customers — 147
Communications Styles — 149
Need for Information and Detail — 149
Organization of Tasks — 152
Locus of Motivation — 155
Level of Initiative — 158
Constellations of Styles — 160
Make the Intangible Tangible — 160
Make the Tangible Intangible — 160
Ten Ways to Make Your Presentation Irresistible — 161
Doing Verbal Demos — 162
Making It Stick — 163
How to Help Your Customer Remember — 163
What Question Came Up? — 164
Follow Up to Close — 164

Chapter 19: Ask for the Order — 165

Ask for a Commitment — 165
Wrap Up the Sale — 165
Closing on the Phone — 166
Get Your Fulfillment Package Out Immediately — 167
Call to Confirm Receipt — 167
Send It Back — 168
Ask for Referrals — 168
The 5-4-3-2-1 Referral System — 168
Thank-You Notes — 169

Chapter 20: Dealing with Objections — 171

Where Objections Come From — 171
When to Handle Objections — 172
No Can Be Cultural — 173
The About-Face — 174
Getting Unstuck on Price Issues — 174

Price Shopping   176
Managing Objections   177
Sales Savers   181

Chapter 21: Serve to Sell Again   183

Your Guarantee   183
Encourage Complaints   184
Lifetime Value of a Customer   185
Twelve Ways to Deal with Angry Callers   186

PART III: MANAGING A TELESELLING DEPARTMENT

Chapter 22: Finding the Right People   191

Recruiting and Hiring Sales Guerrillas   191
Training   193
Monitoring Quality   194
Intervene Often   194
Compensation Strategies   195
Invest in Your Stars   197

Chapter 23: Measuring Your Success   199

Why Measure?   199
Postperformance Checklist   199
Measure the TeleSelling Results   200
Postcampaign Survey   200
Conduct a Mail Survey   200
Customer Surveys   202

SECTION IV: CREATING YOUR TELEPRESENCE

Chapter 24: Creating a Guerrilla Marketing
Calendar   205

Your TeleSelling Calendar   205

Chapter 25: Staying in Front of the Customer   211

Fork Over New Customers   211
Using Advertising Specialties   211
Candy Jar   213
What Time Is It?   214
Buy Them a Snack   214
Postcards While on Vacation   214
Notepads   214
Send a Series   215
Bill Stuffers   215

Chapter 26: Make Your Sales Letters Sizzle   216

Your Sales Letter   218
Special Reports   219

Chapter 27: Just the Fax   220

What to Fax   220
Unsolicited Fax (Don't Do It)   221
Broadcast Fax   222

Chapter 28: Creating Effective Newsletters   223

Develop Your Own Style   223
Printing   225
How Should You Mail?   225
Who to Mail to?   226
How Often?   226

Chapter 29: Become an Author and an Authority   227

Write for Trade Magazines   227
Write a Booklet   229

Chapter 30: Electronic Brochures   **231**

Audio Brochures   231
Videotapes   236

Chapter 31: Marketing Yourself On-Line   **238**

Netiquette   239
Three Steps to Generating Business on the Internet   241

Chapter 32: Videoconferencing and Other Modern Miracles   **246**

Satellite Paging   250
Cellular, PDC, and Emerging Technologies   250
Save on Cell Phone Charges   251
Toll-Free Numbers   251
Toll-Free versus 900 Numbers   253

Appendix   **255**
Web Addresses   255

Bibliography   **259**
Books   259
Audiotapes   264
Video Training Materials   265
Magazines and Journals   265

Index   **267**

Introduction

A guerrilla who works for a software company in San Jose, California, sells an integrated accounting platform for medium-sized manufacturing companies. It's not cheap. Sticker price is about a quarter of a million dollars. But it does everything: accounts payable, accounts receivable, payroll, inventory, job cost, forecasting, the works.

His target account was a rapidly growing company in San Jose, where he secured an appointment to show the product to their accounting department. Well, the accountants loved it! They said, "This is going to save us *so* much time; it'll pay for itself in six months, but we can't make the decision. You have to sell it to Information Services, because they maintain the platform."

So he goes over to the IS department, and shows them the product, and they fall in love with it. "This is going to save so much time, and it will run our existing hardware, but it's not in the budget."

Now, this is where most salespeople would give up, but not this guy. He calls directly on the company president, and runs smack into the president's secretary, who had the personality of your average rottweiler. Very protective!

He phones, he faxes, he sends Federal Express; nothing is getting through. Finally, in desperation, he sends the CEO a box—about the size of a shoebox—by courier, so he has to sign for it.

The CEO puts the box on his desk, opens it up, and inside is a live pigeon and a note; "After exhausting every other means of communication available to me I've resorted to this. I have a software product that will save your company a lot of money. I'd like to buy you lunch. Put the name of your favorite restaurant on the pigeon's leg before you release it. I'll be there."

Well, what is he going to do? He's got this pigeon pecking at his paperwork. So he picks up a post-it, puts it on the pigeon's leg, and he pitches it out the window.

The next day, curiosity gets the best of him. He can't resist the temptation to go to the restaurant just to see if this guy is for real. Sure enough, there's a reservation in his name, and he's escorted to a table in the back where our guerrilla is lying in wait. They have a laugh about the carrier pigeon; the guerrilla walks out of the restaurant 40 minutes later with a signed letter of intent authorizing the purchase of the new software.

■ THE REAL ENEMIES ARE TIME AND DISTANCE

Woody Allen said, "Eighty percent of success is showing up." Yet, competing in the global markets of the twenty-first century requires salespeople to project themselves to a constituency of customers, prospects, influencers, decision makers, and end users scattered across six continents.

The cost of an industrial sales call has skyrocketed, more than doubling in the last decade. Out of an average 53-hour workweek, the typical salesperson spends less than eight hours a week actually interacting with customers. They spend 37 percent of their time traveling. The odds of reaching your customer on the phone on the first attempt are only one in five. How do you get your message across when you can't even get your call through? You must exercise the ingenuity and boldness of a veteran commercial mercenary. You must become a guerrilla.

■ THE FUTURE IS TELESELLING

The future is TeleSelling, and salespeople of every stripe will have to learn to create a *TelePresence*. Telephone sales is one of the fastest growing segments of the sales profession, but there's a lot more to it today than traditional telemarketing.

The modern sales guerrilla will also have to deploy the phone, fax, voice mail, E-mail, audio and videotape, Web sites, paging, cell phones, and personal communications system (PCS) to maintain constant contact with customers and give them the information they need to make informed purchase decisions at the speed of light. Your TelePresence includes everything that touches your customer remotely, from your business card to your E-mail address. And today's business climate changes too fast for customers to wait for a salesperson's visit.

Recently, while standing in line at the baggage-check line in SFO, Orvel met Bill Yeack, vice president of marketing for Synon, a software company that produces applications development engines for AS-400 and PC network platforms. They struck up a conversation and by the time they had checked their bags, Orvel had checked his calendar, and they had a date hold to provide four days of guerrilla sales training for their offices in Marin County, California, and in London. On the way to the plane, Orvel used his cell phone to call the lead into the office. Our staff Fed-Exed a packet of tapes and literature to Bill, then called his office the next day to verify that he had received the material.

Orvel found out later that Bill was also considering two other sales-training firms. When asked, "What won us the contract?" Bill explained that he had visited our Web site, and while he thought it was "content rich, but graphically challenged," he also checked the hot links to several of our client references. Everything *together*, telephone, FedEx, and Web, gave us the credibility he was looking for. It established us as a player in the industry. Our combined *TelePresence*, rather than just a barrage of personal follow-up calls, gave us the winning edge.

■ CREATING A TELEPRESENCE

The secret to getting the sale when you can't be there in person is creating an effective TelePresence. It begins with the concept for your product or service and extends to everything that your customer sees, hears, or feels that represents you or your firm. It's how and what your customers think of you, whenever and wherever they think of you.

Your TelePresence is a combination of all of the marketing weapons in your arsenal. It should be consistent with your image and your identity. When deployed effectively, your Tele-Presence creates an atmosphere of rapport and trust. When ineffectively deployed, it can tarnish your reputation, damage your credibility, and even destroy your business.

This book goes far beyond the boundaries of traditional telephone sales. Sure, we will show you how to make outbound calls that get through to the decision maker. We'll show you how to leave compelling voice mail messages that get your call returned every time. We'll show you how to create fabulous faxes and exciting electronic presentations that will win customers. We'll share secret tips for saving money on your cell phone, and new ways to make your pager a vital link to your customers. We'll also explore how modern technologies—including computers, satellites, fiber optics, microwaves, color printers, laser copiers, and on-line communications—can combine to effectively project yourself far beyond the boundaries of your current territory.

Although the telephone has traditionally been the salesperson's ally, it has lately become our nemesis. With voice mail, E-mail, and snail mail standing between us and our customers, the modern sales guerrilla must mobilize *unconventional weapons and tactics.* This book was written for the everyday salesperson taking care of customers every day. It's for you if you're being forced to manage more accounts in a bigger territory in less time than ever before. It is not designed for the call center, yet professional telemarketers can benefit greatly from its advice.

■ WHO WILL GET THE MOST FROM *GUERRILLA TELESELLING?*

This book takes a solid here's-what-you-do-to-be-successful approach, with lots of real-life examples. These concepts get results. This information will help you make more money by serving more customers, in more places, in more ways than you ever dreamed possible. The effect on your productivity—and your net income—will be exponential.

Guerrilla TeleSelling is written for salespeople, sales managers, marketing managers, and entrepreneurs who need to establish, manage, or expand new or existing telephone sales operations. For these people, this book answers critical questions.

➤ Sales Professional

This material is for sales professionals at all levels who dread making cold calls. It's also for the sales professional who wants to be more effective on the phone. The tactics have been tested in hundreds of training seminars conducted by the authors for client companies all over the world and have been proven effective in thousands of sales situations.

➤ How to simultaneously conduct a presentation with a prospect in one city, an engineering team in another, and a financier in a third, all at the same time, without leaving home

➤ How to use TeleSelling to confirm appointments and get ushered in past the security desk, straight to the buyer

➤ How to most effectively use the telephone to help manage time, territory, and client relationships

➤ How to use voice mail as a sales tool, instead of a sales barrier

➤ How to get the prospect to review your literature and grant you an appointment on the spot

➤ How to save money on prime-time cellular service

➤ Sales Manager

Guerrilla TeleSelling is for the sales manager who's been with the company for a while, whose boss says, "We want you to set up a telemarketing department. Round up half a dozen or so people and do what you can. We've given you a budget of $10,000."

➤ How to avoid costly fines and judgments by understanding what the law allows.

➤ How to attract, screen, interview, and train effective telesales personnel.

➤ How to develop effective scripts.

➤ How to prepare your sales force to use TeleSelling effectively.

➤ Where do you go for information on TeleSelling?

➤ Marketing Manager

➤ Telemarketing is a significant portion of this year's marketing allowance. How will you guarantee the program's success?

➤ How can you make sure this major investment will move the company forward—and increase the value of your stock options?

➤ **Entrepreneur**

➤ What kind of equipment will you need, from computers and software to desks and headsets?

➤ How can a small company compete with larger companies?

➤ How can you use technology to bolster your TeleSelling efforts, including E-mail, voice mail, and fax on demand?

Part

I

Getting Ready for Business

Why TeleSelling?

TeleSelling is hot!

Every week, over 100 million sales calls are made by phone. Every year, these calls generate $370 billion in sales. Effective use of the telephone is critical to millions of people's livelihoods. Today, over 40 million Americans work formally or informally at home. These modern telecommuters rely heavily on the telephone for contact with clients, customers, and coworkers.

As much as one-third of the members of chambers of commerce are home-based businesses. Major corporations are moving large numbers of staff to working out of their home. Notable trendsetters are Xerox (with 5,000 home-based workers) and IBM (where most of their sales staff are home based.) In informal polls we've conducted of sales professionals nationwide, 40 percent office out of their home. Over 80 percent of the workers in America are employed by companies with fewer than 50 employees. These firms depend on the telephone to conduct business efficiently.

■ THE CONSUMER BACKLASH

The owner of a major-league ball club is suspended for offhand racist remarks. A candidate for attorney general has her career cut short by an obsolete tax law. GM is fined $105 million for a faulty design, then sues NBC for staging a fire for a news story. The new liberal administration is clearly turning toward conservative values of home, hearth, and family, calling for mandatory registration of lobbyists and major campaign finance reform. A new energy tax will help reduce the federal deficit while cutting carbon dioxide emissions.

No more business as usual. Managers in both the public and private sectors are struggling to define new boundaries of what's right and correct, fighting to curb waste, fraud, and inefficiency.

The message is clear: to function in the hypersensitive business climate of the twenty-first century, professionals in *all* fields must conduct their affairs under a new, more stringent set of moral, ethical, and social standards. American consumers have been victimized by fraudulent schemes, mostly via phone, and Congress has responded by passing laws to protect them.

■ KNOW THE LAW

The newest revision to the Telephone Consumer Fraud Protection Act (TCFPA) [47 USC 227] of 1994 went into effect on January 1, 1996.[1] After this date, a single mistake by a sales representative could cost your company up to $10,000. The legislation demands that sales organizations maintain a "written policy, available upon demand, for maintaining a *do-not-call* list." The law imposes a fine of $500 on an unwanted sales call by phone. And, if it can be shown that the call was made willfully or knowingly against the wishes of the consumer, a judge can impose a fine of up to triple that amount. As a legitimate business that sells ethically, you must still be cautious not to break the law.

The Federal Trade Commission and your state's attorney general have a great deal of power to prosecute fraudulent or abusive phone salespeople. In the past, these agencies were lucky to get back even some of the money that consumers lost. Under the new TCFPA guidelines, they can now impose fines of $10,000 per violation. These rulings apply to business-to-consumer, but not business-to-business, calls. Check current state and federal *business-to-business call* guidelines.

Angry citizens are using the law to force telemarketers to pay them for the inconvenience of unsolicited calls. The *Pri-*

---

[1]See the complete text of The Federal Trade Commission Telemarketer Guidelines at http://www.ftc.gov/bcp/telemark/out.htm. Or write Correspondence Branch, Federal Trade Commission, Washington, D.C. 20580.

vacy Journal, a monthly newsletter dedicated to privacy issues, reports that dozens of recent lawsuits for repeated telephone solicitations have been won or settled out-of-court.

One angry customer, when he orders a product or service, attaches his check to a telemarketing agreement forbidding the company to call him or to give out his unlisted number. By endorsing the check, the company signals agreement with his terms, including the statement that his time and telephone are available on a for-hire basis of $500 per call, the amount stipulated in the federal law. Have your accounting department watch for these endorsements. Have them forward a copy to your sales manager.

➤ Some of the Rules You Must Follow

1. You must maintain a call log.
2. You may not call consumers before 8:00 A.M. or after 9:00 P.M.
3. You must maintain a database of people who have asked you not to call again.
4. You may not call anyone on your do-not-call list.
5. You are required to state up front that this is a sales call and what products or services are offered.
6. For promotions or sweepstakes, you must clearly state that there is no purchase necessary and disclose the odds of winning.
7. You must have a written policy on managing your do-not-call list that you can send out on request.

The written policy should include, but is not limited to:

1. How do-not-call requests will be captured.
2. How quickly these names and telephone numbers will get into the database.
3. Where appropriate, how the do-not-call request will be forwarded, in a timely manner, to the person, business, or entity on whose behalf the call was made and its affiliated companies.
4. How the accuracy of the database will be maintained.

Consult your own legal counsel for more details on your written do-not-call list policy.

It may be difficult to avoid making sales calls to restricted numbers. Some states and consumer organizations maintain databases of phone numbers not to be called. For example, over 35,000 people have paid $10 to be on Florida's official do-not-call list.[2] The Direct Marketing Association maintains a do-not-call list that is free for the asking.[3] The Securities and Exchange Commission has been charged by Congress to watch the more than 5,000 securities firms that have 500,000 employees. Securities dealers must keep a centralized do-not-call list.

If you feel this do-not-call provision does not apply to you because you have an existing relationship with the individuals you call, think again. Although the federal statute creates an exemption for established business relationships, the FCC requires that the requests of established customers be honored. Once an established customer asks not to be called, the established business relationship exemption no longer applies.

■ YOU MUST BECOME A GUERRILLA

With the new attitude of consumers, it's difficult to reach them by phone. Sales professionals are finding that they can't reach home-based businesses with face-to-face sales calls. They must use the telephone to make the initial contact, or they don't get a shot at this exploding market. Because of the way traditional telemarketing is conducted, those who are on the phones burn out rapidly, so sales firms must constantly recruit and train new people. The shortage of good people is the most frequent complaint of those who must sell via telephone.

The telemarketing books we've reviewed agree that using the telephone effectively is an essential part of doing business in the future. But these authors are still advocating many of the

---

[2]For a list of guidelines by state, see the American Telemarketing Association's Web site at http://www.ataconnect.org, or contact them at 4605 Lankershim Boulevard, Suite 824, North Hollywood, CA 91602-1891. Phone: 818-766-5324 or 800-441-3335. Fax: 818-766-8168.

[3]Direct Marketing Association, 1111 19th Street, NW, Suite 1100, Washington, D.C. 20036-3603. Phone: 202-955-5030. Fax: 202-955-0085. http://www.the-dma.org.

manipulative, high-pressure tactics of the past. Even though this traditional approach burns people out, yields low closing ratios, and alienates the public, many firms stick to the telemarketing approaches of old. These managers must learn that *telemarketing* doesn't close the business, TeleSelling does.

TeleSelling is getting the business when you can't be there in person. Combined with other marketing vectors, TeleSelling substantially increases your bottom line. TeleSelling can be a cost-effective way to close lots of new business. You can personally reach thousands of far-flung customers. TeleSelling offers person-to-person effectiveness at a fraction of the cost of a face-to-face sales call. TeleSelling is unique in that it allows businesses to capture data from buyers and nonbuyers alike. You quickly gather important information about your product, your prospects, and your offer. With TeleSelling, you can test a concept, product, offer, list, prospect pool, or demographic in a just a few hours. You can get accurate, measurable results right away. You can make on-the-spot changes and try new approaches with immediate response.

Chapter 2

What Makes Guerrilla TeleSelling Unique?

■ WHAT'S A GUERRILLA?

Just as a lightly armed, fast-moving band of ragtags can paralyze an army, the sales guerrilla relies on *information* and *surprise* to gain a tactical advantage. Guerrillas embody the spirit and dedication of a veteran mercenary. They are willing to do the unconventional. They often do the opposite of what the competition expects.

➤ Be Exceptional

No one today has resources to waste on inefficient selling tactics like random cold calling or half-hearted follow-up. Consumers will no longer settle for shoddy quality or unresponsive service. They have more choices than ever, and you have to be positively exceptional to maintain their loyalty. To win the business in today's brutal battlefield, you must become a guerrilla.

Guerrilla Selling®[1] is not so much a collection of techniques as it is an attitude, an approach, a philosophy of doing business. Guerrillas build a constituency of dedicated followers by consistently maintaining the highest standards of quality, service, and business principles. The guerrilla looks beyond the commission to the greater good. They often do the very last thing their competitors, or even their customers, expect. They tell the truth at all times, at all costs. Guerrillas rely on *time, energy,* and *imagination* instead of the brute force of a big-budget mar-

---

[1]Guerrilla Selling is a registered trademark of The Guerrilla Group, Inc.

keting campaign. These are the three arenas where no one can outspend you.

➤ Set High Standards

To insure that decisions and dealings will stand the test of time, guerrilla managers apply the litmus test of *fair-care-share*. Is it *fair* to all concerned? Do I really *care* about these people, and have I demonstrated my caring? Have I done my *share* and a little bit more? Like the mountaineer's motto, "Leave the campsite cleaner than you found it, and always leave some wood for the next fire." Follow these principles consistently, and you can't go wrong.

■ SETTING YOURSELF UP TO WIN

It has been said that sales is the world's second oldest profession, but attitudes are changing. The classic view of the won't-take-no-for-an-answer pitch master is giving way to a new view of sales and a new breed of business professionals.

Old way: Sell hard.
New way: Sell smart.

Technologies like laptop computers, fax/modem boards, and satellite-direct pagers make it easier than ever to be in the right place at the right time. Never before has timing been such an important part of the selling process. Customers want to deal with you at their convenience, not yours, so guerrillas meticulously manage their time and expedite everything. Reach for the phone instead of the fax, send a handwritten fax instead of a letter. Use E-mail instead of snail-mail.

Old way: Effective selling requires the right technique.
New way: Effective selling requires the right outlook.

For the guerrilla, the customer is an ally, not an adversary. Because every customer is unique, there is no one right way to sell. Instead of trying to persuade the prospect to want what he has, the guerrilla tries to discover what the prospect *already* wants, then sells to that.

Old way: The salesperson helps the customer make a decision.
New way: The salesperson helps the customer solve a problem.

Guerrillas are problem solvers. They ask. They listen. They take careful notes. They are creative, flexible, and always on the move. By aligning with the values and goals to which the prospect is already committed, the guerrilla makes the best alternative obvious.

Old way: People buy low price.
New way: People buy high value.

If your customer tells you that price is the only consideration, or even the most important consideration, they're being less than totally frank. Guerrillas know that there is always an underlying motivation behind every buying decision, so they try to isolate what the prospect values and sells to those criteria. The guerrilla constantly looks for ways to add value through quality, convenience, and service. On the battleground of price, everyone gets bloodied, so the guerrilla moves the battle for business to the higher ground of value.

Old way: Never let the truth get in the way of the sale.
New way: Never let an untruth get in the way of the relationship.

Guerrillas know that the number one reason people buy from them is *confidence,* so they consistently *under*promise and *over*deliver. Deception is futile. Prospects have more access to information about your company and its services than ever before. The customer will ultimately find out anyway. Even the tiniest white lie can undermine the relationship, so guerrillas are ruthlessly honest and openly disclose the disadvantages, as well as the advantages, of their offering.

Old way: Prospect constantly for new customers and new business.
New way: Take care of your existing customers, and new business will flock to you.

These new boundaries are nothing new to the guerrilla. They have always known that the truth is one of the most powerful weapons in their arsenal. They know that while the customer may not always be right, they are always the customer. If someone is dissatisfied, guerrillas ferret out the cause and correct it. They guarantee everything unconditionally. They recognize the fiduciary obligations they have to their employer and their community as well, and they conduct all of their affairs in ways that are socially, economically, and environmentally responsible. This sense of responsibility, that we're all in this together, gives them the advantage of credibility in their relationships with vendors and customers. Instead of selling "what's in it for me," they sell "what's in it for *us*." By stressing mutual benefit, guerrillas create a strong human bond that transcends commercial interests.

These new standards will change our definitions of quality and service as well. In a Japanese factory, if someone spills coffee on the floor, it's counted as a quality fault and is tallied toward the team's total quality management (TQM) ratings. If someone is late for a meeting, it's a quality fault. Doing a good job is elevated to an ethical standard, a matter of honor. This count-everything approach to TQM is an important reason why Japanese companies have been able to outgun American manufacturers.

The same principle applies to service. That means that no one should be left on hold for more than a few seconds; all orders should be filled the same day; and every vendor should be paid immediately. Guerrillas reward every customer by giving them more than they expect, more than they paid for, or always charging slightly less than the original estimate, thereby building a loyal clientele.

➤ Become Fanatical

The most powerful weapon in your selling arsenal is your own excitement about what you're doing. Guerrillas don't just sell bricks, they're building a city! The guerrilla has a good word for everyone and never complains.

■ TELESELLING IS A UNIQUE ENVIRONMENT

When you call your customer, you have no idea what's going on in their lives. You can't see their facial expression. It's difficult to assess if they're happy, sad, lost, confused, angry, or relaxed. Anyone at anytime can interrupt your conversation. You don't have the option of asking them to close the door or hold their calls. Because all you have is the audio channel and less than one-third of their attention, you must work much harder to make your point.

■ FIVE REASONS WHY THE SKILLS THAT USUALLY MAKE SALESPEOPLE GREAT WILL KILL THEM OVER THE PHONE

1. In a normal sales call, you make a strong impression, because you physically occupy the customer's attention for a period of time. With TeleSelling, you'll get a few seconds or minutes, and your impact diminishes substantially. To compete, you must develop new skills and tools to remotely create favorable impressions.

2. It's more difficult to see if your competitors have been calling. You can't check the visitor log. You must have your facts completely straight about your competitor's products, because you won't get a second chance if you are proven wrong.

3. Demonstrations are difficult or impossible. You can talk a prospect through a procedure over the phone, but the impact is only a fraction of what it would have been if you were there in person. If you're a strong demonstrator closer, you may have difficulty getting the business over the phone without developing new skills.

4. During an in-person sales call, prospects will give you their attention for 30 minutes to a few hours. On the phone you won't have that much time. The average telephone conversation lasts seven minutes (teenagers excluded). You must learn how to compress your message.

5. The trend in commercial businesses is team buying, in which individuals bring their expertise together in making decisions, usually for major capital equipment. Even simple purchases, such as office supplies, involve an average of three people. When you telesell, it can be difficult to talk to all of the players as you would in an ordinary in-person call. You'll work harder to get all the names and to contact all the influencers involved.

■ THE 17 THINGS THAT DRIVE BUYERS NUTS AND HOW TO AVOID THEM

This data is based on surveys that we've done during live training sessions. Here's what annoys callers most in roughly their order of importance:

1. *An obviously canned pitch.* Today, people view themselves as being unique and want the goods and services they purchase to reflect that uniqueness. An obviously scripted pitch turns away savvy buyers. Instead, guerrillas ask lots of questions, and they tell their story after determining the caller's concerns.

2. *People who don't know the products.* Prospects are underwhelmed when they're looking for answers and all they hear is, "I don't know." Service Intelligence used 15 mystery shoppers to call six major software companies. Once they got through, they asked a question taken from the Frequently Asked Questions (FAQs) list on the company's Web site. A quarter of the time the technician gave the wrong answer or declared the problem unsolvable. Guerrillas know that regular product training creates a competitive edge. Make certain your staff is trained on what you sell or can refer the caller to the right person for more details.

3. *Being interrupted.* Let callers talk! Men are the worst offenders when speaking to women, frequently interrupting the conversation. Let your prospects complete what they're saying, and don't try to second-guess what they'll say next. If you jump ahead, you'll miss important information—details that could mean the difference between you making a sale and your competitor getting the business. This is tough to do when you've heard the same question again and again, and you already know the answer. Start every conversation as though you have no idea what your customer wants.

4. *Background noise.* "When I hear lots of other people speaking in the background, I know I've just been called by a telemarketing company," grouses a friend. "I ask, 'How many other people are making calls, too?'"

When they reply, she says, "Then there are plenty of other people you can talk to. Good bye." Guerrillas call from a quiet place, knowing that customers want to feel like they're the only person in the world that you're calling.

5. *Refusing to end the call.* We have no idea why it's so popular for companies to end a call with, "Well if you change your mind, call us at 1-800- . . ." And we haven't gotten anyone to admit that it increases sales. Guerrillas know that when the caller has heard enough, they'll either want to buy or want to move on. Keeping customers who are not interested on the line is a waste of your time, and it leaves them feeling uncomfortable about your company.

6. *Sloppy pronunciation.* There is a psychological connection between the quality of the company and the quality of speech used by that company's representative. Guerrillas stack the deck in their favor with careful diction and pronunciation.

7. *Throat clearing.* Some people have a habit of clearing their throat while others are speaking or just before they speak. This is very distracting, and some people think it's rude. Ask your colleagues if you frequently clear your throat. Or listen for throat clearing when you speak. If you have this problem, see your doctor. Continuous throat clearing is also very hard on your voice, and it can indicate other problems as well.

8. *Discourteous behavior.* "Could you hold please?—(click)" is one of the biggest annoyances in this category. Others include, "He's out, can you call back?" and a cold, "I don't know." Add to this list hanging up too soon when the caller has an afterthought. Guerrillas always wait for the caller to hang up before disconnecting.

> Guerrillas always assume that the caller can hear, even if they're on hold. Dave called for technical support and during the conversation, he had to get some information, so he muted his headset. The tech thought he was on hold and proceeded to rant to a coworker about "this idiot on the line," complete with expletives. Dave calmly took note of the whole diatribe, returned, and said, "May I

speak to your boss please, John? I just heard what you said about me; I was on mute—not hold, and my goal is to make sure that you never refer to a customer that way again."

9. *No handoff.* Often, callers are transferred to the next department and have to reexplain the situation. When this happens several times in a single call, customers get irate. If they don't get mad, they get even. Guerrillas always hand off the conversation, preferably in a three-way call, so the customer can hear the handoff procedure.

> "Mr. Levinson, I need for you to talk to Lori in the accounting department. With your permission, I'll get her on the line right now, introduce you, and fill her in on what's happened. Will that be alright?"
>
> "Sure!"
>
> "Lori, this is Suze. I've got Mr. Levinson on the line with us."
>
> "Hello, Mr. Levinson. I'm Lori."
>
> "Let me explain what's happened so far. . . ."

10. *Long, convoluted voice mail menus.* One of our clients in the health care field found that even four menu choices caused confusion. The reason: ill people can only concentrate on one or two things simultaneously. If you're selling to a group with less than perfect health, only offer one or two choices. Guerrillas keep menu systems simple and easy to understand.

11. *Being called at a bad time.* No one is waiting by the phone, hoping it will ring, wishing it's a salesperson. Seventy percent of all inbound calls interrupt something more important. Guerrillas remain sensitive to this and always test if it's a good time to speak before proceeding.

12. *Not taking "no" for an answer.* Although it's true that on one-shot telemarketing calls objection responses increase sales, guerrillas know that "no" doesn't mean "forever," just "no for now." Use the guerrilla sales process described in this book, and you'll say "no" before they will.

13. *Free things that aren't really free.* With the recent changes in telecommunications laws, this is now treading on dangerous territory. Guerrillas never use this tactic.

14. *Make me wrong or stupid.* "You should have called earlier, before the warranty expired!" or "That wasn't very smart of you!" or "That's not our policy." Guerrillas understand the customer's point of view and work to a mutually satisfactory solution. Because one in five dissatisfied customers will tell 20 people about it, make your customer feel right and smart for buying.

15. *Left on hold forever.* It's easier for your caller to hang up and call the next listing in the phone book. Guerrillas check every 20 seconds, because that's the limit of the average caller's patience.

16. *That awful music on hold.* Orvel called a local car dealer, checking on availability of a specific model. He was placed on hold and found himself listening to a local radio station. He heard a commercial for a competing dealer, hung up, and called them instead. Guerrillas never let some disc jockey decide what their customers will hear. Choose a suitable on-hold message, and as a last resort, choose music that reflects the identity of your business.

17. *Automatic hold cues.* Web guru Wally Bock[2] tells a story, "Some years ago I called a tech support hotline. Usually what happens is you automatically get put on hold for a long time. So, imagine my surprise when a real person answered on the third ring. I outlined my problem, and it quickly became clear that it was well beyond the tech's skill level.

    "How long have you been in tech support?" he asked.

    "Oh, I'm not in tech support, I'm in accounting."

    "But you answered the phone."

    "Well, I was walking through. The phone was ringing, and no one else was here. I want to help our customers, so I answered it."

---

[2]http://www.bockinfo.com.

Think about the things that callers do that drive you crazy. Ask your TeleSelling staff to do the same, and you'll make sure that you don't drive your callers nuts. Being courteous, knowledge-able, and polite to every caller is just the first step. Guerrillas know that *excellence* is the price of admission in the new global economy.

Chapter

Setting Goals and Objectives

If you don't know whom you're calling, any number will connect you there.

Why are you going to get on the telephone and contact people? A strategy is an overall plan of action developed to accomplish clearly stated objectives. The guerrilla needs to be familiar with the main telephone strategies.

■ 11 TELEPHONE SALES STRATEGIES

In 1967, Eugene B. Kordahl and Donald Hoffman, two of the original members of the Phone Power/Telemarketing Professionals with the old Bell Telephone System, identified the first seven telemarketing strategies used in the telemarketing industry. In *The Annual Guide to Telemarketing*, Mr. Kordahl and Arnold L. Fishman found 4 more strategies, for a total of 11, as the ones most commonly used by companies today.[1] They are:

1. Sales programs to handle existing accounts
2. Opening new accounts
3. Suggestion selling on incoming calls
4. Qualification of prospect list

---

[1]Eugene B. Kordahl and Arnold L. Fishman. *The Annual Guide to Telemarketing.*

5. Activating marginal, old, and forgotten accounts

6. Introduction of new products and services

7. Lead generation using direct-response, toll-free numbers

8. Outbound contacts—business reply cards, coupons, and letters

9. Follow-up on direct mail campaigns

10. Full account management methods by territory, product, and size

11. Coordination of order entry and customer service procedures with marketing and telesales programs

■ TELESELLING

You close a sale by being in the right place, at the right time, with the right people, with the right offer, doing the right things that make you the right choice, right now. Your sales objectives let you put together all of those rights.

Guerrillas create objectives designed to do the right thing for the salesperson, the customer, and the company. The challenge in TeleSelling is that you're a sight unseen. The first objective is the correct positioning of your company. Guerrillas invest in positioning, and they do everything in their power to optimize their position. You want your prospects to gladly accept your call.

■ WHAT ARE YOU WILLING TO SPEND?

What is the *allowable acquisition cost* of a customer? Given the value of a customer over their lifetime, what can you afford to spend to capture that customer? If a prospect doesn't buy, it doesn't mean they won't provide quality referrals. Factor this into your acquisition cost.

➤ Calculate Your Customer's Lifetime Value (LTV)

Think about your average customer. How much do they spend with you each time they buy? How often do they buy from you? How many years will they do business with you? Multiply out these numbers, and you'll know how much money they'll contribute to your business over their lifetime. This is their LTV.

Another way to determine your company's LTV of a customer is to take your annual sales, divided by the number of active accounts in AR, then multiply that number by five. Your average customer will be with you for about five years.

$$\frac{\text{Annual sales} \times 5}{\text{Number of AR accounts}} = \text{Lifetime value (LTV)}$$

For example, a gift boutique's corporate client purchases an average of $1,000 per quarter. Their average customer buys from them for five years. So the LTV is $1,000 × 4 × 5, or $20,000.

The true business value of that customer is even greater. If that boutique can get just one referral per year from that corporate client, they will direct 5 × $20,000, or $100,000 worth of additional business their way. Pretty amazing for a $1,000-per-quarter customer.

Research these numbers for your firm, calculate the LTV of your customers, and make sure everyone knows what the numbers are and what they mean.

➤ Calculate Your Return on Investment (ROI)

Divide the LTV by the cost to acquire and manage that lead, multiplied by your closing ratio.

$$\frac{\text{Close \%} \times \text{LTV}}{(\text{\$ Lead acquisition} + \text{\$ Lead management})} = \text{ROI}$$

■ HOW MANY PEOPLE SHOULD STAFF YOUR CALL CENTER?

Determine the likely closing ratio from sales history, and then check your predicted outcome against your sales goal.

$$\frac{\text{\$ Sales goal}}{\text{\$ Average sale}} = \text{New customers needed}$$

$$\frac{\text{New customers needed}}{\text{Closing ratio}} = \text{Number of prospects needed}$$

$$\frac{\text{\% Callers interested} \times \text{Total list size}}{100} = \text{Number of prospects available}$$

The number of calls per hour that your staff can make effectively depends on the quality of the list and level of detail needed to qualify and close prospects. You can estimate the quality of your list by reviewing the list demographics. Then test the list with your best salesperson to get an idea of its value. You could make 12 contacts per hour or 1 contact per day. Guerrillas will optimize their numbers by role-playing likely sales scenarios with a stopwatch to determine the time required for an average call. Remember to factor in time for breaks.

$$\frac{\text{Average calls per hour}}{\text{Calls per salesperson per hour}} = \text{Number of salespeople needed}$$

Guerrillas choose their battles. After running the numbers, do they all add up? Will this plan deliver the profits you need to make it worthwhile? If not, abandon your plan now. Does the forecast suggest that you need more people, better offers, or more prospects? If so, make the necessary adjustments to make certain that you have enough people to handle the calls and enough calls to challenge your people.

■ 11 WAYS TO GET YOUR CUSTOMERS TO BUY MORE FROM YOU

As you plan your sales goals, remember that your best sources of additional business are your current customers. You can increase your profits by five to ten times when you just call on the people that already know you. If you don't have things to sell to them, starting looking! Once the relationship is established and you have proven your worthiness, customers will buy almost anything offered.

➤ 1. Ask Them for More

Ask your customers to buy more. "You know, Cathy, you've placed an order for nine cases. If you add just one more case, you'll earn the ten-case discount."

Ask your customers to buy more often. "I know that sometimes you run out. Would it be convenient for you if I called on you a little more often?"

Send customers customized coupons. Create coupons with your computer and printer especially for each customer, giving them an incentive to buy a little more than normal.

Ask customers to pay more. Informal surveys of our audiences show that 70 percent feel that they are undercharging their customers by at least 10 percent. If your gross margin is 30 percent, and you raised your prices by 10 percent, you'd have to lose 33 percent of your customers before you'd lose a penny of your current profits. Work less, make more.

➤ 2. Find Out What Else They're Buying

What do your other customers usually buy that this customer is not buying from you? They may assume that you don't offer what they're looking for. What else is your customer buying that you could sell to them? Guerrillas look for opportunities to *cross-sell*.

Create *fusion-marketing* partnerships. You can increase the number of salespeople looking for business without increasing your payroll. Find noncompeting companies who also sell to your customers. These companies will have relationships with customers you want and vice versa. For example, a lawn service provider finds customers for a sprinkler installer by asking his customers, "Gee, what's the biggest problem you have with your sprinkler? Would you like my partner to stop by and fix that?" And the sprinkler installer says, "Wow, this is a beautiful lawn! What's your biggest problem keeping it looking good? Would you like my partner to stop by and do that for you?" They practically close the sale for each other.

What kind of tools, supplies, accessories, training, consumables, or disposables do they need? What about maintenance, security, and repairs? Do they need design services, consulting, and printing?

➤ 3. Become Their Sole Supplier

One guerrilla calls his best customers and asks, "What would you need to feel comfortable with me being your sole supplier?" Buyers are often shocked by the question. After closer examination of his performance, they grant him the business to take advantage of quantity discounts. Yet they sometimes respond with, "You already are!" "Great! Why?" This gives him lots of great ideas for talking to those who aren't buying everything from him.

➤ 4. Invite Them to Come Back

Make a *return appointment*. It's as easy as saying, "See you tomorrow!" or including a coupon good for a purchase the next day, week, or month. While flying home for the holidays, Mark passed the airport shoeshine stand.

"Shine, Mister?"

"Nope, I'm off the road for three weeks!"

"See you in three weeks!"

Remind your customers that you're ready when they're ready. Send them a postcard with a reminder or special offer. The best offers are for added value instead of a discount. "Call us and ask for the Spring Deal, and you'll get a bonus gift with your purchase."

➤ 5. Order Things Just for Them

A compact disc store in Denver makes an unusual offer—if they don't have the title you're looking for, they'll special order it and send it to you within two days. They'll even give you a 10-percent discount for your trouble. Very guerrilla. Most stores charge full retail, and many charge extra for special orders, but these guerrillas realize that they actually save money. This small store has to order stock every couple of days anyway, and they've leveraged that fact into a reputation for outstanding service. It also means less capital tied up in inventory, making them competitive with the bigger, better-stocked stores down the street.

➤ 6. Don't Become Attached to What You Sell

What you sell may no longer be appropriate or desirable for your customers. Even if you love your product, get comfortable with the changing desires and tastes of your customers. They love doing business with you because you stock what they want.

➤ 7. Do More for Them

Find out what the customers *do* with what you sell, and do it for them. How do they augment it? How do they improve it? The secret to increased profits is increased service and increased value. Can you put components together into a subassembly? Then do those things for them, and charge for the privilege.

➤ 8. Increase Your Convenience

➤ Look for ways to increase your customer's convenience every way possible. Even the slightest increase can encourage larger and more frequent purchases.

➤ Make packaging easier to use, easier to dispose of, or easier to recycle. Make packaging do double duty when it's empty, such as plastic pails or glass canning jars.

➤ Offer delivery for a fee, or build it into your price. Many customers are tickled when vendors bring goods and services to them directly, either at work or at home.

➤ Consider an automatic shipment program, replenishing customer stock. Adjust shipments as needed for weather, seasonal, or process changes.

➤ 9. Let Them Do Multiple Things at Once

What do your customers do or buy before and after doing business with you? Can they do those tasks or make those purchases with you? Examples include offering postal services at grocery stores, banks with stockbrokers, and printers who manufacture envelopes and stuff them with statements.

➤ 10. Do Everything Immediately

If customers perceive that you respond to their requests instantly, 95 percent of the time they'll do business with you again. The secret to repeat business is to never make your customer wait.

Many businesses feel it's impractical to offer immediate service because of the increased costs for inventory, personnel, and accounting, yet customers are quite willing to pay extra for immediate service. You can charge more, and customers will pay more. Consider a multiple-tier pricing structure based on delivery, more expensive when done this instant, less expensive when done later.

➤ 11. Be More Fun

Xerox found that 2 percent of their dissatisfied customers would do business with them again, 6 percent of their satisfied customers would do business with them again, and 66 percent of their extremely satisfied customers would do business with them again. If your competition has satisfied customers, you can capture them by making them *extremely* satisfied!

The average American watches over six hours of TV daily because they're bored and want more fun in their lives. In a recent survey, 70.9 percent of people polled would switch vendors if the new company was more fun to do business with. When you add entertainment to your sales process, you'll capture the imagination and buying power of your customers. Witness the explosive growth of theme restaurants like Rainforest Café or the popularity of kids' play areas at McDonald's Restaurants.

Before investing in a TeleSelling operation, be clear about your business's goals and objectives. Do you want to expand your market share, expand your territory, or just improve service?

Chapter 4

How to Stay Motivated

If I lose my money, I lose a lot. If I lose my friends, I lose even more. If I lose my courage, I've lost it all.

—CERVANTES

■ THE MOST COMMON CAUSE OF FAILURE

Most salespeople give up too soon. The typical salesperson's greatest fear is being seen as stupid or wrong. When customers say "no," it's uncomfortable. But no one's ever died from being uncomfortable. Salespeople need to understand that even good prospects will say "no" several times before they say "yes." Lands End mails an average of 11 catalogs to a new address before they get the first order from a new customer.

Most salespeople quit too soon:

48 percent quit after the first contact.

20 percent quit after the second contact.

7 percent quit after the third contact.

5 percent quit after the forth contact.

4 percent quit after the fifth contact.

Yet 80 percent of customers say "yes" *after* the sixth call.

■ THE BIGGEST WEAKNESS OF SALESPEOPLE

Assuming that salespeople really understand their product, most don't really understand their customer. Today, they have to do a lot more *reconnaissance*. They have to know who all the potential influencers are, all the way down to the janitor or outside consultant. And they have to focus on solving the customer's problem, rather than pitching their technology. Guerrillas always focus on solving the problem rather than pushing the purchase.

We recently interviewed Shawn Haynes, Manager of the Associates Program for the world's largest on-line bookstore, Amazon.com.[1] He explained, "Everyone is out there putting content on the Internet and trying to figure out how to get paid for it, without considering the value equation of the transaction. We offer 2.4 *million* titles on-line, while a B. Dalton or Walden's store might offer 140,000. We offer discounts of 20 percent, 40 percent, and more, just like the big stores, but we also give you the capability to electronically *browse* through all those books. We include many hard-to-find and out-of-print books. We ship same-day or next-day. We can give you automatic E-mail notification of new releases by topic, title, or author. That's the value we offer, and that's why people are flocking to us to buy their books."

◼ WHAT HOLDS PEOPLE BACK FROM SUCCESS

Some people consider selling to be too much work. It's true. Selling is hard work with potentially substantial rewards. If you think selling is too hard, we advise you to get another job. Here are some common reasons why people fail at sales.

➤ They Don't Want to Sell

Do you approve of selling? When you hear a sales presentation, do you feel uncomfortable? Do you want to sell? Does what you're selling excite you? For how long do you want to sell? If you feel that selling is a stopgap until you find a real job, you may not really want to sell.

Do you hang out with people who don't approve of selling? Does your boss approve of selling? Does your family approve of selling? Do your friends approve of selling?

If you realize that you have a lack of support for your sales career, you need to decide how you'll deal with it.

---

[1]http://www.amazon.com.

➤ They Feel They Don't Deserve Success

Some salespeople don't feel that they deserve the success they've earned. They create convoluted procedures and take needless steps to feel like they get what they deserve. If this is the case, we recommend professional help.

➤ I'm Going to Be Yelled At

Most salespeople have had bad experiences. They were yelled at, lied to, or told in no uncertain terms what a miserable person they are for selling that stuff. That comes with the territory. One percent of the public will hate you, no matter what you do. What was your worst experience? What are the odds of it happening again? What would you do if it did happen again?

What you *say* to yourself about prospecting has a powerful impact on what you *feel* when prospecting. What you feel when prospecting has a powerful impact on what you do about prospecting.[2]

➤ We Don't Have What They Want

Sell to people who obviously need you. Our colleague Van Carpenter points out, "Solution selling means <u>s</u>ell <u>o</u>ur <u>l</u>ine <u>u</u>nto <u>t</u>hose <u>i</u>n <u>o</u>bvious <u>n</u>eed." There's plenty of business; all you need to do is find it.

➤ It's Got to Be Perfect

Customers don't necessarily demand perfection, but they do demand excellence. You create relationships when you admit that you're human. Acknowledge your foibles, and your positive claims become that much more credible.

➤ How to Get Unstuck

Some salespeople want success, but they don't want the pain or discomfort associated with achieving success. Part of their desire drives them forward, and another part of their brain holds them back. They oscillate. They're stuck. When you feel stuck—can't get on the phone, can't make that call, can't start writing—here's a process to get unstuck.[3]

---

[2]Dudley, George W., Shannon L. Goodson, and David K. Barnett. *Earning What You're Worth?* Dallas, TX: Behavioral Sciences Research Press, 1986. 800-343-4659.

[3]Scheele, Paul. *Natural Brilliance.* Wayzata, MN: Learning Strategies Corporation, 1997. 800-735-8273. http://www.naturalbrilliance.com

Release
Let go of the stuck feeling. Sit back in your chair. Take a breath, and exhale to let go of your stress and tension. Realize that you're not doing what you want to be doing, or something is missing that prevents you from moving forward and making calls.

Notice
As you sit back, take notice. What's happening? What are your feelings? What's in your mind? What's on your desk? Become a reporter of your surroundings. Do this with no emotion or judgment, just observe what's happening.

Respond
Based on what you've just observed, make a choice. What you choose to do isn't as important as making a choice. Just do it.

Witness
Now witness what's happening because of your new choice. Look at it from your perspective, then from your customer's perspective, and from a third party's perspective. If you need to, sit back and witness what's happening. Do this without judgment. Witness what things about your choice worked and what didn't.

Repeat
If you're still stuck, repeat the process. The key to success is to have no emotional attachment or response. This is business. Your job is to get the task done.

■ 27 WAYS TO GET DIALING

1. *You're no worse off.* Right now you have no sales. Start dialing. If someone tells you no, you're no worse off than you are right now. And you could be much better off just by asking.

2. *Just ask.* The magic in selling is that if you ask, you get. Melissa Swett, vice president of operations for Easy Spirit Shoes, gives this advice to her sales staff: "Don't say 'no' for your customer. If you don't ask them if they'd like to see the matching purse, you've said 'no' for them. Ask, and let them decide."

3. *Match your demographics.* Who do you find the easiest to do business with? Sell to them. Perhaps you've had experience in that industry or training that makes you an expert. Guerrillas go after the low-hanging fruit.

4. *Say "no" first.* Guerrillas ask questions, and lots of them! (See the 37 Magic Selling Questions in Chapter 17.) Ask questions until you know whether you can help them or not. If you can't, tell them so. Reject prospects you can't help.

5. *Swallow a frog.* Mark Twain said, "When one is about to swallow a frog, it doesn't do to look at it for very long." Call your most difficult prospect first thing, and get it out of the way.

6. *Get a coach.* A coach can get you pumped up for the game. Find someone who can cheer you on. Someone you'll never let down. Someone for whom you're willing to go out and win the big one.

7. *Dream big.* Imagine increasing your sales by a factor of ten! Remember the first time you sold something? It was probably band candy, or scout cookies, or garden seeds. Remember how hard it was to sell $10 worth? And the person who could sell $100 worth was a sales god or had a rich daddy. Can't do it? Right now you're selling at least 10,000 times more than you've sold in the past. The difference between then and now is that today you have a different view of what's possible and better tools and skills. For you to increase your sales by a factor of ten, you need a different view of what's possible and different tools and skills. Start with a big dream, and then you can determine the tools and skills you need.

8. *Expect the sale.* You don't always get what you want, but you almost always get what you expect. Guerrillas know that someone, somewhere, needs what's being offered, so they expect to find them.

9. *No excuses.* An excuse we frequently hear is, "I need a cup of coffee." If you haven't had your coffee and breakfast before you show up to work, you're not ready to work. Make your first ten dials, *then* you can have a cup.

10. *Put it in writing.* Write your goals for the day—how many dials, how many conversations, how many sales. When you get stuck, looking at your goals can get you going again. Your written goals are a commitment to yourself.

11. *Call a customer first.* Make your first call of the day to a customer you've recently served. Ask them, "How's it going?" "Great!" They'll pump you up, letting you know that you can serve another just like them today. If you don't have a customer you can dial, call Mom.

12. *Program two.* Before you go home for the day, program the first two morning calls into your speed-dial memory. When you arrive in the morning, hit your chair, pick up the handset, and push speed dial to get off to a speedy start.

13. *Fasten your seat belt.* One of our colleagues, Steve Miller, puts a belt around his chair and waist. When he's tempted to get up, he can't, and he makes another call.

14. *"This is a cold call . . ."* Tell people right up front that you're cold-calling. You're using the ultimate guerrilla weapon—the truth—which is the *last* thing people expect from a salesperson on the phone.

15. *Never make cold calls.* If thinking about cold calling makes your hands sweaty, your stomach churn, and your knees weak, then don't cold-call. Ask your customers for referrals, or use some other warm-up approach that we suggest in this book.

16. *Research special reports.* Researching and creating special reports give you a reason to talk with people and get introduced without the pressure of selling them. When you've completed the research, call back with the tabulated results, and ask how you could serve them.

17. *Record yourself.* Tape-record your calls. When you're on tape, you'll tend to perform better. Make a habit of taping and listening to yourself every week. You'll be astonished at how quickly you improve.

18. *Tag team telephone.* Use a Y-cord and two headsets, or two extension phones to play tag team. Alternate dials and discussions, debriefing with your partner between

calls. The secret is to focus on positive behavior, and forget the negative. This is a fast way to transfer the best skills between salespeople.

19. *Go public.* Put a big sign in your area: *Quiet, 70 dials in progress. Ask me how I'm doing later.*

20. *Keep score.* Keep a pad of paper by your phone, counting the number of dials, the number of conversations, the number of deals. Compare scores at breaks and at the end of the day.

21. *Thirteen, thirteen, twelve, twelve.* Some guerrillas who have to set their own appointments find that 50 new conversations per week will work well. They dial until they've had 13 conversations on Monday, 13 conversations on Tuesday, 12 conversations on Wednesday, and 12 conversations on Thursday. You can often do this in two or three hours in the morning. Make your follow-up calls and sales calls in the afternoon. Fridays are left open for follow-up and reports.

22. *Head-to-head competition.* Pick a partner and go head-to-head. The person with the most conversations between now and lunch is treated to lunch by the other, or the person who has the most dials gets free coffee from the others. Keep the stakes low and the competitions short.

23. *Blitz 'em.* Everyone gets on the phones. Everyone! From the president down to the janitor. All lines are lit up, and everyone is dialing. If you're not on the phone, you better be in the bathroom. The blitz can last an hour or a week. We've seen companies double their sales during a slump with an all-hands blitz.

24. *Celebrate wins.* Put a bell, horn, or chime in your work area. When anyone closes a sale, celebrate with some noise! Take your congratulations, and get back on the phones while everyone's excited.

25. *Reward yourself.* Give yourself a prize for hitting a target. After ten dials, you can have coffee. When you close a sale, treat yourself to a ten-minute walk outside. At 110 percent of your targets, you buy a new watch.

26. *Get beaten by a jerk.* As long as it's not illegal to be a jerk, they'll be a part of life. Dial until you talk with someone who's a real jerk.

27. *Blow one for fun.* The pressure's on. It's been a long day. Time to blow one, just for fun. "Hello, does someone there speak Vietnamese? We're doing a survey but only with those who speak Vietnamese." Or "We're selling securities that are specifically designed for two-year-olds. Can I speak to your two-year-old, please?"

■ GUERRILLA INCENTIVES

Your boss tells you, "I want you to put together an incentive program to get our new product line going ballistic. And I want results. None of this spend-a-bunch-of-cash-and-get-no-payoff garbage, either. Oh, and make it interesting." Your boss leaves your office, and now you have one more complex project to add to your overloaded schedule. Where do you start? How can you make sure the program works? How can you make it interesting? Start by thinking about what would be the ideal incentive program for you, personally. Then ask your people what they find motivating.

➤ Why Incentive Programs Fail

Many incentive programs reward the wrong behavior or reward behavior that is likely to happen anyway without an incentive. Or worst of all, the reward creates negative reinforcement. It's less effective to offer sports tickets to someone whose spouse hates sports than to offer a romantic evening meal. Prizes are often selected based on the desires and tastes of the person supervising the program. Yet not every employee shares the same affinity for modern art prints or golf accessories.

➤ Any Behavior that Is Rewarded Tends to Be Repeated

Virtually every study on human motivation shows that positive reinforcement of a behavior tends to increase the frequency of that behavior in the future. Conversely, negative reinforcement of a behavior tends to discourage that behavior.

The secret to a successful incentive program is to make the prize a positive reinforcement. One can learn a lot by watching animals in training, a child learning a new skill, or an executive negotiating the first few weeks of a new position. In every case, new behavior is quickly learned and reinforced with small, often subtle, rewards—for a dog, a tidbit for a trick; for a child, a hug and a smile for trying to walk; for an executive, access to information for following corporate protocol.

➤ What's Their Motivation?

You've probably noticed that no matter what you offer, your incentive program doesn't influence some people. About 40 percent of North Americans are primarily internally motivated. They know they've done a good job when they feel like they've done their best. You can recognize internally motivated people, because they are less interested in what other people think or do. They tend to be independent thinkers, not as interested in what you've done for others, but more interested in what you can do for them. They make choices based on personal ethics and morals.

The most effective incentive programs for internally motivated people align with what they're already committed to. A powerful reward could be a donation in their name to their favorite charity.

Externally motivated people are motivated to look good or to do things, because other people tell them they should. They seek acceptance, and an incentive program delivers tangible proof of acceptance.

Sales positions tend to attract externally motivated people who are motivated by quotas and rewarded with commissions and sales contests. Salespeople will work night and day for a $35.00 plaque and a pat on the back. They tend to quit working hard once they've reached their goals.

Externally motivated managers insist that commission is the only way to motivate a salesperson. They would be right if they hired only externally motivated people.

➤ Create a Powerful Incentive Program

Begin designing your incentive program by answering three questions: *Whose* behavior do you wish to influence? *What* behavior do you want to have repeated? And *when* and *where* do you want that behavior repeated?

➤ Whom Do You Reward?

You can reward employees for meeting production and safety goals or sales staff for reaching sales and profit goals. You can reward superiors for their support of the staff or innovation in increasing profits. You can reward your friends for helping you move to a new house or for taking care of a pet. You can reward customers for their loyalty, for purchasing more product more often, or for referring new business. You can reward prospects for paying attention to your sales message or for directing other prospects to your business.

The most successful incentive programs include rewards for people who are influencers or who are important to the program participants. For example, selecting prizes that spouses will find attractive increases their support. Prizes for the team increase morale.

➤ How Do You Know You'll Be Successful?

Here are the elements of successful programs. Use this checklist to make sure your program works.

➤ Successful incentive programs result in *measurable* results. If you can't measure your desired behavior change, you'll never know if your program was a success. Build measurement criteria into your program.

➤ Aim for *permanent* behavior change. You not only want a customer to try your brand, you want them to *switch* to your brand. Price-based incentives attract price-sensitive buyers. You don't want customers who aren't loyal; they'll always switch to the vendor with the lowest price.

➤ Create programs that increase *profits*. Be careful that your people are not going to give away the store to make sales. The only true measure of success in business is profit. Know how much this program can bring to your bottom line.

➤ The promotion must be easy to run and require little or no staff training. If you need a complex document spelling out the rules and exceptions, your program is doomed to failure. A successful promotion can be explained to a 12-year-old in 30 seconds.

The most effective promotions use multiple influence agents. These are the factors that motivate people to do things. Isn't that why you're launching an incentive program? There is more on these influence agents in Chapter 18.

➤ Align with a commitment your participants have already made. The most effective programs let people meet multiple commitments. For example, when Total Petroleum ran "Total Thursdays" in selected markets, you could simultaneously fuel up your car, get a free drink, and donate a few cents per gallon to your choice of charities. The brilliance of this incentive program was that it let people give to charity—something most people want to do—while filling up their gas tank—something to which most people are committed if they're going to drive to work. The program broke all sales records.

➤ Reward Your Employees for Profits

Most progressive companies offer profit sharing, most often by creating a cash pool and dividing that pool by a formula that gives more to the higher-wage earners. In three studies for his graduate degree, Elliott Sampson, senior marketing manager for TAFA (Concord, New Hampshire), discovered that the most effective profit-sharing plan split the pot *equally* among all employees. When the president gets the same share as the janitor, the president will listen to the janitor's money-saving suggestions. Relatively large gains in profitability occur when you reward saving money and increasing profits at all levels.

When you're creating an incentive program to promote other behaviors, such as quality control, waste reduction, or safety, let the participants decide on the reward. You'll discover that they'll usually pick prizes smaller than you had in mind, and they may select social events, like a keg party or pizza night, over cash rewards.

➤ Reward Your Sales Force for Expertise

Perhaps you want your sales force to sell more profitably. The problem with most sales incentives is that they reward behaviors that people are already supposed to exhibit: selling things. Savvy sales managers reward behavior that goes beyond the job description. For example, for your next sales contest, reward competitive knowledge. Have your salespeople study your competitors, their products, and their customers. Hold pop quizzes, and hand out prizes on the spot for correct answers. There's no better way to increase confidence in your product, and your salespeople will be more aware of the competition long after the contest ends.

➤ Reward Your Customers for Loyalty

It's more profitable to sell to an existing customer than to find a new customer, so why not reward your existing customers for their loyalty?

Marketing programs often encourage new customers to buy at the exclusion of existing customers. The offer giveth: "Sign up for a year's subscription at the trade show, and we'll give you a free leather briefcase." The small print taketh away: "Not valid for renewals." Oh, great! Tell your present customers that they don't deserve a leather briefcase for their loyalty. It's enough to make them cancel their subscription and sign up anew.

An unconventional approach is to give your customers a better reward for renewing on the spot, and offer new customers a lesser reward. New customers learn that you appreciate loyalty. When your incentive program focuses on profits, you'll work hard at keeping customers. Your cost of acquiring a customer plummets, and your profits soar.

Instead of giving a customer a restaurant gift certificate as a reward, tell them to take their spouse to dinner and send you the bill. The secret here is to not set a spending limit. The gift is enhanced by your trust in them to spend what they'd like. You'll find they'll often spend less than you had in mind.

➤ Reward New Customers for Saying "Yes"

Often, marketing managers create incentive programs so new customers purchase sooner rather than later. When you understand the buyer's motivation, you'll influence them to buy sooner. People buy to satisfy a personal urge or desire and to fulfill a commitment they've made to someone important in their lives. They won't buy unless there is a compelling deadline to move forward. Pain, hunger, a project deadline, or the desire to have new shoes for the party tonight could motivate that purchase. New customer incentive programs work best when they move up the deadline.

Many salespeople use a discount to impose a deadline. "I can give you a 10-percent discount if you buy now!" Putting an item on sale rewards customers for buying during the campaign. A better approach is offering an added-value reward. Estee Lauder beauty products never go on sale. Instead, you'll receive "a $25.00

value gift when you buy today," and the gift is more of their products. This turns a sample into a reward and drives sales.

➤ Kick Off Your Event

Now that you understand what behavior you want to encourage and you've researched the rewards that are meaningful to your group, you plan a kickoff party to let everyone know about the program. At the party, people make and accept challenges. You stimulate and encourage statements like "I'll hit my quota in ten months," or "I'm going to beat your number, George." Using the power of public commitments, you not only guarantee a program that works, but your boss will be overwhelmed by the success of the program before you've handed out a single prize.

Chapter

Preparing Your TeleSelling Workspace

Create a location that you use solely for making phone calls. You don't open your mail there, you don't eat lunch there, you don't write letters there. You only make calls. This trains your body and your brain that when you're there, you're on the phone and dialing. There are no other distractions.

The location should be quiet, uncluttered, clean, and stocked with reference materials and everything else you'll need to answer all of the questions you'll be asked. You don't want to get up between calls to get what you need.

The best background noise is no background noise. When customers hear the chatter of others in the background, they think—mass telemarketing operation—and you've lost your advantage.

For some guerrillas, the best location would be at home in a spare bedroom. For others, it might be a special corner of their cubicle.

■ ELEMENTS OF THE TELESELLING WORKSPACE

➤ Headset Phones

Increase your energy and effectiveness by using a headset. A telephone headset leaves your hands free to take notes, select materials for a customized information kit, review reference materials, or type at your computer keyboard.

Because you're not hunched over holding the phone, your voice will sound richer and will have more authority. No more stiff neck and shoulders. You will be much more comfortable during long client interviews and "telethon" sessions.

Select a binaural headset with two earpieces. You'll hear much better and cut surrounding noise that can distract you.

If you use a single-earpiece headset, wear the earpiece in your right ear. A survey of 500,000 people found that they process language more accurately with their right ear and process music more accurately with their left ear.[1] It's due to our left-brain–right-brain construction. Because most people are right-handed, they hold the phone to their less accurate left ear. Guerrillas take the advantage by using the more effective ear.

When people stick their head into your office to interrupt you, with your headset on they'll assume you're on the phone. When they say, "You on the phone?" you get to decide how you'll answer.

When you use a headset, your caller will also hear you better. Because the microphone is positioned in front of your mouth, your voice won't fade away or be too loud. You'll hear your caller better. Select a headset that lets you control the volume of your call. No longer will you have to strain to hear or have to ask your caller to speak up—you just turn up the volume.

Look for models with automatic level sensing. Some models will automatically limit the volume when a loud noise is on the line, such as when you accidentally misdial a fax machine (ouch!). Most headset models also include a mute switch. By pressing this button, you can cough, confer privately with others in your office, or say what you really think at that moment. Select a high-quality, professional unit.[2] Expect to pay several hundred dollars for a high-end, cordless headset phone. High-quality corded telephone headsets are priced around $100.

➤ Desk

Select a desk that is large enough to comfortably hold all of the things you will need. You'll want shelves for reference materials and file cabinets for customer records. Select a surface of the correct height for your body structure.

---

[1]Campbell, Don G. *100 Ways to Improve Teaching Using Your Voice and Music.* Tucson, AZ: Zephyr Press, 1992. p. 10.

[2]We've had good luck with Plantronics (800-544-4660), Hello Direct (800-HI HELLO), and Cornerstone (800-262-2480). Call for a free catalog. Check them out as you would any new vendor.

➤ Ergonomic Chair

Plan to invest several hundred dollars in a good, ergonomic chair. Select one that supports your back and has adjustable height. Good chairs are one of the best investments you can make in office productivity.

➤ Mirror Image

Put a mirror next to your phone. Not a little mirror, a BIG mirror, big enough that you can see your head and shoulders in it. Watch yourself in the mirror while you're on the phone with clients and customers. Even though it may sound a bit narcissistic, this tactic will give you a face to interact with and help to focus your attention.

And put a sticker in the corner of your mirror that says, "SMILE?" Remind yourself to smile while you're speaking.

➤ Get Up and Boogie

Put an extra-long cord on your headset that lets you roam your office. Better still, consider using one of the new wireless headsets that give you complete freedom of movement.[3] You will be much more efficient when you're not tied to your telephone. You don't have to put your caller on hold to look something up, get their records, or look out the window.

Stand while you're speaking on the phone. Give your caller a sample of your energy and excitement when speaking to them. Walking around keeps you awake and alert. When you gesture as you speak, your voice changes ever so slightly, yet your customer subconsciously detects these changes. They'll feel that you're more excited and more confident about what you sell, yet they won't quite know why.

■ BIOLOGICAL FACTORS

➤ Light

Good lighting is essential to productivity. If you have a choice, natural light from windows or skylights is best. Install Wide-

---

[3]If you want to be completely wireless, check out Hello Direct's executive headset. Pull down the microphone to answer your phone; put it back up to hang up. 800-HI HELLO.

Spectrum or Natural Light fluorescent lamps, or supplement fluorescent lighting with incandescent light.

➤ Temperature

The best working temperature for making calls is between 70° and 72°. Invest in a small digital thermometer (available at Radio Shack for about $10) to monitor the temperature in your work area.

➤ Water

Keep bottled water available in your work area at all times, and drink frequently. Don't worry about having to go to the bathroom—you lose a pint of water through your breath every hour that you talk.

■ BUILD A TRAINING RESOURCE CENTER

Advanced training for your TeleSelling sales team can make a tremendous difference in effectiveness. Training can take many forms: books, audiotapes, videotapes, competitive reconnaissance, classroom instruction, one-on-one coaching, peer review, and even tag-team selling with a veteran. A thorough treatment of advanced sales skills is covered in our previous book, *Guerrilla Selling—Unconventional Weapons and Tactics for Increasing Your Sales.*[4]

➤ Books

Assign required reading before hitting the phones. Use the bibliography in the back of this book as a shopping list for your library. With paperback books, you can practice *razor reading* by cutting the book apart at the spine and distributing chapters or sections to your team members. Instruct them to review the material and do a verbal book report at your next sales meeting.

➤ Magazines

Guerrillas regularly subscribe to the magazines, journals, and newsletters that serve professional selling. These include *Sell!ng* magazine, *Personal Selling Power, Sales & Marketing Management,*

---

[4]Jay Conrad Levinson, Bill Gallagher, and Orvel Ray Wilson, CSP. New York: Houghton Mifflin, 1992.

Potentials in Marketing,[5] *Entrepreneur, Success,* and the *Guerrilla Marketing Newsletter.*[6] Check with your reference librarian for examples. Many of the associations listed in the Appendix publish articles and newsletters on sales skills as well.

➤ Audiotape Training

The average commute in America is 22 minutes. Provide skill-sharpening audiotapes for your sales team to review while driving to and from work.[7]

➤ Videotape Training

Nine out of ten homes in America have a VCR, and many now have two. If you make training videos available to borrow, your salespeople are more likely to take them home and study them on their own time.[8]

➤ Outside Consultants

If you are inexperienced at managing a TeleSelling team, consider using an outside expert to facilitate your preparations. Whenever possible, preview their work to be sure they're delivering training that matches your company's values. A reliable source for sales trainers is the National Speakers Association.[9] Check their membership list, or ask your speakers bureau for recommendations.

➤ Competitive Reconnaissance

What you don't know *can* hurt you. Consider this: what if you spent weeks with your R&D, marketing, and sales staff, creating your next product introduction, and one month later, you read in the trade press about a similar announcement from your competition? How would you feel? What would your boss say? What would your customers think?

---

[5]To subscribe, call 800-328-4329.

[6]To subscribe, call Guerrilla Marketing International at 800-748-6444.

[7]For a free copy of the audio cassette, *Ten Characteristics of a Sales Guerrilla,* by Orvel Ray Wilson, CSP, call 800-247-9145.

[8]See the Appendix for titles, or call for a free catalog: 800-247-9145.

[9]http://www.nsaspeaker.org, or call 602-968-2552. Ask for a copy of their free membership directory.

There are good reasons why otherwise savvy companies don't know enough about their competitors. Most people who have been assigned the task of gathering competitive intelligence don't look forward to the job. They feel it's a painful, long, drawn-out, pointless process. They don't know how to start, where to go, whom to call, or what to ask. Or they may be concerned about the ethics of posing as a potential customer.

Gathering competitive intelligence is actually fun, easy, and can make you a hero in your own company. Call each of your competitors, and simply ask the receptionist, "I was wondering if you could help me with some information? Could you send me a copy of your (catalogue, brochure, price list, presentation materials, samples, etc.)?" Collect these materials in a ring binder, and use them to review your competitors. You'll avoid common mistakes, and you won't be doomed to repeating the failures of your predecessors. Your well-thought-out plan won't be shot down, because you can demonstrate that you know what the competition is doing.

Chapter 6

Controlling
Interruptions

If making outbound sales calls represents only a part of your workday, you must discipline yourself and others not to interrupt you during this mission-critical activity. Guerrillas control their interruptions to maximize output. Interruptions take several forms. Here's how to manage them.

■ STANDING MORNING MEETINGS

Use a single, 10-minute meeting to collaborate with staff and colleagues, distribute tasks, update company news, and set the schedule for the day. Everyone stands for the meeting.

■ SACRED HOUR

Set aside a single hour per day, such as from 7:00 to 8:00 A.M., when no meetings, visits, or conversations are permitted. This is your sacred hour to plan your day, prepare your work, and accomplish critical tasks.

A company in Colorado instituted this policy, and the union leadership went ballistic. "How *dare* they try to impose an hour of silence on our members." By the time the protest came up for arbitration, the rank and file were saying, "We love this! We're getting more done in that one hour than in the whole rest of the day!" Of course, the protest was hastily withdrawn.

■ CLOSE THE DOOR

If you have a door, close it. People will assume you're either busy or out. Schedule a time when you're off-line to have your door open for people to visit you.

■ FACE THE WALL

If you live in the world of partitions and cubicles and don't have a door, arrange your workspace to face away from the door.

■ CLINIC TIME

Open-door policies have killed productivity. Having access to managers creates team spirit, yet always having access to managers creates chaos.

Set aside a clinic time when all are welcome to come visit and discuss their issues. "You're welcome to come visit me and talk about *anything* you want, at *any* time, as long as it's between 3:00 and 4:00 P.M." Insist that people only visit you then. Many issues will resolve themselves before clinic time rolls around.

■ BY APPOINTMENT ONLY

When people drop in, say, "I'm working against a deadline. Could you come back and see me at 3:00 P.M. today?"

■ INTERRUPTION LOG

Track interruptions with a simple log. Record when you're interrupted, who interrupts you, and the nature of the interruption. You'll quickly identify your key interrupters and can then create a strategy for reducing or eliminating the interruptions.

■ BLURTING

These interruptions are self-inflicted. You glance up when someone walks by your door and say, "Hihowareya?" Then they stop and tell you. Now you've lost five minutes just listening to prattle about last night's TV shows. Resist the temptation to glance up when someone walks by your desk. Wait until they demand your attention before granting attention.

■ BIO BREAKS

When you take a break for biological needs, if you're stopped in the hall, say, "I've got to get back to a call. Can we talk this afternoon?"

Managing Pressure and Stress

Most people have about four good hours of telephone work in them per day. Guerrillas maximize their effectiveness by managing the pressure and stress of responding to customers or making outbound calls.

■ MUSIC

Music can help manage your mood, boosting you up when you're feeling down. What's the best music to listen to while you work? Whatever you like, be it Bach, the Beatles, or Garth Brooks. Keep the volume low enough so that your customers can't hear. Headset adapters are available that let you listen to music while you're off-line and automatically switch off when you're on a call.

■ MOISTURE

Water has healing properties. Drink lots of pure water. Dehydration will cause you to fatigue quickly and elevate the risk of losing your voice. Other ways that water can reduce stress: wash your hands and face, moisten and comb your hair, take a hot bath or shower. The sound of water helps you relax: sit by a fountain or stream, watch an aquarium, listen to a recording of ocean surf.

■ MOVEMENT

Walk, run, dance, stretch, move! Exercise is most beneficial in the morning when it revs up your metabolism for the whole day. Stress builds up muscle tension, particularly in the neck, shoulders, and lower back. Stand and do this series of stretches: reach your hands up to the ceiling, up, up, up. OK, now reach out to the walls, out, out, out. OK, now bend and touch your toes, bend, bend, bend. There. Doesn't that feel better? During your break, don't sit. Walk!

■ MASSAGE

Trade shoulder rubs with a coworker. Relax calves and legs by working them against a foot roller or a bag of marbles on the floor. Treat yourself to a massage after a particularly stressful week.

■ MEDITATION

Sit quietly and reflect. Recall a favorite beach or mountain meadow. Take your mind off work, and recharge your spirit. Take quiet time to reflect, think, stare out the window, and consciously coast for a while. Close the door, redirect the calls, and take a cat-nap. A rest as short as 10 or 15 minutes can be very refreshing.

■ MENU

Be aware of what you eat. Two items in most diets that compound stress are caffeine and refined sugar. Caffeine triggers the release of adrenaline into your bloodstream. If you're tense, a cup of coffee may increase the sense of stress. Refined sugar tends to drive your insulin levels up. In a short while, your blood sugar will fall, making you feel uncomfortable, adding to your stress levels. Your body depends on the fuel you feed it. When you select quality foods, there's no stress in digestion. When you choose over-refined foods, your body is under stress to extract the nourishment. If you have a stressful position, the better the quality of the food you eat, the easier it will be for you to manage stress.

■ MIRTH

Read the comics. Have fun. Laugh. It releases powerful brain chemicals that stimulate creativity, relaxation, and regeneration. Check the Internet for the joke of the day. Fax cartoons to coworkers. Swap funniest-customer-of-the-day stories.

Chapter

Your TeleSelling Voice

Think as the wise men do, but speak as the common man.

—ARISTOTLE

■ HOW TO TALK ALL DAY AND STILL SOUND GREAT

A properly produced voice should not tire or lose volume or intelligibility however much it is used, except in circumstances that interfere with proper voice usage, such as mental or physical exhaustion, emotional trauma, or the type of severe cold caused by a virus that attacks the vocal cords.

—DR. MORTON COOPER[1]

Don't you love listening to a person with a nice voice? A great-sounding voice is not deep, but resonant. A voice that's forced deep damages the vocal cords and creates the subconscious impression that the speaker is a phony.[2]

---

[1]Cooper, Dr. Morton. *Change Your Voice Change Your Life.* New York: Harper & Row, 1984. p. 116.

[2]Mayer, Lyle V. *How to Sound Like a Million Dollars.* New York: Walker and Company, 1986.

56

The secret is to speak in your natural range. The best way to do this is to say, "Umm-hummm, one." Your pitch when you say, "one," is at your natural resonance. Other words to test your natural resonance are: hello, really, beautiful, right, ready, no, go, do.[3]

Here's an exercise that lets you use your entire oral anatomy: tongue, teeth, jaw, and lips. The fun part of this exercise is that you get to open a bottle of wine. Place the wine cork between your teeth. Then practice exaggerating your mouth movements by speaking as clearly as you can while holding the cork between your teeth. Do this for five minutes. Now remove the cork, and notice your improved articulation.[4]

➤ No Put-on

When speaking on the phone, people sometimes put on a special phone voice. Don't! Talk to your customer the same way you would over a cup of coffee. A put-on voice creates a barrier.

➤ Breathy versus Too Tight

Avoid the breathy, Marilyn Monroe voice. Although it may sound sexy, it flattens the voice and weakens your authority. A breathy voice sometimes becomes unintelligible. Your customer can hear that you're speaking, but they may not understand what you say. When your customers don't understand you, they subconsciously devalue who you are.

A breathy voice can damage your vocal cords. With the air escaping through them, the vocal cords are loose and out of control. With this loss of control, the cords bang together and become irritated. Even a few minutes of breathy voice can cause damage that will take a day or two to heal.

At the opposite end of the spectrum is the too-tense voice. Think drill sergeant screaming. Yes, you can be loud all day, but a too-tense voice is rough and grating, sounds pushy, and creates distance. Guerrillas want a relaxed-sounding voice that's not overly tense.

---

[3]Cooper, Dr. Morton. *Change Your Voice Change Your Life.* New York: Harper & Row, 1984. pp. 22–7.

[4]From the audio series *Acting Skills for the Real World.* For more information, contact our speech coach Sarah Reeve at 800-REEVES1.

➤ Nasal versus Denasal

A nasal sound, such as -*ing,* is important for clearly pronouncing words containing *n, m,* or *ng.* If nasal sounds are used for pronouncing other syllables, the speaker appears less intelligent, whiny, and irritating. Think country music singer. At the opposite spectrum is the completely denasal voice. Think Rocky Balboa. Guerrillas who use a mostly denasal voice sound intelligent and interesting.

➤ Frontal versus Throaty

A frontal voice produces the sound at the tip of the tongue and teeth. Think Church Chat Lady: clear, precise, prissy. A throaty voice uses the back of the throat instead of teeth and tongue. This sounds like a local hick and reduces credibility. Think Goofy or Gomer Pyle. Guerrillas select a voice that uses their entire mouth, teeth, and tongue.

➤ Muffled versus Orotund

People who speak with a muffled voice don't move their lips. They're hard to understand and are judged to be imprecise or lazy. An orotund speaker uses their entire oral cavity to create a rich and resonant sound. Consider the deeply resonant voices of Orson Wells, Richard Burton, or James Earl Jones.

➤ Up Pitch versus Down Pitch

Traditionally, English speakers end a questioning sentence by raising the pitch. Recently, it's become popular to end all sentences with the pitch up. This unconsciously signals uncertainty and insecurity. Guerrillas end sentences with the pitch down to convey confidence and knowledge. You can also increase your authority by asking questions ending with the pitch down.

Shouting doesn't have to do with volume as much as it has to do with raised pitch. When you raise the pitch of your voice, you'll sound like you're shouting.

For maximum comfort and vocal variety, start a sentence with your pitch down, move the pitch up at the most important words, and decline the pitch until reaching the end of the sentence.

➤ Flat versus Thin

A flat voice is low pitched with little variation. Think Eeore from *Winnie the Pooh.* It conveys the impression that the speaker is depressed, unexcited, and bored. A thin voice is high pitched, like Betty Boop. It conveys the impression that the speaker is flighty, uneducated, and powerless. Select the right pitch for your physiology.[5]

➤ Rate

Speak at a speed of 150 to 180 words per minute, with 160 words per minute being ideal.[6] Measure this by recording your conversation and counting the words spoken in one minute. People can think at speeds of 400 to 500 words per minute, so you'll have to say things that prospects find interesting, or they'll start mentally working on their vacation plans.[7]

➤ Pauses

When you listen to the radio, notice that disc jockeys hate dead air; they never let a second go by without saying something. Well, you are not a disk jockey. Pauses are powerful TeleSelling weapons. Pause to let your customer think. Pause to underscore an important point. Pause to add drama and to heighten suspense. Your pauses will sound much shorter than they feel, so let them go on for a bit longer than you think they should.

➤ Vocal Energy

Guerrillas match the energy of their customers and then move it up just one step. Here's how to practice. Have a normal conversation with a friend. On an energy scale of one to ten, calibrate that at five. Now, move that energy up to a six. Feel the difference a slight increase in energy delivers? Guerrillas are sensitive to their customers and always deliver the appropriate vocal energy.

➤ Dynamic Range

Dynamic range is the change in volume available to you, and it can swing from the quietest whisper to the loudest shout. Guerrillas understand the wide range available, and they use that

---

[5]For a free audio tape of this section, *The Guerrilla's Power Selling Voice*, illustrating the voices and exercises, call 800-247-9145.

[6]Fairbanks, Grant. *Voice and Articulation Drillbook*. New York: Harper & Row, 1960. p. 115.

[7]Pike, Robert W. *Creative Training Techniques Handbook*. Minneapolis, MN: Lakewood Books, 1989. p. 34. 612-829-1954.

range to create the greatest impact. Some telephone trainers teach that you should start the conversation with excitement and enthusiasm. If one comes on strong at the beginning of the conversation, the only way the energy level can go is down. Start out near the middle of your dynamic range, and move up and down through it. Move up to emphasize; move down to transfer control to your customer.

■ KEEP YOUR VOICE HEALTHY

➤ Let the Phone Do the Work

Don't shout or strain your voice on the phone. Let the microphone do the work for you. If you aren't being heard, adjust the headset microphone closer to your mouth or turn up the sensitivity. Or hang up and call back, this time with a better connection.

➤ Drink Water

When you speak, you lose a pint of water per hour. With that kind of fluid loss, you'll become fatigued and develop a hoarse voice within a few hours. Avoid caffeinated beverages, such as coffee, tea, or colas, which tend to dry out your voice. Avoid carbonated beverages as well. You don't need the sugar, and the carbonation will make you burp. Keep sipping at water throughout the day. For optimum health and extra flavor, add a little fresh lemon.

➤ Wash Your Hands

Wash your hands before you start your shift. The most common source of viral and bacterial infection comes from your hands. You'll be touching your face, rubbing your eyes, and licking your fingers to turn pages. Wash and you'll reduce your chance of getting sick or affecting your voice.

➤ Avoid Throat Clearing

Throat clearing causes your vocal cords to bang together, bruising them and causing damage. To avoid damage, hum before clearing your throat. Sipping water with lemon can help.

➤ Never Scream

You can permanently damage your voice by screaming. This is most likely to happen at sporting events, concerts, or nightclubs. When you go to the ball game, let the other fans scream and shout. Save your voice for work. Learn to whistle loudly instead.

➤ Don't Compete with Loud Noises

If you're talking to someone and a jet flies over, stop, point up, and wait for it to pass. Save your voice for your customers.

➤ No Smoking

Smoking irritates your vocal cords and increases the likelihood that you'll cough and clear your throat. If you make your living with your voice, don't smoke.

➤ Diaphragm Breathing

Breathe from your diaphragm instead of your shoulders. Try this. Put one hand on your stomach, the other on your shoulders, and breathe in. Your hand should move out, and your shoulders shouldn't move at all. Breathing with your diaphragm gives you the best vocal control, range, and variety.

➤ Danger Signs

If you have excessive throat clearing, coughing, regular voice fatigue, or chronic hoarseness, see your doctor. These could indicate something that, left unchecked, could result in the loss of your voice.

■ HOW TO WARM UP YOUR VOICE

Just as athletes warm up before they play, guerrillas warm up their voices and bodies before hitting the phone. Here are some exercises that do the trick.

➤ The Cat and the Lion

This exercise simultaneously loosens up your face and vocal cords. Make a tight prune face, and squeak out high-pitched cat-like sounds. "Mew-mew-mew-mew." Now make a large lion face, and make low lion-type sounds. "Grrowelllll." Alternate five times.[8]

---

[8]Grassburg, Lynn. Speech, 1994. 303-331-2737.

➤ The Motorboat

With this exercise, you bring blood to your lips and warm up your vocal cords. Make the sound of a motorboat with your lips and voice, just like you did when you were a kid playing in the sandbox. Alternate between the low, engine-idle sound and high, revving sounds. Continue revving for 30 seconds.

➤ A-E-I-O-U

The exaggerated vowels warm up the muscles of your face so that you can speak with distinctness and clarity. Say the vowels while really exaggerating your mouth. Repeat five times.

➤ A Good Yawn

A couple of good yawns warm up your jaw muscles.

➤ Jiggle Your Jaw

Let your jaw hang slack, and move it around with your hand for 10 seconds.

➤ Stick Out Your Tongue

Limber up your tongue. Stick it out and wiggle it for 15 seconds. Be careful who's watching!

■ WARM UP YOUR BODY

Get your body ready to work, too. Here are some exercises to get you in peak condition.

➤ Tense and Relax

Tense and then relax your muscles to get warmed up. Hold the tension for a count of five, then relax for a count of five. Start with your face, then shoulders, then stomach, then arms, then hands, legs, and feet.

➤ Shake It!

Shake your hands for ten seconds. Give them a good shake, yet not so hard that you get hurt. Now shake your feet, one at a time. Shake your legs, one at a time. Now the blood is flowing!

➤ Tai Chi

This Eastern martial art is wonderful for getting your body warmed up and under control. Check out an instructional video from your library to learn more.

■ BE UNDERSTOOD

Here's a list of the words people commonly mumble. Guerrillas pronounce them with extra care to avoid misunderstanding.

➤ Mispronounced Words

Commonly mispronounced words include:

Axe for ask
Faks for facts
Gimme for give me
Hep for help
Nuc-u-ler for nuclear
Pit-shur for picture
Wanna for want to

➤ Dropping Plosives

A plosive is any sound that causes air to forcefully leave the mouth. Without the plosives, language becomes hard to understand, and the speaker sounds uneducated and unsophisticated. Avoid these!

b—*pro'ly* for probably
d—*ol'* for old
g—*runnin'* for running
k—*dar'* for dark
p—*lam'* for lamp
t—*liddle* for little or *hones'* for honest

➤ Sliding Glides

A glide is a verbal sound that you dwell on longer than the others. Dropping a glide sounds uneducated and unsophisticated.

l—*fi'm* for film, *he'p* for help, *E'vis* for Elvis
r—*wate'* for water, *fou'* for four
w—*oo-ell* for well

➤ Speaking Naturally

Use contractions naturally. Contractions have an easy, flowing, informal sound that's important to the guerrilla approach. For example, say these words and listen to the difference:

I am	I'm
You are	You're
We will	We'll
They are	They're
Let us	Let's

Being informal does not mean being sloppy. And just because informal speech doesn't follow all the rules of grammar, it doesn't mean that you can make mistakes.

➤ Avoid Slang

Although contractions add to the naturalness and comfort of the telephone conversation, *slang* does not. In general, slang is irritating; using it detracts from your presentation. Avoid careless replies such as "Yeah," "Yep," or "Uh-huh" when what you want to say is "Yes."

Greeting Inbound Calls

Have you ever called your own office, and the voice that answers sounds like, "Hello, what the hell do YOU want?!" They don't *say* that, but that's the message that's transmitted.

A well-known chain of muffler shops discovered that nearly one-half of the customers who had called for an appointment were not showing up. Suspicion fell on the mechanics and the way they were answering the telephone. After all, they were busy; the call was an interruption of their work in the shop; their hands were dirty; they really didn't want to take this call. The company invested in a four-hour telephone skills training for every mechanic. In fact, today, you are not allowed to answer the phone unless you've completed this training. The no-show rate on appointments fell to just 17 percent.

Many companies spend thousands on marketing to get prospects to call and thousands on equipment and training to deliver their goods and services. And yet, every call is filtered through the least-trained, least-paid, least-respected person in the company—the receptionist. Guerrillas know that the person answering the phone is the first salesperson a prospect contacts; therefore, guerrillas train, motivate, and compensate the receptionist accordingly.

■ COMPANY AND NAME

Orvel was standing at the front desk of a hotel recently and listened in as the night-shift clerk answered the phone in a clipped, rushed breath, "Itsa flock duster day ud win um hardens odel this is on hold speed king ow mayai hell-poo?" After listening to this greeting three or four times and reading the promo card on the countertop, Orvel finally worked out a translation. The clerk was saying, "It's a Blockbuster day (referring to the free-video-rental-with-room-stay promotion) at Windham Gardens (the name of the hotel). This is Ronald speaking (his nametag). How may I help you?"

Whoever wrote that copy didn't realize what a tongue twister it was (just try to say it three times fast!), and Heaven help the poor customer who didn't have the slightest clue.

Our advice is to keep it simple. Let your caller know where they've called and with whom they're speaking. This is the classic, "American Amalgamated, this is Debbie."

■ NEVER THE SAME WAY TWICE

Scripted greetings are repeated until they become rushed and robotic. Encourage your staff to change the script around from call to call.

"Good morning, American Amalgamated, this is Debbie."

"Hi, this is Debbie at American Amalgamated."

"This is American Amalgamated. My name is Debbie. How may I be of service?"

"Good afternoon. You've reached the central switchboard at American Amalgamated. I'm Debbie. How may I direct your call?"

By changing up the time of day, company name, receptionist's name, and the offer to serve, you keep the greeting fresh and natural sounding, which projects a more friendly, professional atmosphere for the call.

■ TONE AND ATTITUDE

The tone and attitude projected should be, above all else, friendly and helpful. Put a smile in your voice. It's easier for a prospect to hang up and call the next number in the yellow pages than to put up with a surly service provider.

If this is a concern for you, call your own office and tape-record the conversation, then sit down with the offending individual and play the tape, giving them the benefit of a customer's perspective.

■ HANDLING HANDOFFS

One of the things that drive customers nuts is being handed off from one person to another. This is especially true if they've just told their whole story and then have to start all over again with someone else.

In an ideal world, the same person who answers the phone would handle the call all the way through. But things are seldom ideal.

When you do have to hand off a customer, ask permission to put them on hold, get the person you need on the line, and bring them up to speed, saving the customer the frustration of telling their story again and again.

■ ASK PERMISSION

Always ask permission before putting a caller on hold, and wait until they have a chance to respond. You don't want to treat them to, "Hold please! (click!!)" Tell them how long they can expect to hold. Avoid phrases like, "Would you hold just a second?" These things always take longer than just a second.

People will normally wait on hold about 20 seconds before becoming impatient, *unless* you tell them that "it will be a minute or two," in which case, they will wait up to two minutes.

If they're going to be holding for more than a couple of minutes, offer to call them back instead. "This may take several minutes. Would you like to hold, or is there a convenient number where I can call you right back?"

■ INTERNATIONAL CALLERS

When speaking with international callers, you really need to focus your attention. They may speak with an unfamiliar accent or use words that you don't understand, and they could respond differently than you expect.[1] The key is to speak slowly and pronounce your words clearly; give them time to understand what you're saying. A common mistake is raising the voice, as if shouting would somehow make the message more intelligible. Instead, slow down, rephrase, and simplify the sentence. And don't make jokes. Humor seldom translates as intended.

---

[1]A great resource for understanding international behavior is the book, *Kiss, Bow, or Shake Hands,* by Terri Morrison, Wayne A. Conaway, and George A. Borden. Holbrook, MA: Adams Publishing, 1994.

Chapter 10

Increase Your Caller's Satisfaction

Several years ago, we were hired to develop a sales-training program for the customer service representatives (CSRs) of one of the "Baby Bell" companies. These are the people who answer when you call the phone company regarding new service, a change of service, or billing questions.

Because they were answering more than eight million inbound calls per year, senior management decided that these inbound calls were a sales opportunity, and in January, they put the whole group through a sales-training program offered by another vendor. The session taught them to pitch ancillary services, like Call Waiting and Caller ID, using traditional high-pressure sales methods.

It backfired. Sales actually decreased, and by May, the unit was 28 percent short of their goals.

This makes perfect sense when you consider that these CSRs had a very high level of technical knowledge and an average seniority of 15 years. They were *very* good at serving customers, yet did not see themselves as salespeople and resented being recast into that role. The resulting role rejection[1] actually caused them to shy away from sales opportunities.

The approach we took was contrary. Instead of telling the CSRs how we thought they should do it, we modeled the best practices of their top performers.

---

[1]For more information on the psychology of call reluctance, read *Earning What You're Worth?* by George W. Dudley and Shannon L. Goodson, with David K. Barnett. Dallas, TX: Behavioral Sciences Research Press, 1986. 800-343-4659.

We divided the group of 65 CSRs into three subgroups, according to sales performance: the Sales Stars, the Sales Duds, and Everyone Else. Our premise was, "Let's document what the Stars do that is different from what the Duds do, then train Everyone Else to handle calls more like the Stars."

Next, we used the office's isolated observation room, which is designed for eavesdropping by supervisors to evaluate the performance of the operators. We then listened to over 100 hours of calls being handled by the Stars and the Duds (ignoring Everyone Else). We looked for the contrast between the behaviors of the two groups. As a result, we isolated behaviors observed to be the customer's *satisfiers* and *dissatisfiers*. For example, the Stars frequently used the customer's name in the conversation; the Duds did not. The Stars routinely reported on their progress, whereas the Duds hung silently on the line while searching computer records or updating information, leaving the customer in limbo. Conversely, the Duds would frequently leave a customer on hold for extended periods while performing tasks off-line, whereas the Stars used their three-way–calling capability to let the customer listen in while they worked out technical details with central switching.

Next, we redesigned the evaluation criteria used to evaluate the CSR's performance. Our goal: let's encourage the satisfier behaviors and discourage the dissatisfiers in five areas: courtesy, problem solving, sales attempt, clerical accuracy, and apparent customer satisfaction with the call outcome.

We created a new *Contact Evaluation* form that the supervisors would use to evaluate calls (Figure 10.1). We told everyone the plan and gave every CSR a copy of the form to post next to their computer. The game became, "Score as many points as possible on every call."

The supervisor awarded five points for every occurrence of each behavior, then totaled the points, subtracting dissatisfiers from satisfiers. The strategy was to drive the net score as high as possible. This avoided making people wrong, while gently introducing and encouraging the desired skills and behaviors.

On a simple, short call, a CSR might only score 15 points, whereas a long, involved call might score well over 100 points. The supervisor then granted a separate, subjective evaluation, together with suggestions for improvement, and would debrief the call with the CSR.

CONTACT EVALUATION

Customer Name _____ Rep _____

Observed by _____ Date _____ Time _____

Check ✔ as many items as possible. Award **5 points** for **each occurrence.**

Courtesy

	Uses customer's name
Unnecessary HOLD	Avoids HOLD
No explanation of HOLD	Asks permission to leave the line
	Acknowledges and thanks on return
Ten-second silent pause	Reports on progress
Uses company terms or jargon	Clear, direct explanation
Overexplaining (specify)	

Problem Solving

	Isolates problem quickly
Blame or excuse	Accepts responsibility
	Demonstrates active listening

Sales Attempt

No sales attempt	Increases customer awareness of products
Assumes need	Asks a qualifying question
	Asks for opinion of product
	Suggests additional products or services
	Offers to send demos
Inappropriate example used	Relates benefits to individual customer
	Attempts to answer objection
	Asks for the order

Clerical

No file update	Customer file updated
Poor notation	Complete notation
	Uses off-line time productively

Satisfaction

Avoidable callback required	Recaps contact and action commitments
	Customer offers gratuitous commendation
Customer mistreat (specify)	Closes properly
_____ Total don'ts	_____ Total do's
_____ × –5	_____ × 5

Subjective Rating _____ Net Score: _____

Suggestions:

Figure 10.1 Contact Evaluation Form.

Supervisors observed randomly selected calls over the next few months. The objective and subjective measurements reinforced the effective sales behaviors that we had isolated, and by October, the office had not only caught up the deficit, but had achieved 128 percent of its total sales goal for the year.

To control against the Hawthorn Effect,[2] we then installed the new system of observation and evaluation in a second office not involved in the original study group. Within two months, sales at the second office more than doubled.

This method of evaluating and training CSRs to sell ancillary services was subsequently adopted by the company systemwide.

■ EVALUATING YOUR SALESPEOPLE

➤ Dissatisfiers

These behaviors clearly created distance between the CSR and the customer. They are listed on the left side of the Contact Evaluation form and, in effect, generate penalty points.

Courtesy
Unnecessary hold. Puts the customer on hold when it could have been avoided, or to avoid being distracted by the customer's conversation.

No explanation of hold. Puts the customer on hold without explaining why it was required.

Ten-second silent pause. Lets the conversation stall, allowing more than ten seconds of dead air.

Uses company terms or jargon. Uses unspecified acronyms or insider terminology that the customer is not likely to understand.

Overexplaining (specify). Offers the customer background details that are not relevant to solving their problem. Document the example.

---

[2]The psychological principle that any behavior that is being observed will tend to increase in frequency.

Problem Solving

Blame or excuse. Blames another department, or worse yet, the customer, for the problem. Using phrases like, "That's not my department," or "We have no control over the weather," or "You should have called us sooner."

Sales Attempt

No sales attempt. Customer service representative didn't even try, conceding that in some cases it may not be appropriate to attempt a sale.

Assumes need. Selling blind. Suggesting products or services without asking lifestyle questions to establish that this customer has an application for this product.

Inappropriate example used. Illustrates an application for a business customer using a residential example or vice versa.

Clerical

No file update (six months). Customer records that are more than six months old should be updated while the customer is on the phone.

Poor notation. Uses acronyms or uncommon abbreviations in customer records. If the supervisor can't make sense of the notation, neither will the next CSR who works with this customer.

Satisfaction

Avoidable callback required. Customer service representative has to call the customer back to complete the transaction, because something was missed the first time around.

Customer mistreat (specify). Anything interpreted as rude, brusque, or condescending to the customer. Supervisor must specify verbatim what was said and explain why they felt it was inappropriate.

➤ Satisfiers

The satisfier is often the opposite of the dissatisfier, but not always. These behaviors are listed on the right side of the Contact Evaluation form and generate positive points. Also notice that there are many more opportunities to generate positive points than negative points.

Courtesy

Uses customer's name. "Thank you for calling, Jane," or "Yes, Bill, I can help you with that."

Avoids hold. Completes the call without putting the customer on hold.

Asks permission to leave the line. Before putting the customer on hold, asks, "May I put you on hold?" or "Would you mind holding for a minute while I check on that?" Waits for a response before proceeding. Better still, gives the customer the option, "Would you like to hold, or would you prefer for me to call you right back?"

Acknowledges and thanks on return. When returning to the line, says, "Thank you for holding," or "Thank you for your patience."

Reports on progress. Avoids dead-air time by frequently commenting on the action currently being taken, as in, "I'm reviewing your billing history now . . . OK, now the next page . . ."

Clear, direct explanation. Uses common terms that the customer understands.

Problem Solving

Isolates problem quickly. Probes and questions customer to isolate what needs to be done. Only proceeds to the next step after verifying what the customer wants.

Accepts responsibility. Uses "I" or "we" instead of "they," "them," "those," "they're," or phrases like, "I'm sorry. I apologize for the error. I won't be able to get a crew out there until Tuesday."

Demonstrates active listening. Accurately reflects, repeats, or rephrases the customer's request. "So if I understand you correctly . . ." or "So what you really need is . . ." or "So you were told that . . ."

Sales Attempt

Increases customer awareness of products. "Did you know that we also offer . . . ?" or "Were you aware that you could . . . ?"

Asks a qualifying question. Examples might include, "Do you have teenagers at home?" "Do you ever work out of your house?" "Do you have a computer or fax machine?"

Asks for opinion of product. "What did you think about . . . ?" or "What has been your experience with . . . ?"

Suggests additional products or services. For example, "With two teenage boys in the house, you might want to consider installing a 'Teen Link.' This is an extra line with Call Waiting and Toll Restriction."

Offers to send demos. "Can I send you some literature about that?" or "We have a booklet that clearly explains how to use those features. Would that be useful?"

Relates benefits to individual customer. As in, "Since you sell real estate, being able to get your business calls at home after hours could be very valuable."

Attempts to answer objection. Creates new value in contrast to conceding the objection. Instead of saying, "Yes, it's annoying to have your conversations interrupted by Call Waiting," saying something like, "Some people do find Call Waiting annoying, until they get accustomed to it. You always have the option of ignoring the incoming call, and most customers like being able to make a call while waiting for another important call."

Asks for the order. Any attempt, no matter how feeble, to ask the customer to buy. "Would you like to try that today? Can I activate that service for you?"

Clerical

Customer file updated (six months). Reviews and updates customer information if it's more than six months old.

Complete notation. Notes make it clear to another CSR what was said and what was done.

Uses off-line time productively. Completes required clerical housekeeping between calls rather than at the end of the day.

Satisfaction
Recaps contact and action commitments. Reviews with the customer what has been done and what will happen next.

Customer offers gratuitous commendation. Award these points if the customer compliments the way the call was handled. "I really appreciate what you're doing for me," or "You have been very helpful!"

Closes properly. Says, "Thank you for calling."

■ PUTTING THE CUSTOMER IN CONTROL

People love to buy, but they hate to be sold. Salespeople know how we love to wander through a new store or browse the pages of a new mail-order catalogue. And when we make a purchase, we'd all like to think that we're the savvy ones who decided to buy. We don't want to feel pushed, cajoled, or bamboozled by an overpowering salesperson. This feeling comes from our need to be clever and in control of our decisions.

➤ "Have it your way."

Shopping malls, supermarkets, and hamburger restaurants cater to this very human need to *do it my way, at my own speed.* A guerrilla never forgets how much people need to be in control and how much customers want to take credit themselves for making the purchase. It can be argued that some stores have gone too far by not providing enough competent people to help customers.

Guerrillas give control back by letting customers set their own agenda. In the first telephone contact, guerrillas use phrases like: "I'm not really sure if you could use our product . . ." or "I'm not sure how I can help you; perhaps you could help me out?" In the initial sales meeting they might say, "Now, let's see, what were we going to talk about today?" or "What exactly did I say on the phone that got me this appointment?" By acting naive, the guerrilla puts the prospect in a helping mode, feeling they are in full control.

➤ **"Are we done?"**

A guerrilla offers to end the discussion whenever it appears that the product doesn't match the customer's wants, needs, or budget. A guerrilla might say, "I'm sorry, our best guaranteed delivery is 20 days, although I've often seen 10-day deliveries in your area. Can we work this out, or should I be on my way?" Put in those terms, the prospect's objection more often leads to compromise.

➤ **"What's next?"**

When a presentation is completed, guerrillas ask, "What would you like me to do now?" or "What do you see as our next step?" Because the guerrilla gives the customer the opportunity to ask for the order, the prospect gets all the purchasing credit, preempting buyer's remorse.

■ ARE YOU BEING POLITICALLY CORRECT?

We were entertaining neighbors for an evening of pizza and TV when one of those awful ads came on. You know, the ones with the fast-talking pitchman and those knives that will slice up a brick. "Call now," he said. "Operators are standing by."

I turned to my friend Gail and joked, "Standing by? Why are they standing? Why don't they give these women chairs?" She glared at me and asked, "So, what makes you think they're *women?*"

The next day, I heard about a listener who wrote to National Public Radio in response to their story about New York's St. Patrick's Day parade. The correspondent informed them that the term "paddy wagon" was based on the turn-of-the-century slang "paddy," a pejorative for "Irish." I'm sure the editors meant no offense, and from the letter's tone, I'd judge that none was taken, but the message is clear. There is a growing public sensitivity to the use of language in the portrayal of women, ethnic groups, and even the aged (or should I say "chronologically challenged").

As industry leaders, guerrillas must reflect this new sensitivity and pay close attention to these issues in our publications, newsletters, and particularly our marketing materials. When our language does not reflect social realities, we risk driving away potential clients and customers. Although you may not even notice the occasional slip, it can send a subtle sting. Worse yet, it reinforces obsolete attitudes. It would be far better to use socially (and linguistically) correct forms in the first place, such as "seniors" instead of "the aged."

Our error was perhaps the most common, often made unconsciously, of reinforcing sex-role stereotypes. Speak and write to show women participating equally with men. Women are computer programmers and engineers, and men are nurses, receptionists, and even operators-standing-by. Avoid occupational terms containing the suffix -man when the job could be held by either gender. A "businessman" is referred to as an "executive," "entrepreneur," or "manager." The "fireman," "mailman," and "policeman" become the "firefighter," "mail carrier," and "police officer." Instead of being approached by a "salesman," you'll buy from an "agent," "sales representative," or "salesclerk." And guerrillas never use "chair*person*" or similar forced compounds. The "chairman" is replaced by "the chair," "coordinator," "moderator," or "presiding officer."

Also, watch for the semantic exclusion of women when the intent is to mean adult human, male or female. In place of "mankind," refer to "humanity," "human beings," or just plain "people." The "best man for the job" may not be a man at all, but the "best person for the job." "Man-made" products are "synthetic," "manufactured," or "artificial." These differences may seem trivial to the "common man," but "ordinary people" will often take notice.

Another common trap is the use of the masculine pronoun when referring generally to a member of a mixed-gender group. Because of the shortage of common-gender, singular pronouns, speakers and writers often make this mistake by referring to students, executives, authors, and so forth, as "he." For example, your conference brochure might say, "A delegate can take advantage of many hotel amenities. *He* can enjoy golf, swimming, or tennis . . ." Some writers resort to "he/she" or "s/he," but guerrillas avoid these artificial and awkward contrivances. One solution is to pluralize these references: "*Delegates* can enjoy golf, swimming, or tennis . . . *They* . . ." Better yet, restructure the sentence to avoid the situation: "Golf, swimming, and tennis are all available right at the conference hotel."

Avoid demeaning references such as "lady lawyer." If the adjective specifying gender is inconsequential, leave it out. Use "attorney" or "counselor" instead. Never say, "I'll have my girl do it." Delegating to a "secretary" or an "assistant" is far more appropriate. Men, remember that women prefer the word "woman" to "lady," "female," "gal," or other slang. Even when trying to be polite, referring to a group of "ladies" can sound condescending. Use "women" instead, except in the context "ladies and gentlemen."

Finally, give some of your characters ethnic identities by using Hispanic or Asian names, but even here, avoid racial stereotypes like Jose the janitor, Vladimir the cabdriver, or Ahmed the convenience store clerk. Portray both women and minorities in positions of authority, responsibility, and power. Follow these guidelines, and your marketing materials will be more believable and more convincing. And you're right—it should have been "announcer," not "pitchman." No offense.

■ THE COMMUNICATION GAP BETWEEN MEN AND WOMEN

Men and women live in the same world, but when they try to communicate, it seems as if they're from different planets.[3] Guerrillas are sensitive to these differences.

Women make suggestions indirectly, whereas men make direct commands. Perhaps you've been in a situation in which the woman says, "Are you hungry?" and the man responds with, "No." He interprets her question literally and responds by directly answering the question. But what she's really saying is, "I'm hungry. Can we please stop and eat?" but the man didn't interpret it that way. That's why women frequently complain, "He just doesn't *listen* to me."

Men focus on report talk: news, sports scores, factual data. When men introduce themselves, they talk about their accomplishments and credentials. Women focus on rapport talk, they talk about family, relationships, and personal matters. They tend to be more reserved about discussing personal achievements. Guerrillas use this awareness to read between the lines and pick up subtle implications when speaking with prospects.

---

[3]For more on this topic, read *Men Are From Mars, Women Are From Venus*, by John Grey. New York: HarperCollins, 1992.

Chapter

Developing an Effective Script

The simple guerrilla formula for developing effective scripts is . . . use what works!

■ DEVELOPING SCRIPTED PRESENTATIONS

➤ The Right Words

When developing scripted presentations for use on the phone or in face-to-face sales calls, guerrilla managers never argue with results. They study the people on their team who are producing the most results and model presentations around them.

1. Select your top three salespeople, based on production.

2. Make an audiocassette of those top three people in action and transcribe the tape. It doesn't matter if they are selling over the phone or in person. Effective words will be similar.

3. Create a script using the words, phrases, and voice inflections of the top three. In that script, underline the phrases stressed by these top producers.

4. Distribute copies of the script to each of your other salespeople.

5. Ask those sales representatives to memorize the script, rehearsing until it sounds as though it's delivered straight from the heart.

It's okay for them to eliminate words that seem uncomfortable, substituting equivalent words; however, they should not edit words and phrases that are used by all three top producers.

The guerrilla approach to a TeleSelling script includes the actual words and phrases that will be used. It's 20 percent of your success equation.

A powerful script has three parts: the introduction, the body, and the close. In the introduction, you introduce yourself by name and begin to establish rapport. In the body, you present the logical (for the left-brained callers) and the emotional (for the right-brained callers) reasons that they should buy right now. In the close, you ask the person to respond positively to your offer. When creating your script, be sure that you know:

➤ What the caller should know, do, or feel after hearing your message

➤ Whether the caller could order using a credit card or charge to their account

➤ Whether the caller should ask for your brochure

People are more motivated by their need for security than almost anything else. In direct selling, you create that feeling of security by offering a guarantee or a trial offer. In TeleSelling, elimination of risk becomes even more crucial.

Your introduction is the most important part of your script; it's the first impression that you will make personally. Remember that your introduction is like the headline of a news story— it captures your caller's interest and makes them want to learn more. Write your close next, because it's your final goal. Create the body last, so that it leads right into the close. Edit the body copy mercilessly, making sure every word and phrase adds to the effectiveness of your introduction. If they don't, scrap them.

Yes, you should ask questions. Yes, you should respond to the answers. Yes, you should read over your opening line and see if it would excite you as a caller. Questions you might ask at the close include:

➤ Are these the results you want for yourself or your company?

➤ Shall we get started?

➤ May I sign you up now?

We know that it's tough to operate from a script if you're a free spirit; however, we also know that free spirits frequently fail dismally at TeleSelling. We've witnessed several tests of scripts versus outlines, and the scripts win every time. The winning combination for guerrillas is a potent script coupled with potent training. What they win is sales, relationships, customers' hearts, and profits.

■ KEEP TESTING

Watch your top producers. They will instinctively make changes when the script doesn't work as well as they know it can. Test those changes with a sampling of other sales representatives. Have one or two of your superstars test variations of the script to see if they can do better. Changing just a few words can increase sales by 10 percent or more.

■ THE RIGHT WORDS WORK

➤ Killer Words and Hidden Meanings

Some common words and phrases actually transmit hidden messages that undermine your authority and destroy your credibility. Because we use them unconsciously as a matter of habit, the effect is subtle and pernicious. Forewarned is forearmed.

Purge these from your TelePresence, both on the phone and in your correspondence with customers.

Killer Phrase	Hidden Message
Actually, honestly, frankly . . .	So, you've been less than honest with me so far?
Don't you think?	You want me to validate your thinking? What I think is more important than what you think.
Am I right?	You're not certain that you're right. You're trying to get me to agree with you.
Hopefully . . .	You're pessimistic about the outcome.

This is what we call . . .	Ok, just call it what it's called. I'm so stupid, I don't know what it's called.
The point is . . .	You're uncertain what the point really is. If you have to recap, you didn't make it clear.
I think . . . I know . . . I believe . . .	You don't *really* know, now do you.
I wasn't going to say this, but . . .	Well, what made you change your mind?
What I'd like to do is . . .	You're not certain I'll cooperate.

➤ Telegraphs

Telegraphs are preamble phrases commonly used to give your listener a preview of what you're about to say. Because they solicit confirmation in advance, they weaken your authority.

Killer Phrase	Hidden Message
This is funny . . .	You're afraid I won't find it amusing.
What a great story . . .	Oh really. Let's just see how great it is.
I might add . . .	Or you might not, it's not that important.
This is important . . .	Then the rest of your message is not important.

■ RULES OF POWER TALKING

The specific words we use shape the vision that people have of us. They affect how people will cooperate or not. The words that come out of your mouth also go into *your* ears and, thereby, shape your internal image of yourself as well.

Simple word substitutions can have a major impact on your sales, your personality, and even your business.[1]

Change from, "I'll *have* to . . ." to "I'd be *glad* to . . ."

Don't waste people's time by telling them what you *can't* do. Tell them what you *can* do.

---

[1]Walther, George R. *Power Talking*. New York: Berkley Books, 1991.

Tell yourself and everyone else what you *will* do, not what you'll *try* to do.

Drop preamble phrases like, "Let me be *honest* with you," or *"Candidly . . . ,"* or *"Truthfully . . ."* that undermine your integrity.

Instead of saying, "I was wondering if you *can . . . ,"* say *"When will you . . ."*

Substitute the word "challenge" or "opportunity" for the word "problem," and concentrate on exploring opportunities.

Substitute the word "invest" for "spend" when talking to someone about how you'll use your money, or theirs.

"But" is a conflict word that discounts whatever it precedes, as in, "I love you, but . . ." Use "and" instead.

"Disagree" is also a conflict word. Instead use, "I see your point. My position is . . ."

When you want people to cooperate, don't ask yes/no questions, use multiple-choice questions instead. Routine sounding phrases can communicate implicit subtextual messages that may make your prospect feel pressured or uncomfortable.

➤ "Talk to" versus "Talk with"

"Talk to" implies talking down to someone. Instead of saying you will "talk to" someone, say you will "talk with" them.

➤ "I Will Call" versus "I'll Be Giving a Call"

"I will call . . ." implies that the prospect has no choice and takes away their feeling of control. "I'll be *giving* you a call . . ." makes them a willing recipient.

➤ "Tell" versus "Let You Know"

The word "tell" can trigger a defensive reaction. People hate to be told. Instead, say, "I'll be giving you a call to *let you know* about . . . ," as if you are letting them in on a secret.

➤ "Inform You" versus "Share Some Ideas"

Avoid saying, "I'm calling to *inform* you . . . ," implying that they have done something wrong, or something tragic has occurred. A better choice would be, "I'm calling to *share some ideas* about . . ." People have been taught since childhood that sharing is good.

➤ **"See if You're in the Market" versus "Touch Base"**

When arranging to make a future contact, it is not helpful to ask, "May I call you again in three months to *see whether you're in the market* then?" That approach makes people feel pressured and uncomfortable. It is better simply to ask, "May I give you a call in three months or so *just to touch base?*" This soft-sell approach is almost never turned down.

➤ **"What I . . ." versus "Let's"**

When you say, "What I want to do . . . ," the listener's subconscious is likely to scream, "I don't *care* what this person wants; it's what *I* want that counts." Instead, use the inclusive form, *"Let's* go over this . . . ," implying cooperation instead of competition.

➤ **"What You Must Do" versus "What You Might Want to Do"**

When you say, "What you must do . . . ," "What you have to do . . . ," or "What you need to do . . . ," it can trigger negative reactions. The person thinks, "I don't *have* to do *anything.*" You are more effective when you make suggestions, such as, "What you *might* want to do is . . . ," or "Perhaps you may want to . . . ," or "Might I suggest that . . ." These guerrilla suggestions allow for a choice and relieve the pressure.

➤ **"Allows" versus "Makes It Possible"**

It is unwise to say that a product or service *allows* the prospect to do something, because *allow* suggests that permission is required. You'll obtain better results when you say that a product or service *makes it possible* to do something, using words that indicate that doors are being opened.

➤ **"Change Your Mind" versus "Reach Another Conclusion"**

You face a touchy situation whenever you impart information that might make people change their minds. Generally, people are admired for sticking with decisions. The challenge is to give them an opportunity to change their minds without feeling wishy-washy. If you want to give them a graceful way to reconsider, avoid saying, "Here is some information that will make you change your mind." Instead, say, "Here is some new information; perhaps you might reach another decision." Or, "You might draw another conclusion."

➤ "Scheduling Appointments" versus "Arrange a Meeting"

Do not say to a prospect that you wish to "schedule an appointment." The word *appointment* reminds people of a visit to the doctor, dentist, or lawyer. The word *schedule* may remind people how busy they already are, and they may react negatively to adding to an already full calendar.

Instead, suggest *arranging* the time to *meet* or *get together,* to *drop by,* or to *stop over.* Such additions are inviting rather than pressuring.

■ THE TEN MAGIC WORDS

Response! That's what you want when you TeleSell.[2] To get a response, you must first make sure your letter, postcard, or self-mailer gets read, and that the sales script is attention grabbing. The best way to make this happen is to use the right words—and use them strategically, logically, and with integrity. Here are ten magic words that work better than any others in creating long-lasting sales success.

➤ Free

Everyone on the planet, from the richest tycoon to the poorest pauper, likes to get something for free. People will spend money to get something else for free!

GreenIdea, an innovative software company, provides a program that allows a corporation to display its most important messages to employees every morning as soon as they turn on their computers. They offered a "**free** demonstration disk at your request." GreenIdea got an impressive 10 percent response to the letter—and made $130,000 in sales from the first 100 letters mailed!

---

[2] *10 Magic Words* is courtesy of David Garfinkel. Contact David at 415-564-4475 or garfinkel@aol.com.

➤ You/Your

After their own names, the words people most like to hear (or read) are "you" and "your"—especially in phrases and sentences that offer them a benefit they want.

SportGems, a sports memorabilia company, wanted to attract buyers from major retail chains to its trade show booth. "Come by because you have reserved in **your** name a beautiful football-shaped clock ready for engraving." As a result, the company got an $80,000 order from one of the nation's largest retailers.

➤ Announcing
➤ Introducing
➤ New

These words all have a *news quality* to them. By putting them in front of other words, you are in effect trumpeting out, "What you are about to hear is *news!*"

For example, you might say right now you are learning "The **new** way to TeleSell so you can get all the business you want!" Just by using "new" as the second word, we have added immediacy to this phrase, and, at a subconscious level, we have made it carry all the urgency and excitement of *news*.

➤ Secrets

People are intrigued by secrets. What do you know that your prospects don't know, that could help them get more of what they want?

The word "secrets" can work in any business. Suppose you had a pest control company. You could use the teaser, "**Secrets** of keeping your restaurant's kitchen infestation-free." That would certainly get their attention and compel them to listen longer.

➤ How to

Though, in fact, it contains two words, the phrase "how to" functions as one. And it's powerful. Why? Because people are naturally curious about new ways to do things.

For example, a business that provides rapid Internet training could make this promise to busy executives: "Learn **how to** save time on the Internet. We'll show you in less than an hour."

➤ Guaranteed

If you have an unusual guarantee, you can get a lot of mileage by emphasizing it in your copy. And even if you only have an industry-standard guarantee, you will attract additional attention and increase your business merely by mentioning it.

How sure am I of this? To quote Men's Wearhouse Chairman George Zimmer, "I **guarantee** it!"

➤ Magic

It's a powerful selling word, because it romances the imagination of your prospects. And it works like . . . magic!

Compare these two offers:

1. The aloe solution to remoisturize dry skin
2. The magic aloe solution to remoisturize dry skin

Notice how much more intriguing the second headline is?

➤ Easy

Find something "easy" about what you sell. For instance, what's **easy** about doing business with you (there must be something!) or performing a household chore after your product or service is involved? With your answer in mind, lead your discussion with a statement emphasizing how easy it really is!

To sum up: You can use these words not only in your phone script, but in every piece of marketing copy you write. They're versatile . . . they're well known by your prospects . . . they're easy to use . . . and best of all, they're . . . *FREE!*

■ AVOID SUPERLATIVES

Think of words like "beautiful" and "exciting." The ideas are good, but you've heard them so often they've lost their impact. We're conditioned to tune them out. Another example would be superlatives, words expressing *extremes*, like "best," "highest," "fastest," "newest" (any word that ends in "-est" is a superlative), as are words like "perfect," "fantastic," and "outstanding."

Instead, convey what is *appealing* about your product or service. Is it efficient? Spacious? Convenient? What makes it that way? If it is beautiful, what makes it beautiful? Shape? Color? The way it's put together?

■ USE EVOCATIVE LANGUAGE

You can create vivid, enticing pictures in your prospect's mind by using evocative words. These are words that evoke or draw out the appealing qualities of your subject. By using evocative, descriptive language to complement factual information, you stimulate people's imaginations and, therefore, their desire for your product, service, or idea.

The exciting thing about using evocative language is that it allows for flexibility and individuality. There is no right or wrong way—there are just different ways. Everyone has slightly different associations with words, which means that the particular descriptive language you use will always be a little different from what anyone else might choose.

■ KEEP CUSTOMERS MOTIVATED

Sometimes, words or phrases that we use increase the distance between our prospects and ourselves and decrease their motivation to listen. Avoid these common mistakes:

Demotivators	Motivators
Make them stupid.	Make them feel clever.
Criticize them.	Praise them.
Tell them what to do.	Ask what they think they should do.
Make them feel threatened.	Make them feel safe.
Make them feel intimidated.	Make them feel powerful.
Use unclear language.	Present your case clearly.
Unfamiliar words.	Speak their language.

■ YOUR CALL GUIDE

A call guide is a carefully prepared script. It focuses on a step-by-step approach to dealing with eventualities that might occur during the call. Your entire TeleSelling team creates the best call guides. A call guide can help less-experienced salespeople be instantly successful. Computerized call guides are highly sophisticated sales tools, because they permit sales representatives to stay with the caller, no matter which way the conversation goes.

Your call guide provides clear and concise answers to normal questions and concerns, yet it is flexible enough to deal with the unexpected. A prospect might say, "You're too expensive." This opens a window of opportunity for the guerrilla, who may respond to such an objection by saying, "We can show you how the product will pay for itself in two months." Many objections are actually buying signals. When answered in the correct manner, these can lead directly to sales.

➤ Objection Buster

The best time to answer an objection is before it arises, the preemptive strike. While developing your script, brainstorm with your team to develop a list of your top ten most frequent objections, and then collaborate with your sales veterans to develop scripted answers, solutions, and resources that everyone can use. Include these branch responses in your script. The same technique can be applied to common complaints and problems that callers are likely to bring up.

Buy a flip-up page photo album, the kind with individual picture sleeves that can flip up and down to reveal the photos, that has one-eighth of an inch showing across the bottom of each individual picture sleeve. Write the name or text of each objection across the bottom edge of a three-by-five-inch card, so that when you slide it into one of the picture sleeves, you'll be able to see it. Put the answer to that objection on the rest of the card. If you need more space or want to include a diagram or picture, place another card in the sleeve right before, so you're looking at two cards at once. Now, when a prospect raises an objection, you simply scan the edges of the picture sleeves, find the right card, flip it up, and read the answer. Give this Objection Buster album to your sales staff, and watch sales soar.

This tactic instantly cures call reluctance. New hires and nonsalespeople won't be afraid to call, because they'll already have access to the answers to the hard questions.

Lead Management Systems

We said earlier that less than 4 percent of sales are closed on the first call. It takes an average of nine impressions to take a prospect from total apathy to purchase readiness. That's why *follow-up* is a critical part of the selling process. Guerrillas use a systematic and organized approach that lets them make the sale. Because there are so many approaches to follow-up systems, find one that works for you.

■ COMPUTER-BASED SYSTEMS

For the most effective sales follow-up system, a computer is the best choice. Computers free you to take care of sales without the concern of remembering commitments.

■ ARE COMPUTERS WORTH THE MONEY?

Sales and Marketing Management's seventh annual "Survey of PC Users and Sales" reports that almost two-thirds of the survey respondents say that they recoup their investment in sales force automation in *only eight months.* Firms with fewer than ten salespeople had the fastest payback, and firms with more than 100 sales representatives had the slowest payback. Twenty-three percent say they don't see the need to develop quantifiable measurements. Some used PCs to keep up with competitors, and others use them to give salespeople a more professional look. MIT's Sloan School of Management's survey of 400 of the Fortune 500 companies found an average 54 percent ROI on computer purchases.[1]

Inc. magazine conducted a fax poll as a follow-up to their "Guide to Office Technology" issue. Most readers reported that they depend on their computers, faxes, and other high-tech office equipment. Seventy-three percent asserted that their investments in new office technologies have absolutely paid for themselves in increased productivity, while another 21 percent acknowledged at least some productivity payoff.

We recommend a PC, preferably a laptop. Guerrillas buy their own, knowing that owning their own tools is part of their commitment to the sales profession.

There are a number of great contact management systems available. These programs allow you to create and manage a database of your customers and prospects. You'll track the important details, such as your prospect's name, address, all their phone numbers, secretary's name, birthday, important events, how to pronounce their name, and their E-mail address. You can track where the lead came from, so you can thank those who refer you business. You'll be able to identify if they don't want to be called by phone, so you can mail to them instead.

Contact managers offer call-tickler reminders, mail merge, broadcast fax, call reporting, forecasting, performance measurement, call statistics, and hundreds of other features to measure your success.

The difference between these programs will be how user-friendly they are, which features are most important to you, and how much they can be customized. Also, consider the local availability of training and support. Most contact managers, like ACT! and Telemagic, automatically dial the number through the computer's modem. Others, like Relationship Manager, have a custom-built library of letters that can print automatically for mailing to prospects and customers.

■ DUAL SYSTEMS

One hot trend is to have a full contact manager on your desktop or laptop computer, and a personal digital assistant (PDA) with

---

[1]Taylor, Taylor C. "Computers Bring Quick Return." *Sales & Marketing Management* (September 1993): p. 22.

the records and information you need for the current day and week. A docking station automatically transfers the data back and forth, keeping the two systems synchronized. We like the 3COM PalmPilot®.[2] It fits in your shirt pocket and allows you to stay on top of activities, and it eliminates the large, bulky, paper-based system. Also, it's easy to take notes with this pen-based entry system. Most important, it lets your entire staff stay up-to-date without lengthy meetings to synchronize paper records. Over 3,000 companies are writing custom applications for the PalmPilot.

■ DAILY PLANNER

Daily planners, such as DayTimer®[3] and FranklinCovey®,[4] are very popular. Your planner should include daily planning sheets, used in conjunction with a monthly planner, to track appointments and other commitments. Guerrillas keep at least two to four weeks of daily sheets in their planner at all times. When they add another set of daily sheets, they transfer needed information from the monthly planner onto the correct daily sheet. Create a customer and prospect section in your planner as well. This section allows you to keep important notes and dates, as well as names, addresses, and phone numbers.

■ INDEX CARDS

This system works well if you have a limited budget and have to get going right away. For a few dollars at your office supply store, you can get started with your first follow-up system. Buy three-by-five- or five-by-eight-inch index cards, a file box, and two sets of tabs: a set for the months of the year and a second set numbered 1 through 31. Staple your prospect's business card to an index card, stapling more cards as your records on the firm grow. Place the prospect's card behind the month or day corresponding to the date you want to call. A week before the first of the next month, transfer cards out of that month's section into the day cards.

---

[2]http://www.3com.com/palm.

[3]http://www.daytimer.com.

[4]http://www.franklincovey.com.

Although an index card file is the easiest system to develop, it's the most difficult to keep up-to-date and cumbersome to use. The problem with this system is that the information is limited, and it is easily neglected if not maintained daily.

■ BINDERS

Three-ring binders will work to keep up with clients and prospects. File sheets alphabetically with all of the vital information required for that particular account and notes taken during conversations. This system works best if you are working with less than 100 prospects at a time. Use a page of detailed to-do lists to complete commitments you've made.

Create preprinted blank client information sheets with your computer printer or at Kinko's. You'll manage telephone inquiries easily, comprehensively, and professionally. Include room for name, address, various contact numbers, a series of questions,[5] and lots of room for notes. Leave space for follow-up information. You'll have an at-a-glance look at what the prospect or client wants, what commitments you've made, and when to take the next step.

If you are not using a follow-up system that works, we suggest that you start using one right away. Remember, if your prospects recognize that you can't follow up to sell them, they will be certain you can't follow up to serve them after they buy.

---

[5]See the 37 Magic Selling Questions in Chapter 17.

Chapter 13

Whom to Call?

The people that you call will be the people you need to stay in contact with or prospective customers. When you speak with your customers or prospects with which you have a relationship, ask them, "What's the best way for me to stay in contact with you? Would you prefer E-mail, fax, regular mail, or an occasional phone call?" Then ask them, "What's the best number for me to reach you?" Often, you'll get a back line, lab extension, home phone, cell phone, or pager number.

Your best list is your customer list. Call the people who already know and love you. It's five to ten times more cost-effective to resell to an existing customer than to find and sell to a new customer.

■ WHO'S INVOLVED IN THE DECISION

Guerrillas understand that few purchase decisions are made in a vacuum without the decision maker consulting others. You've got to identify the players and contact them, or you'll be left out in the cold. Here are the people involved in a decision-making process, either directly or indirectly.

➤ Gatekeeper

The gatekeeper is the receptionist, secretary, nurse, administrative assistant, spouse, or voice mail. The gatekeeper answers the phone and guards the door to the rest of the organization. They are trained to say "no," and they don't have the authority to say "yes."

Salespeople usually treat gatekeepers with disguised contempt. Sure, representatives are nice to their face, yet many salespeople do everything they can to minimize the gatekeeper's power.

Gatekeepers, however, have great influence on the decision-making process, because they decide who gets consideration. More than one gatekeeper has killed a deal by mentioning, "They're real jerks. Are you sure you want them working with our customers?"

Guerrillas treat gatekeepers with deference and respect. Treat them as if they run the company, because they do. So, sell to them first. Let them know what you can do for their organization, what problem you can solve, and how you can make their headaches go away. Ask them for a favor, "Will you help me? I know that you know who's the best person for me to speak to. What's the best way for me to approach them? What drives them crazy?" Ask them when is the best time to call. Ask them when other salespeople usually call, so you can avoid those times. Ask them if you can call in advance to see what the decision maker's schedule looks like that day.

The gatekeeper is an incredibly valuable resource. They know the politics, and they will tell you things that no one else will.

➤ Influencer

The influencer is someone who has technical or financial knowledge about what is being purchased. An influencer can be someone who has successfully used your product, or has read good reviews about your products, or is skilled at analyzing your type of products. They influence because of their respected knowledge and wisdom.

The influencer can be a nurse, a technician, an engineer, a CFO, a consultant, or a spouse. You find influencers by asking, "Who else, besides yourself, is involved in making this decision?" Even if you think you've found the decision maker, continue to ask everyone else this question.

Once you've identified the influencers, ask them, "What process do you use to make your decision?" or "How will you know who's the best vendor?" or "What criteria do you use to make your recommendation?" Once you know their decision process and criteria, you'll know exactly what to show them, what to do, and what to say for a favorable decision.

➤ Economic Buyer

The economic buyer places the order, sends out bids, issues a purchase order, or is the end user. This could be a buyer, purchasing agent, CFO, owner, or spouse.

The economic buyer may be charged with getting the best possible price for what you sell, so they may bid you against your competition. All things being equal, the economic buyer chooses the lowest cost. Guerrillas ensure that nothing is equal. Buyers will almost always choose reliable delivery over lowest price. Win them over by illustrating that you'll deliver at a fair price.

➤ Decision Maker

This is the person who ultimately makes the final decision and is responsible for the choice made. They can say "no" when everyone else says "yes" and vice versa. Most salespeople are taught to find the decision maker and sell to them. Yet most decision makers are not influenced by salespeople. Decision makers are influenced by their staff—willingly or unwittingly. The decision maker will be most influenced by you when they regard you as a professional colleague.

Approach the decision maker with a summary of what their staff suggests. "Your staff has reviewed this product, and here are their comments." Have them review your product, and ask for their commitment. When the staff is on your side, the decision maker will almost always give you the nod.

➤ User

The user is the ultimate decision maker. Users can sabotage the purchase decision. Guerrillas invest time with users to understand their concerns. They then offer the decision maker solutions that preempt user issues and instill confidence in the ultimate success of the purchase decision.

➤ Spy

The spy is someone who, for reasons of their own, wants to see you succeed. The best spies are people whom you have served well at one place, and they have moved to a new location. They want you to serve them like you did before.

Guerrillas recruit a spy by seeking the advice of a non-decision maker. These people are flattered by your attention and will tell you things that no one else can or will.

➤ The Decision-Making Team

When you get all of the team pulling your direction, the purchase decision will go your way. If you miss even one member of the team, you can lose to a better-prepared salesperson.

■ HOW TO FIND LISTS OF NEW PROSPECTS

First, write your Guerrilla TeleSelling plan, and set your objectives. How will you know when you're successful? What will be your allowable cost per lead? What will be your allowable cost per closed sale? What will be your profits from the campaign?

Define your target prospects. Whom do you want to call on? If you've sold this product before, what are the characteristics of the buyers of this product? What are the demographics? Where do they live? What type of sales approach was successful in selling to these customers?

If you haven't sold this product before, what similar product have you sold? What success secrets can you borrow from that previous campaign? If you haven't sold anything like this before, ask yourself who is most likely to want to buy this, who can afford to buy this, and who can be motivated to buy this.

➤ List Brokers

Call two or three list brokers to obtain lists covering your target prospects. You can find list brokers in the yellow pages. The best list brokers are experts on specific markets. You don't pay extra for your broker's services, because the company who owns the list pays them a commission. A good list broker will make you money, because they will steer you toward lists that have a high success rate.

Pay top dollar for your lists. When it comes to lists, the more expensive the lists are, the better they tend to be. Lists of top decision makers that are clean and current are expensive when compared with lists compiled from the yellow pages. Most expensive of all are *hot lists*—lists of people who have just purchased products or services similar to what you sell. Your list will be the least expensive part of your campaign. Spend what you need to get the best possible list.

If list brokers are unable to provide the names of decision makers in your target market, you'll need to make calls into the company and learn whom you should talk to. Successful Tele-

Selling depends on speaking to the right people. Sure, it costs more to find out who they are, but the results are always consistently better and always more profitable.

➤ Associations

Consider using association membership lists. Birds of a feather flock together. Find out what flocks your customers belong to and use that association's list to find more customers like them. Although many associations will rent out their lists, you may have to join the association to use the list. Check Gail's *Encyclopedia of Associations* at your local library reference section for more information on associations.

➤ Wait until the Last Minute

Get your list only when you're ready to begin dialing, and only get as many names as you can call in the next 30 days. Business lists go bad at the rate of 1 percent per week. At the end of the month, 4 percent of the people on that list have moved on.

■ USING A DATABASE TO SELL

A database is a collection of information organized especially for rapid search and retrieval. A database management system manages the way in which a database is maintained and the method in which data is made available to computer operators. You can search the data fields to select market segments and succinctly target prospects. For instance, you can call prospects whose purchases exceeded a certain dollar amount last year. You can use the database to mail to customers in certain locations or industries. Database management converts your prized prospect and customer list into a gold mine that you can use to get more business.

And database management can go much further. All types of details about your buyers can be recorded and integrated with layers of demographic, financial, and lifestyle data from outside information brokers. This is called data enhancement. Knowing who received which mailing when; which prospect received a raise, or promotion, or got married; the right time to follow up calls; and who knows about company announcements—all have an impact on your sales success.

This information can then be used to understand your customers' buying habits. Guerrillas know it's profitable to truly understand how a certain prospect buys so that they can tailor their sales presentations accordingly.

Bank of America, one of the fastest-growing banks in the country, extracts customer data from bankcard, checking, and savings accounts. The information is then used to target mail, or telesell, new products and services.

■ QUALIFY AND TEST LISTS

Quality databases are accurate. All names should be spelled correctly, all corporate titles exact. Addresses should be checked, and account information continually verified. Ask your list broker for a sample of the list for you to test. Request an "n" sampling, in which every nth name is selected. For example, if there are 50,000 names on the list, and you only want to test 500 names, you'd ask for every 100th name—n equals 100.

Call the list, and test to see if the people you've selected are responsive to your offer. If not, choose a different list sample. Some guerrillas will take samples from four or five lists and test them simultaneously, moving to the best list as soon as it's identified.

Keep track of the number of nixies, the phone numbers that are disconnected or at which the person is no longer there. Most list brokers will refund nixies.

■ PRECALL LETTERS

Mary Pekas found a substantially increased success rate with cold calls when sending out a precall letter. She sent out handwritten notes to prospects (she paid housewives and senior citizens by piecework). The note simply stated that she would be calling them to ask a few questions. "If you do not want the phone call, please call and let us know, we'll honor your request," the note continued. Ninety-nine percent of the people called said that the note increased their willingness to take her call.

Part

II

Guerrrilla Tactics That Get the Business

Chapter 14

Opening Moves

■ PRECALL SALES MEETING

Set aside 15 minutes before you hit the phones to review your TeleSelling goals and objectives with your team. Let them know exactly what is expected of them and what you consider acceptable daily sales performance. Take time to refresh and review critical TeleSelling skills and procedures for lead management. Use a quiz-show game or other device to make the review fun and interesting. Award prizes for the right answers.

■ DAILY DEBRIEFS

Immediately after the close of the sales day, call a team meeting to discuss and review the day's progress. Measure performance by tallying that day's number of leads gathered, contacts made, and dollars closed. Discuss new information gleaned about your competitors. Announce any changes in your strategy. Finally, select a salesperson of the day. They get a trophy for the day or a small gift.

■ HOW TO ORGANIZE YOUR TELEPHONING FOR APPOINTMENTS

1. Set a specific time to call each day—preferably from 9:00 A.M. to 10:00 A.M.

2. Plan to call at least 30 people a day. Make a tally mark for each person you call so you know when you reach 30. If a person isn't in or even hangs up on you, it still counts as one of the 30. Thirty calls should result in reaching 15 people, which should yield eight set appointments. Make 30 calls daily, and you will get many solid appointments. The more practice you get, and the more you master these techniques, the more your ratio of appointments to calls will increase. Don't just call three people, stop, and think that you can't get an appointment. No one can succeed on a few calls.

3. Once you start your 30 calls, don't stop until all are done. These calls go fast if you don't stop to talk or go for coffee in between. When you get an appointment, dial another number immediately. There's power in calling for the next appointment immediately after closing one.

4. Always have preset appointments for the next day. If you always have appointments, then, when you're tired or unmotivated, you can't make excuses and spend the day at your desk. After you start talking to the prospect, you'll get energized.

5. Call back at the end of the day to reach all the people you couldn't get to in the morning. Maybe they were in morning meetings or take their calls in the afternoon. Call after the secretaries go home, between 4:00 P.M. and 5:00 P.M. or later.

6. Don't call during your peak selling time. From 10:00 A.M. to 4:00 P.M. is not the time to call. Be with clients then.

■ MAKE 1,000 EXTRA CALLS A YEAR

Before you get out of the car at night, program the first two calls of your next day into the memory of your cell phone. Do the same when you arrive at the office, programming the last two calls of the day so you can make them on the way home.

This is a particularly effective tactic for motivating you to make calls that you've been reluctant to make. By making them an automatic part of your commute, you'll make the time more productive and talk to people you otherwise wouldn't reach. That's four calls a day, 250 business days a year, and you'll make 1,000 extra sales calls a year!

■ CALL A CUSTOMER FIRST

Your first call of the day should be to a customer you've served well in the past 30 days. Ask them whom they've talked to about what they've just bought. Remember when you bought your last new car? For the next month, you drove the gang to lunch, showing your new prize to anyone who would pay attention. And some of your envious friends said, "That's nice! I need to get me one!" If your salesperson had placed one call, they could have sold another car.

Guerrillas go back within a month to pick up that easy business that's there for the asking, "Who has mentioned to you that they'd be interested in something like this?"

■ THE GOLDEN SELLING HOUR

Call between 9:00 A.M. and 10:00 A.M., their time. According to the American Telemarketing Association, you are five times as likely to reach your prospect on the first attempt than at any other time of day. Remember to adjust when calling across time zones.

Guerrilla sales managers never hold meetings between 9:00 A.M. and 10:00 A.M., because this is the prime, golden selling time.

■ CALL EARLY

If you call a prospect at 7:30 A.M. and you don't get voice mail, the boss, the CEO, or the owner is most likely to answer. The top officers are getting a jump start on the day before the rest of the crew shows up.

■ CALL LATE

Friday afternoon, most salespeople are off playing golf, giving up on the rest of the week. Yet the boss, the CEO, or the owner is still at their desk, knocking off that last project before heading home for the weekend. Their secretary is gone, leaving them available to take your call.

We've found Friday afternoons to be a great time to reach top officers, because there's no other salesperson competing for their time.

■ THE BEST TIME TO REACH YOUR PROSPECTS

Accountants: Standard business hours, except between January 15th and April 15th.

Bankers: Before ten in the morning and after three in the afternoon, Monday through Friday.

Clergy: Between Tuesday and Friday.

Dentists: Between nine and eleven in the morning, Monday through Friday.

Doctors: Before nine-thirty in the morning or after one-thirty in the afternoon, Monday through Friday.

Engineers: Between one and five in the afternoon, Monday through Friday.

Executives: Before nine in the morning, during the lunch hour, and after one-thirty in the afternoon, Monday through Friday.

Farmers: Between noon and one in the afternoon.

General contractors: Before nine in the morning, during the lunch hour, and after five in the afternoon, Monday through Friday.

Grocers: Between one and three in the afternoon.

Heads of businesses: Before nine in the morning, during the lunch hour, and after five in the afternoon, Monday through Friday.

Homemakers: Between ten and eleven-thirty in the morning, between two and four in the afternoon.

Lawyers: Between eleven in the morning and two in the afternoon, and between four and five in the afternoon.

Nurses: During the half hour before or after scheduled duty hours (usually 11 to 7, 7 to 3, and 3 to 11, these will vary from person to person). You might want to call the hospital to get more details on the shift schedules.

Pharmacists: Between one and three in the afternoon.

Teachers: Between two in the afternoon and six in the evening, Monday through Friday.[1]

■ SNAPPY ANSWERS TO STUPID QUESTIONS

Secretaries and receptionists often attend half-baked, half-day seminars on telephone skills in which they're taught to ask certain questions. Here are some answers to make your day.

Guerrilla: "May I please speak to Ms. Murphy?"

Secretary: "Can I ask who's calling?"

Guerrilla: "Certainly!"

Secretary: "Who shall I say is calling?"

Guerrilla: "I am."

Secretary: "Who are you with?"

Guerrilla: "Uh, actually, right now, I'm alone."

Secretary: "You're a real comedian."

Guerrilla: "Yes, I am. That's why my associates love doing business with me."

Secretary: "And what do you want?"

Guerrilla: "I want to talk with Ms. Murphy."

Secretary: "And where are you from?"

Guerrilla: "Originally, California."

Secretary: "What is the nature of your call?"

Guerrilla: "It's my job."

Secretary: "May I tell her why you're calling?"

Guerrilla: "Sure. You already know?"

Secretary: "Will she know what this is regarding?"

Guerrilla: "Absolutely not! Can she read minds?"

Secretary: "And this is regarding . . ."

---

[1]Pekas, Mary D. *Basic Telemarketing—Skills for Sales and Service Productivity.* Eden Prairie, MN: Paradigm Publishing International, 1990. 605-785-3971.

Guerrilla: "It sure is."

Secretary: "Ms. Murphy isn't available. Is there someone else you could speak with?"

Guerrilla: "OK. Who else is there?"

Secretary: "What *was* your name?"

Guerrilla: "Well, it *used* to be (maiden name), but then I got married, and . . . that's a long story."

Secretary: "Can you spell that?"

Guerrilla: "Yes, T H A T."

Secretary: "Can you spell your name?"

Guerrilla: "Since first grade!"

Secretary: "May I leave her a message?"

Guerrilla: "Sure. What do you want to tell her?"

Secretary: "And why *exactly* are you calling?"

Guerrilla: "It's about her order."

Secretary: "What order?"

Guerrilla: "My question *exactly!*"

Secretary: "Please tell me your name."

Guerrilla: "You first."

Secretary: "Would you like to leave a message?"

Guerrilla: "Would she like to call back?"

Secretary: "Are you always this difficult?"

Guerrilla: "All I did was call for Ms. Murphy! Is that difficult?"

■ HOW TO GET UNLISTED ADDRESSES

If your prospect has registered to vote, their address is a matter of public record. Check your voter's registration office.

■ GUERRILLA COLD CALLS

Guerrillas know that cold calls are made for two reasons: to find people that are ready to purchase but haven't made the decision and to start a relationship with a prospect, so they know you're ready when they're ready. Finding someone who's ready on the first call will happen less than 4 percent of the time; therefore, a guerrilla knows that closing sales with a single cold call is a bonus, not the goal.

➤ Guerrilla Prospecting

Guerrillas do thorough reconnaissance before calling a decision maker. Instead of calling and asking for an interview, they might call customer service (CS) and ask for help. The CS people can tell you about their biggest headaches, and they'll be more forthcoming than the purchasing agent.

Make friends in low places. The only person in the building with a set of keys that will open every door in the place is the janitor. Ask about what's happening, what's changing, and who's shaking. Ask how a company like yours might be able to help, and always ask, "Who else, besides yourself, will be involved in making the decision?" Sell end users first, then work your way up.

➤ Add Value in Advance

A guerrilla in Texas clips articles that may be of interest to executives of prospect companies; he sends them a clipping as part of a three-step prospecting system. "Enclosed is an article about opportunities in (topic). I hope you find it useful."

He follows up a week later with a letter and another article. "I hope you found the article about (last topic) of interest. Enclosed is a related item that you might find useful."

The third week he sends a third letter that says, "I'll be in your area on Thursday and would like to introduce myself and my firm. I'll be calling to arrange a mutually convenient appointment." Eight out of ten executives he calls agree to meet their one-way pen pal face-to-face.

➤ Not Your First Words

Openers to avoid when you're talking with people whom you don't know:[2]

How are things?

How goes it?

---

[2]Ibid.

How is the world treating you?

What's going on today?

What irons do you have in the fire today?

What's new?

What's the good word?

What's up?

How are you?

What's new in your world?

These openers can be used with people you call on regularly. When you know someone, you can genuinely care about how they are or what's new. If you don't, these phrases create a feeling of insincerity.

■ YOUR FIRST CONTACT

Unfortunately, people have built up a strong resistance to sales calls. As soon as they recognize the caller as a telemarketer, they are likely to hang up. There are two exceptions: if the person calling doesn't act like a telemarketer, and if the person or the company they represent has a right to be calling.

Guerrillas seek to *disqualify* prospects. You should only spend time with people who are likely to do business with you and who are receptive to listening to your message *right now*.

No one is sitting by the telephone, waiting for it to ring, hoping it's a salesperson. Seventy percent of all inbound calls interrupt something that's more important, which is why people screen their calls.

➤ Match Them

When they answer the phone, match their rate of speech and tone of voice. This will instantly reflect their state of mind. You'll know if they're pressured or relaxed, if they're angry or calm, if they're hurried or methodical.

➤ "Is This a Good Time to Speak?"

The next step is to find out if they are psychologically receptive to your call. Next, open the conversation with, "Is this a good time to speak?" Don't offer your name, and don't offer your company name. Just check to see if they can take your call.

You'll get one of three answers. The first could be a terse, "No!" Reply, "When would be a better time?" Do not try to push the call through. You can't lose what you ain't got, and you really don't want to talk to them if they're unreceptive. Better to take another shot at them another time.

If they blurt, "Tomorrow!" say, "Thank you," and hang up. Don't even ask if morning or afternoon would be better, they don't have time to give you that information. If they're more relaxed, you could ask for a specific time.

You might be thinking, what if I say, "When should I call back?" they say, "Never!" First, that's unlikely to happen. Second, no matter how brilliant your offer, the odds of you getting that business are low. Next!

When you call back you can ask, "Is this a better time to speak?" They'll remember you, even though they don't yet know who you are. Most likely, the response to "Is this a good time to speak?" will be, "Well, I don't know. What's this about?" This is good! You know they're busy. Guerrillas know that busy people buy things to make their life less demanding.

The third response might be, "Sure, what do you want?" Now you've got about 15 seconds of their attention.

➤ Tell Them Where You're Calling from

Let people know the town and state you're calling from. Some will have been to your town, others will know someone from that town. "This is Susanna Smith with The Guerrilla Group calling from Boulder, Colorado." People are more likely to accept calls that are long-distance. Immediately continue to the next step.

➤ The Nature of Your Call

The next step is to disqualify those that don't buy things over the phone. Guerrillas use the ultimate sales weapon—the truth. Tell them *why* you're calling. Say, "This is a sales call."[3] The last thing people expect from a salesperson is for them to *admit* that it's a sales call. Once you admit you're calling to sell, one reply you might hear is, "I'm not interested!" These people aren't rejecting you; they just don't do business over the phone. Next

---

[3]The FTC now *requires* that certain businesses identify the type of call or face stiff fines. See the whole text of The Federal Trade Commission Telemarketer Guidelines at http://www.ftc.gov/bcp/telemark/out.htm.

dial. Most likely, they'll say, "What are you selling?" You just got ten seconds of their attention.

➤ Your Ten-Second Commercial

Now, *disqualify* them for your goods or services. Give them a ten-second overview of the common problems and headaches that you solve for your customers. This starts with the words, "We're the people who help organizations/companies/families like yours . . . ," then fill in the blank with the solutions to the biggest headaches you solve for your customer. Focus on the problem you solve, not the product you deliver. Guerrillas deliver solutions, not stuff. End the question with, "Who is most interested or is responsible for this?"

For example, at The Guerrilla Group, "We're the people who help organizations like yours increase their sales and profits with unconventional sales and marketing weapons and tactics. Who in your organization is most responsible for developing your sales team?"

If you were a lawyer, you might say, "We're the people who help companies like yours keep more of their money, reduce their legal risks, and get what's rightly theirs. Who in your company is most interested in that?"

If you were selling insurance, you might say, "We're the people who help families like yours make sure that there's enough money to pay the bills and keep the family together, in the event of a disaster or emergency. Who in your family should I be speaking with?"

If you're collecting donations, "We're the people who help flood victims rebuild their lives more quickly, so they can get back to work as proud and productive citizens. Who should I talk to about helping us with that?"

➤ Ask for Help

Call and ask, "I understand that you're the person who can help me with information about your company." Most people are willing to help when asked.

■ I'M BUYING!

One guerrilla who recycles laser toner cartridges calls and says, "I'm not calling to sell you anything. I'm calling to buy your old, used-up laser toner cartridges. Who do I talk to about that?"

The gatekeeper puts him right through to the right person, who is so intrigued that they agree to see him. In the meeting, he finds out how many toner cartridges they go through every month, how much they're paying, and if they would be willing to try a couple of his recycled cartridges in trade for their empty ones. They quickly become a customer.

■ DEALING WITH GATEKEEPERS

A gatekeeper is the first person an outsider contacts. They're one who cannot say yes and one who is trained to say "No!" Gatekeepers can be an executive assistant, receptionist, security guard, spouse, or voice mail. Many people ask us to teach them how to get around the gatekeepers. Yet guerrillas treat the secretaries and administrative assistants with great respect. By controlling access to the decision makers, they can stop you cold. Also, they can be tremendously helpful if you treat them right.

➤ Deliver Respect

Sell to them first. Instead of telling them who you want to see or what you're selling, let them know the problem that you can solve for their company. Ask the magic question, "Perhaps *you* can help me?"

➤ Get Their Name

"Hello, this is Christina Smith with The Guerrilla Group; I'm sorry, I didn't catch your name. Lori? Hello, Lori, I'm a specialist at helping companies like yours increase their cash flow and profits. I have some creative ideas for your company. Now, Lori, I don't know who is best for me to give these to, but I'll bet you do! Who's the best person for me to speak with?"

➤ Call Back to Say "Thanks"

"Hi, Lori, this is Christina Smith again. I just wanted to call and say thank you! You got me through to exactly the right person. They were happy to hear from me, and I wanted to tell you that I'm grateful for your help!"

➤ Send Them Stuff

Send flowers, candy, birthday cards, and thank you faxes. Treat them as if they are the most important people in the world. Show up for an appointment at the beginning of their workday with a box of cookies in hand. Say, "I got here early to beat the traffic. I guess I did! Here, these cookies are for you and the staff." Then strike up a conversation as you wait for your appointment. "Gee, there's an awful lot of construction going on around here. What's happening?" They'll tell you things the boss may not want you to hear.

➤ Seven Things to Do When You Can't Get Through

1. Send their boss a fax complimenting the gatekeeper on their efficiency. "Your assistant, Lori, is incredible! I wish that I had someone that able, bright, and tenacious working for me! Whatever you're paying her, it isn't enough. By the way, I have an idea that I think you'll find valuable. Would you allow me two minutes to offer you several ideas?"

2. Call early or late in the day. If you call at 7:00 in the morning or 7:00 at night, whoever answers the phone is likely to be a senior player. The boss will be there starting or wrapping up their day before the staff goes off duty.

3. Call during lunch hours. Often, a less-protective staff member will answer. This is also a good time to deliberately drop into someone's voice mail.

4. Ask if they would pass on a present to the boss. Guerrillas understand and use the influence principle of *reciprocity*.[4] When you give something to someone, they feel compelled to give you something in return.

5. Keep calling until someone else answers, then make your request. Gatekeepers get sick, go on vacation, or have to run errands. When they say, "I'll put you through," interrupt and say, "Before you do, what is their direct-dial number, so that I don't have to bother you again?"

6. Call asking for information on the company. "I need to find out some information about your company. Whom do I speak with about investor relations?"

7. Call and ask for AR. Accounts receivable wants to talk with everybody. Once they answer, say, "I'm sorry, I need

---

[4]Cialdini, Robert B. *Influence: The Psychology of Persuasion.* New York: Quill, 1993.

to speak with Ms. Taylor. Do I have the right department? Would you please transfer me?"

■ FINDING THE DECISION MAKER

There's nothing more frustrating than trying to get to the person who has the authority to make a decision *today*. We stress today, because you'll never become successful in sales unless you are able to get buying decisions, even small ones, from your clients on the day that you're making the call.

Often, the problem with finding the decision maker is that many people like to feel important, especially prospects operating out of an Ego-driven personality phase. They will often wait until the very last minute to explain that they can't give you the go-ahead until they've talked to their boss. Or, you've run into a potential customer, operating out of a Pleaser mode, who simply avoids making any decisions without checking with others on the team. Perhaps you've just met an Authority prospect who is compelled to strictly follow the rulebook and who has a company acquisition cycle of 30 days with approval by the VP of purchasing, even for inexpensive office supplies.[5]

What's a guerrilla to do? The answer is espionage!

➤ Who Was That Masked Man?

Check to see if the company has a Web site. Some organizations post an organizational chart. Check the date that the org chart was updated. It could be woefully out of date.

When you first contact any organization, ask whoever answers the phone, "Who's in charge of . . ." the operation or department you want. When the person says, "Mrs. Mary Smith is in charge of that," then ask, "And who does Mrs. Smith report to?"

"Tom Riley," and so on up the corporate ladder. Take careful notes, checking name spellings as you go. Now ask who is in charge of buying your product or service. If you don't hear a name that's on your list, ask who this person reports to, and so on, until you hear a name from your first list.

Now that you have a fair understanding of the company hierarchy, start at the top. Remember that the boss can always

---

[5]For more information on the Ego, Pleaser, Authority, and the other four personality phases of The Mind Map, read Chapter 4 of *Guerrilla Selling*.

refer you to the right person. "Hello, Mr. Riley? I'm not sure if I have the right person, but who in your organization is responsible for your print advertising? Who should I talk to?"

"That would be Mary Smith."

"Thank you, sorry for the interruption. Could you transfer me please?"

Then you can talk with Mary Smith and say, "I was just speaking with Mr. Riley, and he told me you were responsible for print advertising and that I should talk to you. Have I reached you at a good time?" Of course you have!

■ FOLLOW-UP CALLS

Imagine this scene: you are in your office working on a project your boss asked you to complete by the end of the day. It's taking longer than you expected, and there have been so many distractions. Your phone rings. It is a salesperson following up on some literature you requested. Your first reaction is to think of the call as an interruption and end it as soon as possible. A guerrilla overcomes this natural resistance by following these simple guidelines:

➤ Go Slowly

"Good morning, Mr. Johnson. This is Janice Dallas calling from Top Dog Security Systems." This opening gives the person you are calling a chance to switch their brains from what they were doing to participating in the conversation.

Words like "Good morning" and "This is" are fillers to help you slow down. Because the prospect's mind was elsewhere, their full attention is not on you. They need this slow pace to comprehend what you are saying. Breaking the opening into two or three sentences serves the same purpose.

➤ Give the Prospect a Headline

After your opening greeting, the headline helps grab the prospect's interest. Tell them the purpose of your call: "I'm calling to make sure you received the literature that you requested on the office security system you are looking for. It should have arrived yesterday in an orange envelope." Tell them what the package looked like. Notice that this headline recaps that they've asked for your information and assumes that they want to make a purchase.

➤ Let Them Think About It

Give the prospect a moment to think about the literature (or other actions they may have taken toward considering your products). You'll be tempted to fill the dead space in the conversation by talking, but you're more likely to get the prospect involved in the conversation if you give him or her a few seconds to think about what you have said and then respond.

About half the time, the prospect will say, "Yes, I got it!" The other half of the time, they haven't gotten to it in their stack of mail.

If they haven't gotten to it, ask them, "Would you like to see if it's in your in-tray, or would you like me to send you another package?" You're illustrating your responsiveness, even when it's not your fault. Almost all will volunteer to look for it.

➤ Ask a Series of Open-Ended Questions

If they have received the package and didn't have to hunt for it, assume that they've looked at the literature. "What did you like best about what you saw?" If they didn't look at it, they'll tell you so. Ask them when they'd like for you to check back. Better yet, ask about their decision deadline, or remind them of the special offer that expires soon.

If they did look at it and like what they saw, you're on your way to making the sale. Use a series of open-ended questions that focus on the prospect's needs, not on your product:

> "How do you handle security now?"
>
> "What do you like best about your current system?"
>
> "What do you like least about your current system?"

For details on questions to ask, see "37 Magic Selling Questions" in Chapter 17.

➤ Present Your Solutions

When you understand the prospect's needs, and the prospect is totally involved in the conversation, it is time for you to present your company and your products as the solutions: "I see, Mr.

Johnson. The big issue in your company is inventory shrinkage in the evening when the guard is off duty. Let me tell you how the Top Dog Security Model 1000 addresses that problem."

You now have everything you need to lead this customer to a close:

1. You got the conversation going by using an effective greeting and then giving a headline that told the prospect what your call was about.

2. You asked many open-ended questions focused on the prospect's needs, which expressed your interest in the prospect and gave you insights into the prospect's needs.

3. You offered a solution that specifically addresses one of the prospect's issues of concern.

■ MAINTAINING RAPPORT

Use the person's name during the conversation to control attention, increase rapport, and acknowledge the caller's identity. That doesn't mean you use their name in every sentence, but use it two or three times during your conversation and again when you part company.

Feel free to use caller's first names if they are your age or younger, unless local culture dictates otherwise. If your caller is obviously older than you, or if you're uncertain of their age, use the last name along with the courtesy title Mr. or Ms. until they invite you to use their first name.

If the name is tough to pronounce, take some time to find out exactly how to say it and how to spell it. Work together to make sure it's right. Your caller will be flattered.

On your notes, include a phonetic version of your caller's name. For example, if your caller's name is Stein, you could say *STYne* or *STEEn*. Write it out, and you'll be able to ask for the right person when you follow up. Some contact management software includes a special "Say:" field for this purpose. If yours doesn't, then add one.

■ CONTROLLING ATTENTION

If there is a sudden distraction, such as a loud noise, or if you hear a baby crying, or a phone ringing in the background, stop and comment on it. You may ignore the distraction, but your customer will not, and you will lose their attention. Comment on the distraction: "Wow, what was that?" or "Do you need to look after your child?" or "Do you need to answer that line?" Acknowledge it, showing your respect and concern. Then you can both return to your discussion.

■ BECOMING A BETTER LISTENER

Listening is a process of hearing, understanding, remembering, and observing what people are telling you.

➤ Hearing
Hearing is the physical process of having the sound waves reach your ears with enough loudness for you to recognize what your caller is saying. Make sure your environment is quiet enough and that the phone connection is clean and the sound is clear so your caller can hear you well. If not, say, "This line isn't clear. May I call you right back? Is that better now?"

➤ Understanding
Understanding is the mental process of grasping the ideas your caller is trying to communicate. The key is never assume that you know what the caller will say. Although you may have asked the same question and heard the same answer a thousand times, you never know when it might be different. You may know your answer, and you may have heard nine others answer the same way, but you don't know their answer. Don't assume anything. Repeat what they said to make sure you understand them correctly. Ask further questions to clarify important points.

Your caller doesn't *feel* understood until they *know* you understand. Demonstrate your understanding with questions that clarify what they've asked and by paraphrasing back what you've heard in your own words.

➤ Remembering
With all the activity going on and all the people you'll talk with, remembering details can be difficult. You intend to remember an important detail, and then you speak with someone interesting, your attention is redirected, and you forget that detail.

■ TAKE NOTES

The dullest pencil works better than the sharpest memory. It's critical to remember what your caller says so you can make the appropriate recommendation and take the correct follow-up action. You don't have to take extremely detailed notes, but you need enough documentation so that if another person picked up the caller's file, they could understand what happened.

Taking notes signals your prospect that you care, that you are attentive to detail, and that the information they're sharing is important. Always ask permission before taking notes, especially if the topic is sensitive. Ask, "Do you mind if I take notes?" This demonstrates that you respect that this may be an off-the-record discussion. If you use a computer terminal, draw attention to your note taking. "You can probably hear me clattering away here; I want to get this information in my notes." Or "Would you slow down a bit, you can hear I'm typing notes." Later, draw attention to them by asking, "According to my notes . . ."

Taking notes accomplishes five things:

1. You focus your attention better on what the caller is saying. You can't simultaneously take notes and think up snappy answers. Guerrillas know the snappiest answers will come from their notes.

2. Your caller knows you're paying attention and listening.

3. You have written details that you can use to resume the next call. ("Looking at the notes I took during our discussion the last time . . .")

4. When you have a record of the conversation, your prospect is less likely to change their mind. "Let's review our notes from our last conversation to see if anything has changed." Their review of your notes recommits them.

5. When people know they're going on record, they tend to speak with higher integrity. One of our clients had customer mistakes and cancellations decline to almost zero when they added a pre-CSR connection recorded message: "Your conversation may be recorded for quality control purposes." Although they didn't actually record

the conversations, customers assumed that tapes could be used as evidence if they were less than honest.

When asking qualifying questions like, "What do you want in a _____?" write down the caller's criteria words *verbatim*. You will want to use this *exact* vocabulary later when you do your presentation. Guerrillas understand that every prospect feels that "these ears believe most what this mouth says." When you truly understand your prospect's needs and can describe your offer in familiar terms, your offer becomes irresistible.

■ HOW TO HANDLE SENSITIVE SUBJECTS

It's imperative that all salespeople have a single message when asked sensitive questions. These answers are your party line. This list will give you an overview of some of these topics. Training by management on the company platform will help keep the message consistent and help fend off bad press. Feel free to use this list of out-of-bounds topics for your company.

➤ *Financial projections.* Forecasts of orders, shipments, earnings, and related internal data should never be disclosed over the phone. (When asked, "How's business?" the response should be, "Business is great!")

➤ *Operating results.* Don't divulge any sales or profit figures (past or projected) for the company, a product line, or a specific product.

➤ *Market share.* Don't estimate market share. Obvious generalizations are all right ("Our technology positions us as *the* leader in the web-printing marketplace"), but avoid dollar estimates, percentages, or expressions such as "We dominate the market," unless you have irrefutable proof.

➤ *Marketing strategy.* This includes projected marketing plans and expenditures, sales force information, advertising plans, and other information that could aid competitors.

➤ *Legal matters.* Patent information, tax matters, and other legal matters shouldn't be given comment.

➤ *Impending changes.* This means changes in structure, expansion, staffing levels, and the like. If you're in the know, it's tempting to build your ego by dropping hints or leaking information. It's better to play dumb and suggest that the person talk to a corporate officer. Your ego may suffer, but the company won't.

➤ *Products under development.* Until a product is officially introduced, it shouldn't be discussed—either directly or by implication. Any such discussion should be covered by a written nondisclosure agreement, and then, only with a bona fide customer or prospect. If necessary, keep copies of your nondisclosure agreement on hand.

Here are some deflecting replies to these questions:

➤ "I'm sorry, but I don't have the authority to discuss that." Refer the questioner to the right person in your organization.

➤ "That's a good question. What makes you ask?"

➤ "Our company considers that proprietary information. What makes you ask?"

➤ "Good question. Is that important to our doing business?"

Chapter 15

Getting through Voice Mail

The first step in using voice mail effectively is realizing *why* customers have voice mail in the first place. They want to more effectively *communicate* with the world. They want to receive messages from important clients, customers, and vendors. They may also want to screen unwanted calls that would waste their time. So the basis of all of your Guerrilla TeleSelling tactics is to make yours one of those important messages. You're going to learn how you can create messages that do not waste their time, that stimulate their interest, and motivate them to return your call, already receptive to your offer.

■ CREATING EFFECTIVE VOICE MAIL MESSAGES

➤ State Your Business

First, state your business. Let them know right up front who you are, who you work for, and how you can be reached. If your name is unusual, spell it out.

"We're the People Who . . ."

Voice mail is a great place to use the phrase, *"We're the people who . . ."* "This is Harrison Smith, calling from Nextel, in Washington, D.C. We're the people who offer nationwide cellular service, with no roaming charges. This is saving cellular users, like you, thousands of dollars when they travel. If you or your colleagues travel out of your home area, I've got some ideas that can let you use your cell phone more often without concern for the cost. Call me and I'll tell you all about it." Promise an answer to problems that most customers experience. Use the word, "I have some ideas . . ." instead of "I have some solutions. . . ." Prospects know solutions cost money, whereas ideas are free, so they're more likely to call back.

"I'd Appreciate the Courtesy of . . ."

Preface your phone number with the phrase, "I'd appreciate the courtesy of a return call at (number)." This tactic communicates confidence and appeals to your prospect's sense of civility. Because you are direct and courteous in your message, this magic phrase will make them three times as likely to respond. But be very careful of the *tone* you use. Never emphasize one word over another, such as, "I'd *appreciate* the courtesy of . . ." or, "I'd appreciate the *courtesy* of . . . ," or your message will sound condescending.

➤ Good News

Promise some *good news*. Give them the top three reasons why they should be interested in returning your call. Because we hear so much bad news, we are often motivated to listen to news when it's good. Perhaps the good news is that you can offer them a special price on your product or service. "Hello, Mr. Prospect. This is Aaron Wilson calling, and I have some really good news I'd like to share with you. You can return my call at . . ."

➤ Offer a Gift

"I have two extra tickets to the ball game, and I thought you might be interested. Please call right away, even if you can't go, so I can give them to someone else."

➤ Incomplete Message

If a gift doesn't work, guerrillas have to get a little bit more aggressive and leave an *incomplete message*. This is when you disconnect the call yourself in the middle of a word or phrase. "Hi, John. This is Pam Tucker calling again from San Francisco. You can reach me at (phone number). I need to speak to you no later than Tuesday because . . ." (*click!* . . . silence). Curiosity is a powerful motivator, and your prospect will often return the call just to find out what the rest of the message *would* have been if they had gotten it. Two caveats: hit the switch hook with your finger to disconnect versus hanging up the receiver, and leave your phone number before you disconnect.

Some alternatives:

"Your name came up today with John . . . (click)."

"They were talking about you and said . . . (click)."

"I have an opportunity that would make you a hund . . . (click)."

"I'm interested in getting more information about your . . . (click)."

"I was talking to your competition today, and they said . . . (click)."

➤ Make an Appointment

If your prospect sits at their desk and lets the phone ring through to voice mail anyway, try setting an appointment for your call back. The script is, "Hi, I know you're very busy today, yet I've got some great news for you! All I need is a few minutes, and I can tell you all about it. I'll call back at 3:00. If you're at your desk, will you please pick up? Talk to you at three!" When 3:00 P.M. rolls around and their phone rings, they'll know it's you, and if they want to speak with you, they'll pick up the call.

You can also make an appointment for them to call you. The script is, "I'm very busy today, yet I've got some great news for you! All I need is a few minutes, and I can tell you all about it. I'll be in the office this morning between 9:30 and 10:00, and I'll also be available to receive your call between 4:30 and 5:00 this afternoon." Of course, you'll be at the office and available to receive their call *all day*, but because it feels like an appointment, they are more likely to call at the time you specify. By setting different appointment times for different people, you'll greatly reduce phone tag.

➤ Step One

What if you receive the outbound response of, "The voice mailbox you've reached is now full. (Click.)" Just *step one*. For many companies, extensions are physically located close to each other, and extension 341 is likely to be the next desk over from extension 342. So, instead of dialing extension 341, the guerrilla will deliberately misdial extension 342 (adding one to the number of the original telephone extension) and leave the message in a colleague's voice mailbox. When they get this message, which is obviously for their coworker next door, they will either forward it or transcribe it and pass it on. Now your prospect has a paper message that he is more likely to return. If you're really lucky, the owner of extension 342 will be sitting there and transfer the call to their colleague.

➤ Call Another Department

Call the sales department—they'll tell you everything if they think you can buy from them. In a larger company, call the publicity or public relations department—it's their job to give out information. Call AR. They'll talk to *anyone!*

➤ Follow Up with the Fax

Write your prospect a note with a large marker, "Check your voice mail for an important message." Fax it to them.

If you need to leave a detailed message, and someone answers the phone and offers to take a message, ask them, "Would it be easier if I faxed it to you? Would you please see that (prospect) gets it right away?" Your message will stand out among the others on the desk, and you'll make sure that the correct information was delivered rather than relying on the receptionist's shorthand.

Fax your schedule to the target prospect, marked with open dates and times circled. This really gets their attention, especially when they see that you have appointments with their competitors.

Fax a joke or cartoon. WinFax Pro includes a hysterical collection of cartoon cover sheets with their fax software that you can customize with your own captions.

Fax a referral letter from a satisfied customer with a cover sheet that says, "FYI." You'll really get their attention when the referral letter is from a company in the same industry as the person you want to contact.

➤ "Please Fix Your Voice Mail"

Fax an urgent request: "Please fix your voice mail. I've left several messages, and apparently they're not getting through, so I can only assume that it's not working properly!"

➤ "Where Can I Reach Her Today?"

Push zero and ask the receptionist the question, "Where can I reach Mrs. Olson *today?*" or "Where are they hiding?"

"Well, she's working at home today." Or, "She's in the San Diego office today."

"Could I call her there, *today?*" Often, the assistant will give you the number at which your prospect can be contacted.

Ask for the prospect's normal arrival and departure times, or ask their assistant to book a tentative appointment.

➤ The Next-to-the-Last Thing to Leave

The next-to-the-last thing to leave is *your phone number.* Repeat the phone number again at the end of the message so that your prospect doesn't have to rewind the whole message to verify that they have transcribed it correctly.

Write down the number as you dictate it so that you know you're not going too fast. Repeat your number again at the end of the message, this time a little faster, so that they can verify that they've transcribed it correctly. Say it a different way the second time, using teens and hundreds. "One, eight hundred, two four seven, *ninety-one forty-five.*" People tend to remember the number better when grouped this way.

It's important to repeat your number if you're delivering a message by cell phone; there might be a signal dropout while you're leaving the number.

➤ The Last Thing They Should Hear

If you're leaving voice mail, your prospect will know when the message is over. Never close your message with some stupid-sounding phrase like, "Buh-bye." The last thing they should hear is *their name,* what Dale Carnegie called "the sweetest-sounding word in any language."

So now your voice mail message sounds like, "Hello, John. This is Orvel Ray Wilson, *calling from* The Guerrilla Group in Boulder, Colorado. I'd appreciate *the courtesy of a return call* at one, . . . eight hundred, . . . two, four, seven, . . . nine, one, four, five. *We're the people who* conduct the Guerrilla Selling and Guerrilla Marketing seminars all over the world. *The reason I'm calling* is that I have some really *good news* that I'd like to share with you. I'd like to send you some information about our new Guerrilla TeleSelling program and invite you to a special preview session that we're conducting in your area. You can reach me at 800-247-9145 anytime today. That's eight hundred, two four seven, *ninety-one forty-five*. I look forward to hearing from you then, *John*."

■ USING VOICE MAIL TO SELL

Guerrillas see voice mail as a golden opportunity to reach people when they otherwise couldn't. You'll never get a call back if they don't get your message, so guerrillas always leave a voice mail message, no matter what they're selling. Just create a message that is so compelling that people will call you back.

➤ Get Voice Mail

If your customer can't reach you, they may be forced to call your competitor. If you don't already have voice mail in your office and at home, get it. Your customer should never hear a busy signal. The busy signal labels you as an amateur, and it says that you're too busy to take their call, or that you don't care enough to receive their message.

When it comes to your voice mail system, the human touch is always best. The receptionist answers, rings your extension, and monitors the result. If you are not in, she returns and says, "Mr. Levinson is not in. Perhaps *I* can help you? If you prefer, I can take your message, or would you like to leave a detailed message on his voice mail?"

➤ A Three-Minute Commercial

Use your inbound after-hours voice mail recording to broadcast a three-minute commercial about your business. Callers will listen to up to three minutes of your outbound recorded message before hanging up. Write a three-minute, radio-style commercial that lets your customers know who you are, what you sell, and why they should buy it from you.

➤ Answer Common Questions

This carefully prepared script includes your days and hours of operation, street address and directions, mailing address, shipping address, fax number, Web address, and any other pertinent information your prospect may need to reach you.

Early in the message, give them the opportunity to break off and leave a message. Include the phrase, "You can enter the extension of the party you are calling, or press the pound key to begin recording a message at anytime."

➤ Include Your Web Address

"If you'd like full information about our company right now, you can find us on the World Wide Web at www.guerrillagroup .com." Savvy callers can get your full-color information immediately.

➤ Narrow, Deep Menus

If your voice mail system is menu-driven, set it up with narrow, deep menus. Give your prospect no more than four options to choose from before dropping them into a submenu. People hate sitting through the explanation of nine different options, then they can't remember which one they wanted and have to start over.

➤ Specify Your Response Time

Change your outbound message frequently. Three times a day is about right. If that sounds excessive, here's why. Savvy buyers do business with busy salespeople, because they're obviously doing something right. You want your prospects to know that you're busy.

Your message should sound like, "Good morning, this is Orvel Ray Wilson. It's 7:00 A.M., and I'll be in a staff meeting until nine this morning. If you let me know what you need at the tone, I'll get back to you before lunch."

"This is Orvel Ray. I will be out to lunch with a client until 1:30 this afternoon. If you leave a message at the tone, I'll get back to you before 4:00 P.M."

"This is Orvel Ray. This week I'll be in San Francisco, Los Angeles, Chicago, New York, and London, so if you'll leave a message at the tone, it may be a week before I get back to you. If you like, you can come by my office and haul away all of my furniture."

Let them know what to expect from you in the way of response time. Also, ask them to let you know *what they need*, so you can call back with a response, saving everyone time and energy.

➤ Screening Cycle

When you have to work on proposals or other projects against a deadline, you might use a screening cycle. In this outbound message, you say, "This is Mark S. A. Smith. I'm working against a deadline today. I'm checking messages at the top of the hour. Let me know what you need and when you need it; I'll call you back later today." Let them know when to expect your return call.

➤ After Hours

When you're unable to return calls until late in the day, ask for an after-hours phone number. "I'll be traveling to New York today, and will not be available until 7:00 P.M. eastern time. Leave a message, and please include your home number, and I can get back to you tonight. Also, please tell me when it would be too late to accept my call."

➤ Alternate Access

Always include *alternate access*. As hard as it might be to imagine, some people still don't have touch-tone phones. Always allow a caller to automatically roll over to a live person without pushing buttons. Give your prospect some other way to get through to you if the need is urgent. If they can't reach you, they'll call your competitor. Other alternate access options:

> "Press zero, and an operator will come on the line and reroute your call."
> "My pager number is. . . ."
> "My home phone number is. . . ."
> "My cell phone number is. . . ."
> "My assistant's extension is. . . ."

■ GETTING YOUR CALL RETURNED

Guerrillas put their own special spin on every aspect of the selling process, outthinking and outflanking the competition, turning their disadvantages into advantages. Because they are fighting with a muzzleloader, they will wait patiently, calling again and again until they get a clear shot at the order. Here are some guerrilla tactics to get people to return your calls. These ideas have come from our seminar attendees and our colleagues.[1]

➤ The Insomnia Call

Because most voice mail has a time stamp, you can leave messages at odd hours to make a strong impression. "Hi, it's Ted Wilson calling. It's 3:30 A.M., and I was just thinking about your account with us, and I couldn't sleep, so I decided to leave you this message . . ."

➤ "I'm Calling from the Plane . . ."

Next time you're on a plane, use the onboard phone to place calls to people that you wish to reach. "Hi, I'm calling from 37,000 feet on my way to Chicago. I was thinking about you and just had to call." It's well worth the high price to leave an impression. If they're in the office, tell the secretary that you're calling from the airplane, and you'll be put right through.

➤ Take Stock

Buy a few shares of your prospect's stock. Then call and introduce yourself as a concerned stockholder.

➤ Let's Make a Deal

"Look, John, I'll make a deal with you. I won't call unless it's important, but I want you to agree to return my call when I do. Is that fair?"

➤ Who You're Not

"Hi. I'm *not* with the IRS, I'm *not* selling insurance, I'm *not* looking for a job, and I *don't* want to borrow money, but I *do* want to talk to Mr. Smith."

➤ I'm Not Hanging Up!

"Look, this is the fifth call I've made at the times Mr. Smith has suggested. Please put my call through, and tell him I'm not going to hang up until he comes to the phone."

---

[1]Shook, Robert L., and Eric Yaverbaum. *I'll Get Back to You.* New York: McGraw-Hill, 1996.

➤ I'm Just Doing My Job

"It's my job to talk with you, and so sooner or later we'll talk. And I know that you prefer doing business with a company that gets the job done."

➤ You're Getting an Award!

Ask the gatekeeper, "I need to know the correct spelling of Mr. Danajewski's full name. I'm having a plaque engraved with his name for an award."

She carefully spells the name, then asks, "What's the award for?"

"It's the award for the most unreturned phone calls during the past six months."

➤ Will You Call?

"Hello, I was just updating my will and decided to give you a call."

➤ Dan Asked Me to Talk with You

One superstar guerrilla had a mentor—on his deathbed—tell him, "What you do is so important to the world, I want you to talk to everyone possible about it. Tell them Dan asked you to call."

➤ Disregard That

The first message you leave is, "Hi, Jane. Please disregard that last message. If you need anything else, please call me at. . . ." Last message? *What* last message?

➤ File a Missing Persons Report

"Hello, Debbie. Your staff doesn't seem to know where you are, and frankly, I'm concerned. I just wanted to let you know that I've filed a missing persons report."

➤ I'm Using Your Toll-Free Number

"Hi, Jack. This is the last call I'm going to pay for. If you don't call back, I'll start using your toll-free number. So, if you don't return my call, you'll pay for it."

➤ Persistent or Pest?

Our colleague, Larry Winget, uses this one. "There's a fine line between being persistent and being a pest. I want to serve you well, yet never be a pest. Will you please call, and tell me how best to serve you?"

➤ Back-to-Basics Fax

Send a fax with a simple message. "It's imperative that we speak now. Please call me at. . . ." Expect a 90-percent-plus success rate.

➤ Checklist

Fax this checklist for them to return:

- ☐ I don't buy things. I've got enough rubbish already.
- ☐ I don't work here anymore.
- ☐ I'm not interested.
- ☐ I'm out of town.
- ☐ I'm sorry. I'll call you!
- ☐ I'm working against a deadline. Call me after _____ o'clock.
- ☐ I've lost your other message. Call me.
- ☐ If it takes less than five minutes, call me now.
- ☐ This is a power play. Beg some more and I'll call.
- ☐ You're a jerk. Go away!

➤ Find a Minute

One guerrilla sends a box of food, including Minute Rice®, instant coffee, instant tea, instant oatmeal, instant pudding, and instant mashed potatoes, along with a note. "When you use these items, perhaps you'll find a minute to give me a call."

➤ Send a Subpoena

Our colleague, Jeff Slutsky, had a phony subpoena delivered ordering the prospect to appear in his office. A friend delivered it dressed in his SWAT team uniform. Blank forms are available at your office supply store.

➤ Send Them a Telephone

Send them a telephone with important, preprogrammed speed-dial numbers, such as the White House, Disney Studios, CNN, your office, etc. Or program every speed-dial number to be yours.

➤ Balloons

Our colleague, Sarah Reeves, sends customers a helium-filled mylar balloon in a cardboard box. She attaches a note to the ribbon with her message. Days later, the balloons are still floating around.

➤ Kiddy Call

Have your kid make a call. "My daddy is going crazy waiting for you to call him back. Would you please call? As soon as you do, he can take me for ice cream."

➤ This Is a Cold Call

Our colleague, Ron Gabrielsen,[2] has created a reputation as being "The Cold-Call Man." When he calls a prospect, he says, "Hello, this is Ron Gabrielsen from Milwaukee. I'd like to speak with Mr. Jenks. This is a *cold call*."

The receptionist replies, "Does he know what this is about?"

"Absolutely not! This is a *cold* call."

"Can I tell him what this is about?"

"Well, if you did, it wouldn't be a *cold* call, would it? Just tell him he's got a cold call waiting for him."

➤ Happy Birthday!

Guerrillas use *Who's Who*[3] to look up personal details. Get the gang to gather around the speakerphone and sing "Happy Birthday" into their voice mail.

➤ Congratulations

Call with congratulations on their alma mater's win of an important game.

➤ Just Show Up

A guerrilla in Connecticut was having trouble getting an appointment with an important prospect. She told the secretary

---

[2]Contact Ron at 414-784-6669.

[3]http://www.whoswho-online.com.

that she had a little surprise for him and asked what time he usually arrived for work and where he parked his car. She showed up early with two folding chairs, a thermos of coffee, and fresh pastry. When he tried to park in his reserved space, she was sitting there waiting. In the time it took to ride up the elevator, she got the contract.

Chapter

Questioning and Qualifying

Guerrillas focus on the problem, instead of the purchase. You'll sell more when you fully understand your customer's problems.

■ FIND A REAL NEED

A customer calls to buy a fax machine and says, "I've got $500.00 in my budget." Most salespeople would launch into a presentation of $400 to $600 fax machines. Not the guerrilla!

"Tell me how you plan to use this machine; what problem are you trying to solve?"

"Well, customers send us orders via fax," replies the prospect.

"And then what happens to that order?" queries the guerrilla.

"The order is typed into our accounting system, and that work is audited by a second person."

"Are mistakes ever made during this transcription?"

"Sure. Mistakes cost us a lot of money."

"Yes, in our business, too! And how long does it take from the time you receive the fax from the customer until the time you can confidently ship?"

"About a day and a half."

"I've got an idea. What if your customers could fax directly into the computer; and smart software would automatically enter the order into your accounting system; and you had one person doing an on-screen, side-by-side comparison of the computer's work as a double check. How would that speed up the process?"

"We'd cut order entry by at least a day!"

"And based on 20 working days a month, what would that do to your cash flow?"

"Increase that by 5 percent!"

"The good news is I think we can do that for you. My concern is that you can't do it that way for $500. It's closer to $15,000."

"Well, we could pay for that in a couple of weeks."

"What about the people that you don't need for order entry?" points out the guerrilla.

"We need them other places in the company right now!"

"Well, what should we do next?"

➤ Low-Hanging Fruit

It's easier to find people who already want and need your product or service than it is to persuade those who do not. And you'll have virtually no problems with returns or cancellations.

Keep asking diagnostic questions until their need is clear. Ask open-ended, naive questions. "What are you using now? What do you like most about it? What do you like least about it?" These answers give the guerrilla the performance specifications for their product or service, revealing the criteria most important in the decision.

Translate generalities into specifics by using the about-face. Repeat the key word in the prospect's statement in the form of a question.

"We never use your brand."

"Never?"

"We want something cozy."

"Cozy? What does 'cozy' look like to you?"

"Your price is too high."

"Too high? Relative to what?"

By demonstrating a sincere fascination with the prospect's concerns, you become a confidante and arm yourself with inside information.

■ PROSPECTING, GUERRILLA STYLE

Guerrillas know that *time* is the currency of their career. So they guard their time just like their customers guard their cash. When guerrillas prospect, they seek to *dis*-qualify. If someone can't buy, next dial. They actively seek out a reason to end the conversation and move on to the next prospect. Guerrillas look for people who:

1. Have a need
2. Have a budget
3. Have the authority to make a commitment
4. Have a motivation to act now

Most salespeople miss the fourth point—motivation. There are many more people who have a need, budget, and authority, yet they aren't motivated. The job of the guerrilla is to actively seek out those who are motivated.

➤ Disqualify

When guerrillas sense that something so far is missing from the sale, they say, "Based on what you've told me, I don't think I can help you right now. What should we do next?"

"Based on what you've told me so far . . ." tells them that you've listened, and your decision to move on is solely based on the information they've provided. The underlying message is, "Tell me more, or I'm gone!"

"I don't think I can help you now . . ." leaves the door open for future contact.

"What should we do next?" lets your prospect decide the plan of action. They might want to be called in a few weeks; or have you send information for their files; or refer you to the right person; or ask if you know anyone who can help them; or they might say, "You're right! Thank you. Good-bye!" Regardless of their answer, you'll always be welcome back because of your courteous approach and honest methods. Buyers tell us that these guerrillas are their favorite to do business with. "They don't waste my time, and they take great care of me when I need them."

➤ Cover Money Matters Early

People shy away from discussing finances, but not the guerrilla. Ask frankly, "How much have you budgeted to solve this problem, in round numbers?" By asking for an approximate figure, the guerrilla broaches this sensitive topic. Whenever possible, quote exact prices. Help the prospect demystify the money matters, and you make it easier for them to buy from you. Discussing their budget, purchasing priorities, and required payback up front eliminates sticker shock and most price objections.

➤ Get an Early Commitment

Raise an objection yourself, and volunteer to end the meeting. "We have a problem. You said you wanted maple, and we only have this in oak. Are we done?"

The client will almost certainly stop at this point and ask about alternatives. More importantly, you've demonstrated that you put their needs above your own. You've also given back control of the interview. The prospects will be more likely to proceed, because they've committed to continue the conversation. The roles have been reversed, with the *customer* now doing the selling.

➤ Referrals

Even if they do not have a need, guerrillas always ask, "Who else do you know who might have an interest in this? Could you give me their number, please?" Prospects who do not buy from you are more likely to give you qualified referrals. Many businesspeople don't want their competition to have the edge you're offering.

➤ "Asked . . . Promised . . ."

When calling the referral, introduce yourself with, "Dan Johnson asked me to give you a call, and I promised him I would." You'll get a warm reception.

➤ The Special List

You can triple your response rate from any list, from any source, if you start at the *end* of the list and work backwards. Everyone calls on the people at ABC Company and Aaron

Anderson & Associates. The people at Zizivivitz Corporation or Xaxatron Instruments haven't seen a salesperson since the Truman Administration. When you call and say, "I'm selling . . . ," they'll interrupt, "Great! Come on over."

"But you don't even know what it is."

"That's OK. We need *everything!*"

■ GETTING THEM TO KEEP THE APPOINTMENT

You may need to make sales calls by appointment. You have set up several appointments, only to have the prospects cancel. How can you get them to follow through?

➤ "I'm Running Ten Minutes Early . . ."

Call your prospect en route from the car phone or a phone booth. Tell them you're on your way and that you're running a few minutes *early*. "Is that okay?"

Then ask a favor. "Could you please tell me where's the best place to park? Let security know I'm coming. Which door should I come in? And where will you meet me?"

This 15-second call accomplishes several objectives.

Confirmation of Appointment

By agreeing to the minor change, the prospect confirms the appointment, and the courtesy call sends the message that you value their time as much as your own. This guerrilla tactic is particularly useful if the appointment has been set for you by telephone. Because you're already in the neighborhood, "I'm calling from just down the street . . ." or "I'm on my way . . . ," the prospect will feel guilty canceling the meeting.

If the appointment *is* going to fall through, you want to know that while you're still in your car. There are two reasons why appointments are canceled: either the prospects don't *want* to see you, or there's an emergency and they *can't* see you. If they don't want to see you, no matter how brilliant your sales presentation, the odds of closing that business are against you. If there is an emergency, this is a golden opportunity for you to come through as a hero. Ask how you can help.

Begin Building a Relationship Before You Arrive

This on-the-run courtesy call is a golden opportunity to build advance rapport with the new prospect by asking a favor. Asking for their help changes the dynamics of the sales call from salesperson versus buyer to guest greeted by host. They've said "yes" to you twice even before the sales call begins. The advance introduction by phone means you're no longer walking into a "cold" call.

Choice Parking

Have you ever parked in what you assumed was the right place, only to make someone mad or have your car towed? You will park in the right spot every time and often get a prime parking space. The prospect says, "Oh, Charlie Smith is out today, just park in his reserved space."

Demonstrate That You'll Deliver

The greatest fear buyers have is not getting what they need when they need it. By showing up early, you are demonstrating that not only do you keep your appointments, you keep them early. You can deliver.

Change the Rules

Although other salespeople do show up early, guerrillas let their prospects *know* that they will show up early. The guerrilla gets the credit and changes the rules of the game on the other salespeople. You'll get ten more minutes of face time that your competition won't get. Guerrillas create every advantage possible to win the battle.

They'll Meet You Promptly

Have you ever had your prospect keep you waiting in the lobby with the other salespeople who look like they're going to have a root canal, so that they know that you know that they're in control? This phone call kills that behavior, because you've just let them demonstrate that they're in charge.

The 37 Magic Selling Questions

■ QUESTIONING SKILLS

Asking good questions is an art form. Salespeople usually do all the talking and seldom ask enough questions, so we've developed a list of the 37 most powerful questions guerrillas can ask. These questions will automatically take a prospect all the way through the buying process. Your team members should memorize them until they can recall on demand—"What's question number 10?"

These questions really work magic. We've italicized the magic words in each question with an explanation of the strategy behind each one.

1. **What is your main *objective*?** When you understand what your customer is trying to achieve, you can align your proposal with their intent.

2. **How do you *plan* to achieve that goal?** You may already fit into their plan and not even know it. If you're part of their plan, your customer will close themselves.

3. **What is the *biggest problem* you currently face?** If you can help them solve their biggest problem, you will be a big hero.

4. **What *other problems* do you experience?** You may not be able to solve their biggest problem, so what other problems do they have that you can solve?

5. **What are you doing *currently* to deal with this?**

6. **What is your strategy for the *future*?** These two questions, together, give you an outline of the customer's current trajectory. These questions tend to accelerate the decision-making process.

7. **What *other ideas* do you have?** This fills in the blanks and lets you uncover their other thoughts with which you can align.

8. **What role do others play in *creating* this situation?** Anyone who is contributing to the problem is a potential adversary. Find out who they are.

9. **Who else is *affected*?** Anyone who is affected by the problem is a potential ally.

10. **What are you using *now*?**

11. **What do you like *most* about it?**

12. **What do you like *least* about it?** Always use these three as a group. Question 10 tells you what they're buying, from whom, and for how much, revealing both the need and the budget. Question 11 gives you their critical buying criteria. A replacement vendor must be equivalent in these areas to even be considered. This also tells you the thought process they went through to purchase last time. Question 12 tells you where the competitor is vulnerable. If you can offer them everything they like most and fix the things they like least, they *now* have a justification to *change*.

13. **If you could have things any way you wanted, what would you *change*?** People are naturally resistant to change. "Better the devil you know than one you don't." This question inoculates the issue of change. It also allows them to dream and explore possibilities. You can probably do about half of the things they wish for. There is something special about making a person's dreams come true.

14. **What *effect* would this have on the present situation?** This question brings the dream to reality.

15. **What would *motivate* you to change?** This question creates the rationale they will use to justify the change, reducing their resistance later.

16. **Do you have a *preference*?** If they do, you need to know what it is and what it is based on.

17. **What has been your *experience*?** If they have had an unfavorable experience with the competitor, you may be able to exploit it. If they have had an unfavorable experience with your company, you better fix it.

18. **How do you *know*?** Sometimes they really don't know. You want to know where they got their information. Be very careful with the tone; you don't want to sound accusatory.

19. **Is there *anything else* you'd like to see?** This open-ended question encourages them to brainstorm additional options and may reveal additional opportunities for the guerrilla.

20. **How much would it be *worth* to you to solve this problem?**

21. **What would it *cost*, ultimately, if things remained as they are?** These two questions set up the cost justification for the investment you'll ask them to make. Question 20 tells you the most they should be willing to pay, and question 21 tells you the least they should be willing to pay. If they didn't have a budget before, they have a budget range now. Always ask both questions, because some people are motivated *toward* some positive outcome or reward, whereas others are motivated *away from* some consequence or penalty. Whichever question they answer most completely reveals the strategy you should pursue when preparing an ROI presentation.

22. **Are you working within a *budget*?** If so, they should reveal it here. If not, you have the necessary data to create one. A budget is the best indicator of commitment.

23. **How do you plan to *finance* it?** Where is the money going to come from? Can you offer alternative financing?

24. **What *alternatives* have you considered?** Don't be naive. They're talking to the competition. It is perfectly appropriate to ask a prospect who the competition is. You'll know how to present your offering in the best light against that competitor.

25. What benefit would you *personally* realize as a result? People do things for their reasons, no matter how good your reasons might be.

26. How would *others* benefit? The answer to this question creates a justification for what may ultimately be a self-ish decision.

27. How can I *help?* Easily the most powerful sales close in the book.

28. Is there anything I've *overlooked?* This gives you a chance to tie up any loose ends that might tangle and trip you up later on down the line.

29. Are there any *questions* you'd like to ask? Encourage your prospect to get all their questions answered here and now.

30. What do you see as the *next step?* The prospect will tell you what to do to advance the sale: write up an order, check on a specification, make a presentation to a committee, or nothing.

31. Who else, *besides yourself,* will be involved in making the decision? Even if you're meeting with the janitor, always assume they may be a behind-the-scenes influence. Even if you think you've found the decision maker, keep asking this question of everyone else.

32. On a scale of one to ten, how *confident* do you feel about doing business with us? *What would it take* to get that up to a ten? This two-part question will tell you exactly what incremental evidence they need and what form of proof they will require. If they say, "8," then say, "What would it take to get to a 9?" If they say "10," then proceed to writing the order.

33. Are you working against a particular *deadline?*

34. How *soon* would you like to start?

35. *When* would you like to take delivery? These are all time-frame questions. Remember, if they're not motivated by some time frame, they probably will not buy, at least not for a while.

36. When should we get together to discuss this *again?* You usually will not be able to close the sale on the first contact, or even the second or third. Let them define the time frame for the next meeting. If they resist, ask, "How about if I call again within 90 days?" If you ask, "May I call again in 30 days?" 15 percent will agree. If you ask, "May I call again in 60 days?" 45 percent will agree. If you ask, "May I call again in 90 days?" 66 percent will agree; however, extending the follow-up beyond that point is actually counterproductive. Only 67 percent will agree for you to call again after 120 days. These statistics suggest that you should be contacting every active, qualified prospect at least quarterly.[1]

37. **Is there _anything else_ you'd like for me to take care of?** We leave far too much money on the table, because we do not ask this simple parting question.

---

[1]Pekas, Mary D. _Conversational Soft-Sell Telemarketing._ Lake Norden, SD: Telemarketing Institute, Inc. 605-785-3505.

Chapter 18

Presenting Your Proposal

Here are the secrets to getting your proposal noticed, agreed to, and acted upon.

■ EXPEDITE EVERYTHING

Getting things done quickly is one of the most effective tactics guerrillas use for gaining a competitive edge. Give them an opportunity to say "yes" to you before they even get a chance to say "no" to anyone else. Reach for the phone instead of the fax. Send E-mail instead of snail-mail. Fax that letter or proposal. Send sales materials overnight. Give your customers a choice: "I can have that on your desk tomorrow morning by 8:00 A.M., or would 10:00 A.M. be adequate?"

Follow up the same day. "Did you receive the packet I sent? Well, what did you like best?"

■ HOW GUERRILLAS INFLUENCE PROSPECTS AND CUSTOMERS

Professor Robert Cialdini, in his book *Influence: The Psychology of Persuasion,* identifies six factors or influence agents that substantially influence people.[1] When you use any of these influence agents, you will increase your TeleSelling success. You'll have the most impact when you use as many as possible.

[1]Cialdini, Robert B. *Influence: The Psychology of Persuasion.* New York: Quill, 1993.

➤ Consistency

People tend to act in ways that are consistent with their public statements. Taking notes is one way to gain consistency in your prospect's behavior. For a double impact, fax or E-mail your notes to your prospect.

Referral programs are one of the most powerful ways to get customers to stay with you. The secret: when a person who is referred to you buys, the referring person's good judgment is reinforced. Someone who offers advice seldom acts contrary to their own counsel, especially when others follow the advice.

➤ Reciprocation

In every culture, granting a favor obligates the recipient to return a favor. So, guerrillas look for ways to give to their prospects first, then convert them to customers.

The customer handed the shopkeeper a $20 bill to pay for a $10.25 purchase. The shopkeeper returned a $10 bill in change and said, "I didn't want to break your ten." For a mere 25 cents, this guerrilla created a lasting impression that he may not have gotten from a more expensive program.

I'll go out of my way to patronize the little Kwik Mart in the mountain canyon where I live because of the way I was treated by a clerk one day, years ago. It was one of those honey-would-you-please-pick-up-bread-and-milk-on-the-way-home-from-work stops, and I was running late. The cash in my pocket was 40 cents short, but when I offered to write a check, the clerk said, "Oh, don't bother. Just catch me next time." I swear I went out of my way the next day to stop and buy something, so that I could repay that 40 cents.

➤ Social Proof

If everyone's doing it, it must be OK. Forty thousand Frenchmen can't be wrong. Referral programs encourage participants to use social proof to our advantage. Holiday tie-ins are a natural, because the holidays are part of our social psychology. Trade-ins allow you to get the old products out of circulation, increasing the proof that your new product is superior. Testimonials harness the ultimate power of social proof. Microsoft took advantage of this principle when they introduced model-year branding to software with the introduction of Windows '95 (and '98 and on and on). Gotta get the newest model—everyone's using it.

➤ Authority

Most cultures are trained to respect certain authority and respond to their influence almost without question. Deadlines are created and followed. An official product is often more desirable than an unsanctioned one. If you are calling on behalf of their bank, or a well-known charitable organization, or other authority, you'll gain an advantage.

➤ Liking

When a person likes you, they are more easily influenced by you. Sending a gift or valuable information in advance of your call increases your success rate. Allying with associations is an easy way to transfer the existing relationship with the association to your company. Associating with sports teams often creates instant affiliation with fans.

➤ Scarcity

Anything that is perceived as being scarce is also perceived as being more valuable, even though it may not function any better. If what you offer is perceived to be scarce, you'll increase your success.

■ COMMUNICATIONS STYLES

People have different styles of communicating, just as they have preferences for styles of clothing or styles of music. Communicating with your customer effectively requires that you recognize and adapt to their preferred communication metastrategies. Like tuning in a radio, the structure of the presentation must be properly aligned with the prospect for them to hear and understand your message clearly.

You adjust your communication style in each of four categories: need for information and detail, organization of tasks, locus of motivation, and level of initiative.

■ NEED FOR INFORMATION AND DETAIL

The first of these categories describes your prospect's need for information and detail, and it describes the need for explanation and tolerance for specifics. Think of it as a continuum that ranges from the *general* communicator at one extreme to the *specific* communicator at the other. People can fall anywhere along this scale—some have already made up their minds and would rather not be confused with the facts, whereas others need lots of information to make a decision.

➤ General . . . Specific

This spectrum is one of the easiest to recognize. As you listen, pay attention to the level of detail that your prospect uses in the conversation, and expand or contract the detail of your presentation accordingly.

Test yourself: you may be a specific communicator if right now, without looking, you know exactly how much money you have in your checking account. On the other hand, if you haven't balanced your checkbook since 1973, or perhaps you rely on the automatic teller machine method (when the ATM stops giving you cash, you know you're overdrawn), then you are more likely to be a general communicator.

General Communication Style

You can recognize the general communicators, because these people are most comfortable talking in sweeping generalities. They prefer the big picture, the overview, the executive summary. They are impatient with minutia. Getting any real information from generals can be like pulling teeth. General communicators tend to fill in the blanks. They are notorious for making assumptions, because in the absence of hard data, they will fill in the details based on their general understanding. If conclusion jumping were an Olympic event, these people would be gold-medallists. They will offer monosyllabic answers to questions like, "You've been out of the office for a while?"

> "Yes!"
> "Traveling on business?"
> "Vacation."
> "Where did you go?"
> "Nowhere."
> "What did you do?"
> "Nothing."
> "So you just stayed home and relaxed?"
> "Yeah."
> "How was it?"
> "Great!"

Generals have a tendency to think big, without consideration of potentially limiting details. They have big dreams and big goals. They think long-term and may have a ten-year plan and a five-year plan, but they don't have plans for lunch.

When outlining their needs to salespeople, general communicators are often vague. Be careful when dealing with general prospects, because, in their haste to make a deal, important details may be overlooked. Above all, they hate paperwork, preferring verbal or telephone communication to paper or electronic correspondence.

Specific Communication Style

The opposite extreme of this scale is the specific communicator. You can recognize this style, because they have a very high capacity for and need for detail, and they are very precise in their communication. Their conversation is peppered with particular references, like place names, proper nouns, dates, times, and statistics like percentages, quantities, or distances. They have a tendency to think in the short-term, the close-up, and they have difficulty understanding the big picture or seeing the overview. You have to be absolutely accurate, because they're alert to the tiniest omission or contradiction. And you better always be exactly on time.

Be very careful when dealing with specifics, because the intent of their communication can get lost in all this detail fog.

General versus Specific

You run into problems when you put a specific communicator and a general communicator together. The general prospect will simply stop listening and daydream if their need for detail is exceeded. The opposite is true for the specific communicator; unless they have every little bit of information filled in, they have trouble arriving at a conclusion.

The Most Effective Approach with Generals

To communicate with the general communicator, be direct. One of the most frequent mistakes salespeople make is overloading this prospect with irrelevant detail. Start with the bottom line. If they need more information, they will ask for it.

To persuade the general communicator, summarize using charts, graphs, or maps. Look for forms of proof that you can mail or fax to them. For generals, a picture is worth a thousand words, and the more concisely you present your case, the easier it is for them to understand.

To motivate the general, align your proposition with their long-term plan; show them how it fits into their big picture. These people enjoy making decisions, especially big decisions.

The Most Effective Approach with Specifics

To communicate with the specific communicator, be thorough, complete, and precise. They need all of the salient facts and then some. Explain your reasoning and the evidence that supports it before drawing a conclusion. Show them how your product will perform in exact terms using dollars, percentages, and dates.

To persuade the specific communicators, break your proposition down into incremental commitments. These people hate to make decisions, especially big decisions, so give them a series of little decisions to make. Confirm your agreement point-by-point on the color, then the quantity, then the shipping method, and finally the delivery date.

To motivate the specifics, include all the supporting documentation you can get your hands on: computer printouts, brochures, specifications, blueprints, everything. The specific communicators may not read it all, but they have an emotional need to feel like they are getting the whole story.

We have studied the work habits of hundreds of professional salespeople, and we've learned that one of the hallmarks of successful guerrillas is the ability to *shift* from the general to the specific in their presentation. They take the general needs of their prospect and apply them to the specific priorities and criteria that are most relevant. Then, they translate them into general terms that a prospect can understand. Because the guerrilla's communication style fits the prospect like an old shoe, prospects are comfortable making the required decisions and commitments.

■ ORGANIZATION OF TASKS

Another dimension the guerrilla must consider is the need for order and structure. How your customer organizes their world will be a reflection of how they tackle problems. By matching the process they use, you are more likely to arrive at a favorable outcome.

➤ Options . . . Procedures

Think in terms of a scale with options at one end and procedures at the other. Keep in mind that a person can fall anywhere along this scale, and their position on one scale may be completely unrelated to their position on the other scales.

Test yourself. If you prefer to do things step-by-step in routine, repetitive procedures, you may be a procedural communicator. You keep a neat desk, taking out one file folder at a time, working on it until you're finished, then putting it carefully away. What drives you nuts are messes.

On the other hand, if you have the messy desk, piled high with books, papers, and file folders, 14 different projects underway all at the same time, you are more likely to be an options communicator. If some well-meaning colleague cleaned your desk for you, you'd have to kill them. This might actually be justifiable homicide in your state.

Options Communication

You can recognize the options prospect as soon as you talk to them. This prospect is talking on the telephone, writing a letter, eating a snack, and carrying on a conversation with someone else, all at the same time! These folks are multimodal, and they are often good at handling multiple demands and simultaneous tasks. They organize their work as a set of alternatives. If they've got five things on their to-do list, they may start with item number three and work on that for a while, then jump to number one, make a dent in that, then go on to number five, and so on. They are notorious for starting projects and not finishing, so you have to follow up carefully on any commitments they make.

Procedural Communication

The procedural prospect, on the other hand, organizes tasks sequentially or as a checklist. They'll often numerate their conversations, start with item number one, and discuss it till it's resolved. Then, and *only* then, will they go on to item number two. If you interrupt them by changing the subject, it is very stressful, and they may have to start all over again to regain their train of thought. Perhaps you know someone or have worked with someone like this. They'll say things like, "Look, I can only do one thing at a time!"

Options versus Procedures

An individual's communication styles can be either a resource or a liability, depending on the circumstances. A highly procedural secretary will be irritated if your call interrupts her while she's typing a letter. So the guerrilla has to listen carefully to background noises, and if the voice sounds stressed ask, "Have I reached you at a bad time?" or "Do you have to answer that other line?"

The Most Effective Approach with Options

Guerrillas will adapt the presentation to follow the organizational strategy of the prospect. To communicate with the options prospect, be flexible. This customer may interrupt you with questions or comments, and you must give them free reign in the conversation and follow their lead. No canned pitch. Be prepared to follow them on a joyride around the issues. A carefully planned presentation is of particular value here, even if you don't follow it sequentially, because like a roadmap, it helps you get the conversation to the desired destination.

To persuade the options prospect, spell out an array of alternatives, outlining the advantages and disadvantages of each. This prospect must see the alternatives to make a choice.

To motivate options prospects, give them a set of alternatives to choose from, and ask them to make a choice. Be careful not to give them too many possibilities, particularly if they are also general. You can overload them with too many alternatives.

The Most Effective Approach for Procedures

Procedural communicators are not pioneers. They follow the beaten path. They avoid change. There is one right way to do everything—*their* way—and any deviation violates their need for order and correctness. To communicate with these people, stay on track, and numerate your carefully prepared presentation step-by-step. If you digress, use an "as I was saying . . ." transition to get back into your outline. It helps if you can give your prospect a copy of your notes. Fax them an outline in advance so they can check off each issue as you cover it.

To persuade the procedural communicator, structure your case as the only logical choice, given the evidence. If you can lead the procedural to a logical conclusion, based on the facts, it's easy for them to go along with your deal.

To motivate the procedural communicator, do a demonstration or show before-and-after pictures. If they follow some structured routine, find out exactly what it is. If they reorder on some regular schedule, make sure you call on exactly the same day each month to take their order. Whatever you do, be consistent.

■ LOCUS OF MOTIVATION

This dimension indicates where your prospect looks for evidence to confirm that they have made the right choices. Do they look for it internally, or do they look for it externally? Prospects differ in the strategies they use to maintain their motivation, and one of the most important dimensions is the locus of the feedback they depend on for their decisions.

➤ Internal . . . External

Some people look inside themselves for internal confirmation of their decision making, whereas others look outside themselves to the external world for praise and feedback. This distinction will help you communicate in a way that will build powerful motivation.

The basic form of the question that reveals this metastrategy is, "How do you know when what you are doing is working?" or "How do you know when what you have bought is doing a good job for you?" For example, a guerrilla might ask a prospect, "Based on your experience, how do you know when you've found the right vendor?"

Test yourself: you might be externally motivated if you work your butt off for a year to earn a $35 plaque at the sales meeting. Externally motivated prospects will decorate their offices with trophies, awards, and dead animals.

➤ Internal Frame of Reference

A prospect who is internally motivated references their gut reaction, their conscience, or their intuition to validate their decision making. They base their choices on factors inside themselves—a vision, a feeling, or a voice inside their head.

The internally motivated prospect might respond to the question by saying, "You just know when it's right. You get a feeling when you first talk with them. Are they knowledgeable? Is the company's reputation solid? If I'm going to spend five or

ten years with a vendor, the relationship has to be comfortable."
This prospect might be interested in the same vendor as the
externally motivated buyer, but for very different reasons. Their
relationship with the salesperson will be different as well.

➤ External Frame of Reference

Externally motivated prospects tend to respond to the same
question with something like, "I want a vendor that I don't have
to be embarrassed with if something goes wrong." These
prospects are fixing their frame of reference externally, on the
outside world, depending on what others might say or feel
about their choice.

Most Effective Approach for Internals

Internally motivated prospects may be motivated independent
of what's going on in the real world. These people really don't
care what you think (or anyone else, for that matter). Communicate with the internal by asking questions and listening
actively to the answers. Persuade the internal communicator by
soliciting their advice, asking for their opinions, feelings, and
values. "What do you think of this capability?"

Use questions to help them access their own internal judgment, because that's the scale they'll use for weighing the evidence and for making the decision. It makes them uneasy if
you try to load them up with rave reviews. Not only do they
ignore it, they resent it.

Motivate the internal communicator by aligning with their
personal vision, by saying, "Well, I'm sure that you understand
your company's needs better than I do, and I'm really counting
on your feedback as we discuss different options. I'd like to help
you, yet, ultimately, you have to live with your decision."

Most Effective Approach for Externals

People who are externally motivated are dependent on your
input, statistics, and testimonials; they have to have that input
to make a decision.

Communicate with the external by offering opinions, recommendations, and testimonials. They want you to tell them
about your proposal, to make suggestions, perhaps even to prescribe a particular course of action. They expect you to use
external forms of proof, including third-party references, testimonial letters, demonstrations, referrals, and more.

Persuade the externally motivated prospect by appealing to what other people are going to think. The guerrilla could make comments like, "This is the most popular model on the market," and "I can just see your friends green with envy when you take delivery." To sell the external, tell your story and offer third-party testimonials.

Motivate the external by providing constant praise, especially public recognition. They want the salesperson to say, "You are a very savvy customer. Most of my clients aren't nearly as knowledgeable." Send them a Customer-of-the-Month Award.

Managing Motivation

As a manager, it's also very useful to be aware of your own motivational style and those of your subordinates. Externally motivated salespeople often mistake a rejection of their product for a rejection of themselves. They may be overly focused on external evidence, and they may take it personally when a prospect says "no."

Internally motivated salespeople may think they're doing a great job when they've actually missed the boat with the prospect. They're preoccupied with their own thoughts and judgments and may insist on doing things their own way, even when their performance is substandard. They interpret instructions as information.

Externally motivated salespeople need regular praise, recognition, and short-term feedback about their work, and they will ask for coaching even when their productivity is stellar. They will be the ones who strive to win the contests and the awards. They interpret information as instructions. They want participation and input from others on their work. They will work hard to achieve goals set for themselves or to earn recognition or awards. They will bust their chops to make a customer happy or to get their name painted on a parking space.

Internally motivated salespeople will let the weekly sales figures speak for themselves when it comes to recognition. They require careful coaching in the beginning, but once they decide that they know what to do, they may become unteachable. They are somewhat self-managing. After a careful training period, they need to be given a free reign with only periodic checkups. They do not want to be told how they're doing; for them, you're just restating the obvious. They are not as interested in recognition or awards, but they will work very hard to meet standards and goals, particularly those that they've set for themselves.

Which are you? Are you motivated by what others say or think, or by your own gut feeling? Guerrilla TeleSelling requires adapting to the motivational needs of your prospects and striving to appreciate their feelings and intuition, as well as the external feedback on the tote board. Overreliance on one at the expense of the other can lead to disaster.

■ LEVEL OF INITIATIVE

Another dimension to watch for is your prospects' levels of initiative. Do they take the initiative to make things happen, or do they wait for others to get things started?

➤ Proactive . . . Reactive

Proactive prospects like to be in control and to make things happen. They tend to jump in with both feet. They have a bias for experimentation over analysis and tend to act first and ask questions later. *Reactive* prospects prefer for someone else to do the driving and take them along for the ride. They have a bias for analysis over experimentation and tend to relentlessly ask questions rather than act.

Test yourself: what do you do when you approach a yellow traffic light? Reactives stop. Proactives gun it!

The Proactive Style

The proactive prospect wants to take the lead, to be in control, and, in severe cases, may resist the initiative of others, including yourself. Inaction makes them uncomfortable. They prefer to try your product out, but if it doesn't work the way they expect it to the first time, that's enough; they're ready to deal with someone else. They have a bias for products that are new, improved, state-of-the-art, and leading-edge technology. They hate to be kept waiting. You may be proactive if you've ever found yourself standing in front of the microwave saying, "Come on! Come ON!!!"

Most Effective Approach with Proactives

Communicate with the proactive by following their lead, and treat everything as if it were their idea. These people are go-getters. If you promise to send a brochure or catalog, get it out the same day.

Persuade the proactive by offering something that they can say "yes" to. Fill out the order blank, or write up the contract in advance. Just ask for their signature.

Motivate the proactive by initiating, and expedite everything. Once they've made up their mind, they want it delivered yesterday.

With proactives, any actions on your part will be well received. They respect people of like mind and are happy to push things along. They make great allies within an organization, because they tend to ferret out any resistance to a project they've started. Be careful if you talk to those who are also internally motivated; they may make commitments they can't keep.

The Reactive Style

At the other end of the scale, we have the *reactives*. These prospects are not motivated to start things, but, instead, rely on the initiatives of others, so take the lead and make suggestions and recommendations. They have a bias for products that are proven, old-fashioned, and guaranteed. Reactives are afraid to rock the boat; they prefer the status quo and may be resistant to change. You may be reactive if you are still waiting for them to work the bugs out of color TV.

Most Effective Approach with Reactives

Be prepared to sell the reactive prospects with facts, figures, and test results, and take the initiative to offer samples, do a trial run, or, in some other way, get the ball rolling.

Communicate with reactives by advising, suggesting, and taking small initiatives. Also, keep in mind that these prospects resist change, so describe your product in terms of "progression," "evolution," and "improvement," rather than "new," "revolutionary," or "breakthrough."

Persuade the reactive by soliciting the opinions and recommendations of others. Be prepared to prescribe a solution or to get the spouse involved.

Motivate the reactive by pushing gently and involving others. Go over their head for approval if necessary. They may interpret your initiative as being pushy, but they will react to it, either positively or negatively. They require constant attention, checking back, and prodding along, or the momentum of the sale will be lost.

■ CONSTELLATIONS OF STYLES

Guerrillas carefully analyze the constellations of needs when developing their presentation. For the CEO who is general, options, proactive, and internal, the guerrilla may fax a quick-deal memo immediately after the phone call. For the production manager of the same company who is specific, procedural, reactive, and externally motivated, the guerrilla takes the time to write a carefully worded cost/benefit analysis. A *Thank You* card goes to the division manager who is specific, reactive, and internally motivated, itemizing all the little things done to facilitate the demonstration. Another short note is sent to the sales manager who is specific, options, proactive, and externally motivated, congratulating him on the success of his idea. In this way, guerrillas cultivate a favorable motivational environment for their product or service throughout the organization.

■ MAKE THE INTANGIBLE TANGIBLE

People in our seminars often comment, "But what I sell is different. I sell a service, and because it's intangible, traditional presentation methods won't work. How do I adjust?"

Keep in mind that all products have *both* tangible and intangible aspects. An automobile is a tangible bundle of steel, glass, and electronics, but it is also an intangible bundle of prestige, freedom, and safety.

When selling a service, the challenge is to solidify the intangible aspects into tangible forms that the customer can see, touch, and feel. Use presentation aids like faxed information or videoconferences. Invite your prospect to tour your office or plant, where they can get close to the action. One of our clients, a linen service, brings customers into their cleaning plant, where you could hear the noise of the machinery and feel the heat of the steam presses.

■ MAKE THE TANGIBLE INTANGIBLE

The opposite is true when selling tangible products. Because the tangible aspects are somewhat self-evident, salespeople typically emphasize these features. The challenge is to get the prospect to *feel* the intangible benefits associated with the tangible features.

The guerrilla tactic is to emphasize these intangible aspects in your presentation through testimonials, test results, or consumer reports. "The heated leather seats in the car are more comfortable in the winter." "This mutual fund will not only provide a generous rate of return, but it will give you a sense of security as it builds equity for your retirement."

■ TEN WAYS TO MAKE YOUR PRESENTATION IRRESISTIBLE

1. Discuss *specific* benefits your caller would gain that would allow them to meet the needs they've discussed. Customers do things for their reasons, not yours. You might have a hundred good reasons for them to buy from you; their decision will hinge on the three or four reasons that they think are important. Present proof that you can fulfill these few criteria, and you can safely ignore everything else.

2. Show *exclusive* or superior features. Don't waste time on basics. Discuss what your competition can't do, but only if it's important to your caller. Use the magic word "only"—"We are the *only* supplier that has a warehouse within the same-day shipping radius of your plant."

3. Project that your company is a *reliable* vendor. You do this with your professionalism and a positive approach to selling. Negative remarks about your competition imply that you don't really have a superior product and erode your credibility.

4. Position what you sell as having the *right price*. Make sure your caller understands the value you provide for the price you ask. And that doesn't mean the lowest price (more on this in Chapter 20).

5. Demonstrate that the time is right to buy *now*. Do this through special this-week-only pricing or promotions or by immediately solving one of your caller's problems.

6. Use *proof statements*, based on your notes, to match your benefits to the prospect's needs using, "You mentioned

that saving time is important to you. With this new technology, our product takes less time to do the job than what you're using now, saving you hundreds of hours."

7. Support your case with *visual aids*. Yes, you can do visuals. Guerrillas use their Web site or the fax machine to deliver instant visuals. "I'll fax you a chart that shows your savings over the next three months." "Go to our Web site, and I'll talk you through our catalog to help you find exactly what you're looking for."

8. Present an *emotional appeal*. Emotion puts the motion in motivation. Explain not only the features and advantages, but also put the prospect in the picture. Demonstrate how they will personally benefit. Put them in the action. Help them imagine themselves using the product, benefiting from it, and enjoying it.

9. Dramatize with *success stories*. These are especially effective when they're from your caller's industry or location. "Widgets, Inc. has slashed its production costs by 10 percent with this product."

10. Include a *demonstration*. If a picture's worth a thousand words, then a demonstration's worth a thousand pictures. Arrange for a demonstration: have them come to your location, visit their home or office, or send them a videotape.

■ DOING VERBAL DEMOS

If you're explaining processes or procedures, use your Web site or a faxed diagram to preview what you'll be describing. For some callers, this verbal description will be enough.

There are three parts to a quick verbal overview:

1. Review the basic operations, highlighting the areas that are of most benefit to your caller.

2. Stop after each major point to check and make sure your caller is satisfied with what they've heard so far.

3. Ask a trial close after pointing out the key features.

If the caller agrees that the product is attractive, schedule a follow-up visit to do a complete demonstration in the office.

■ MAKING IT STICK

Adults retain only 10 percent of what they hear. Within two weeks of your call, your prospect will have forgotten 90 percent of what you told them. If you can get them to take notes or to jot down numbers, their retention increases to about 50 percent. If you can get them to *discuss* their needs with you, their retention increases to 75 percent or better. This is why guerrillas always engage in a discussion with prospects after they find someone they can serve.

■ HOW TO HELP YOUR CUSTOMER REMEMBER

Recognition is when the prospect will remember you if they're reminded. "Mark Smith? Oh, yes, I remember talking to him." The mention of the name triggers the memory. Recall, on the other hand, is when the prospect spontaneously remembers you when they need you, without anyone or anything reminding them. You know you've done a great job if they think of you when they need you.

Unprompted recall is not nearly as reliable as recognition, so guerrillas never rely on recall alone. They build recognition and keep reminding prospects of how they can be of service. If you want your prospect to remember what you tell them, here are some ways to increase their retention of your ideas.[2]

➤ Primacy

People tend to remember the first thing that you tell them. So make sure that your opening lines have power and impact.

➤ Recency

People remember the last thing they hear, so make your closing statement count.

➤ Outstanding

Anything that is unique makes a lasting impression.

➤ Specifics

People tend to remember specific numbers when it's important to their decision. The more unusual the number, the more

---

[2]Rose, Colin. *Accelerated Learning.* New York: Dell, 1985. p. 31.

likely it is that they'll remember it. For example, asking for a meeting at 11:59 A.M. is easier to remember than asking for a noon meeting.

➤ Principles

If you can create a rule of thumb, people will remember it. For example, financial advisors use the Rule of 72: divide 72 by your annual interest rate, and you'll know how many years it takes to double your money.

■ WHAT QUESTION CAME UP?

During your presentation, questions will arise in your prospect's mind. To make sure that you get all questions on the table, ask your prospect, "What question came up while you listened?" If they do have a question, compliment the question. "That's a great question. I'm glad you asked that. Thank you for letting me clarify that point."

■ FOLLOW UP TO CLOSE

After making each key point, stop and check if you're on track. Ask, "Will that work for you?" After you respond to their question, ask, "Did that answer your question?"

Chapter 19

Ask for the Order

The guerrilla knows that they've done everything right when the prospect closes themselves. Yet, not every prospect will take that initiative. Guerrillas know that sometimes it takes a nudge to get the prospect to become a customer.

■ ASK FOR A COMMITMENT

Guerrillas recognize when to close—when the prospect is ready to make a decision—and not before. They are aware of unconscious, often subtle, buying signals. If the prospect asks, "Can I write a check?" this would be a buying signal (and we're astounded at how many times we've seen trainees miss this one). "Can you deliver on the weekend?" This, too, would be a buying signal. Perhaps the prospect confers with a colleague or spouse; you know they're ready to make a decision.

The briefest comment about a color preference indicates an internal commitment. Changes in voice tone are often important buying signals. If calm matter-of-factness begins to turn to excitement, or if nervous chattering begins to settle down and become more businesslike, these are both buying signals.

■ WRAP UP THE SALE

Summarize with, "That about wraps it up. What do you see as the next step?" Whatever course of action the prospect suggests will move you directly toward the sale.

"From what you've understood so far, is this a product you would be interested in owning?"

"Based on what we've discussed, how do you see this service working for your company?"

"What do you like best about this?"

If the answer is negative, ask:

"What other questions do you have?"

"What are you uncertain of?"

Now, ask questions to identify where you missed their needs.

A negative response means the selling process isn't over yet. It doesn't necessarily mean that the prospect doesn't want your product. It may be that your prospect doesn't fully understand the benefits your product offers.

If the answer is positive, go for the close.

■ CLOSING ON THE PHONE

If you've done a good job of qualifying your caller, determining their needs, and demonstrating how you can satisfy those needs, your caller is just a whisper away from becoming your customer.

There are a number of closing statements you can use over the phone:

➤ *Assumption*—"It seems that this meets your needs. How do we go about getting it into your company?"

➤ *Recommendation*—"Based on what you've told me, I recommend that you buy our ____ model. How long would it take for you to get an order through your purchasing department?"

➤ *Alternate choice*—"I think our company can solve your problem. Would you prefer model ____ or model ____?"

➤ *Summary of benefits*—"To summarize . . . (refer to your notes). How do you see this product fitting into your company?"

➤ *Today*—Give them a compelling reason to act today. "You can take advantage of our special. How would you like to proceed?"

After the prospect agrees, do not continue to sell. You run the risk of confusing the prospect and losing the sale. Besides, it's time to move on to the next caller.

Create your action plan, such as taking the order on the spot, arranging a date and time for a salesperson to follow up, or arranging for a quotation to be faxed. Thank the prospect, and dial the next number.

■ GET YOUR FULFILLMENT PACKAGE OUT IMMEDIATELY

This greatly increases your odds of closing sales. Lead management consultant Mac McIntosh says, "If your literature is immediately on your prospect's desk, they'll be very impressed with your service—impressed enough that they'll want to do business with you. You are demonstrating your responsiveness. People perceive that you conduct all your business that way, and people like to do business with companies that are responsive. According to TARP, a government-funded study, when service is perceived to be immediate, 95 percent of customers will do business with you again."[1]

■ CALL TO CONFIRM RECEIPT

Within a day or two of the prospect's receipt of your packet, call and confirm, "Did you receive the material we sent you?" If no, offer to send another at once, or offer to fax the information immediately. If yes, ask, "What did you like best about what you saw?" The likely response will be, "Uh, I haven't looked at it yet." Then ask, "Well then, how soon should I follow up?" and schedule a telephone appointment. If they have looked at the literature, their response will tell you how close you are to closing. A certain percentage of your prospects will close themselves, then and there. Others will ask questions before ordering, and still others will want you to make a face-to-face appointment. A few will decline your offer, having decided that they don't have a need after all.

---

[1]You can reach Mac at 800-944-5553.

■ SEND IT BACK

Rich Vanderport, National Sales Manager for Credit Acceptance Corporation in Detroit, suggests enclosing a self-addressed, stamped envelope along with your sales literature.

"I call to ask if they've read my material, and when they say, 'No, I haven't gotten to it yet,' I explain: 'If you're really not interested, that's fine, but that stuff is expensive. If you don't mind, would you please mail it back to me?' " Over 90 percent of prospects faced with this choice will exhibit a *polarity* response—that is, they'll offer to do the exact *opposite* of what Rich is suggesting. "No, I'll get to it today," they promise. By asking them to return the material, the prospect feels motivated to act on it without feeling pressured to buy.

Rich says that many times, prospects who don't have a need for his services will use the postage-paid envelope to forward the material on to a colleague who does. He's closed several referral sales this way, and his return rate is practically zero.

■ ASK FOR REFERRALS

There's nothing unconventional about asking for referrals, except that no one does it. When was the last time a vendor asked you for a personal referral?

Ask everyone for referrals. Thirty days after delivery is the best time. It's during that first month when people tell everyone about what they bought. Remember when you bought your last car? You asked your friends, "Want to go to lunch? I'll drive!" And some even said, "Hey, this is a nice car. I ought to check this out!" They were hot, ready to go; all they needed was a sales call. Find this person by asking, "Who else do you know who has just bought a house, had a new baby, or is planning to buy a computer?" Ask specific questions to qualify these new prospects. "Why did you recommend that I speak with them?"

Ask for referrals anytime someone offers you a compliment. Say, "Thank you! Can you think of someone else who would appreciate that same level of service?"

■ THE 5-4-3-2-1 REFERRAL SYSTEM

Here's a referral system from our colleague Mitch Axelrod. Mitch points out that it's not just the questions, but it's the sequencing of the questions that makes this work. Many times people don't ask the questions, because they don't want to know the answers. Guerrillas know why they're successful and why they're not successful. First ask, "Will you help me to help you more effectively? I learn how to serve you better when you can help me with the answers to a few questions."

5. "Why did you buy from me?" You'll learn the reasons, their feelings, and your benefits—often, they are benefits you didn't consider.

4. "How do you feel about the work I've done?" You'll learn how you affected the sale.

3. "What are you satisfied with or pleased about?" These are things that are likely to please other customers. They are also the things you can do to sell to this customer next time.

2. "What would you change or do differently if you had to do it all over again?" You'll learn the things that are keeping you from closing sales with other people. This question can make you lots of money!

1. "How can I better serve you in the future?" Now you know how to sell more to them.

They've just been reminded how well you've served them, so now is a good time to ask for the referral. "I'd rather serve my current customers than search for new ones. Would you be willing to introduce me to three people whom I can serve like I've served you?"

At the very least, these questions will get you a testimonial letter. At best, they will get you an endorsement. Record the interview on tape, and ask if you can send out the tape as part of your sales materials.

■ THANK-YOU NOTES

When you talk with someone particularly interesting, personally write a follow-up note. Let your prospect know that more information will follow in the mail or that you'll be in touch soon. The extra, personal contact that a note gives will take you miles ahead of your competition. Use our THANKS approach:

T—*Today!* Write your thank-you letter the same day, if at all possible, and get it in the mail. The only thing worse than receiving a late thank-you note is receiving none at all. An E-mail thank-you note is inexpensive, easy to get out, and arrives instantaneously.

H—*Handwritten.* In today's world of word-processed everything, a handwritten note especially stands out in a stack of mail. It will probably be the first piece read. A barely legible, scrawled sentence has more impact than a typewritten page.

A—*Active.* Make your note active. Don't start out "Dear John"; say, "It was great to speak with you today, John!"

N—*Next step.* Remind them what is planned to happen next. "I'm really looking forward to seeing the installation of your new equipment. Sincerely, Mary." Make sure your reader knows what to anticipate, what date to check, and when to expect action.

K—*Keep it short.* You only need 25 words or so. A few sentences are enough to make the point and the impression. Write the note in 90 seconds or less.

S—*Specific.* Be very specific on why you're writing the note. For example, "I kept thinking about what you need, and I believe I have an answer. I'll call Monday with my idea." You can be certain that your call will be taken.

Chapter
Dealing with Objections

Nothing will ever be attempted if all possible objections must first be overcome.

—SAMUEL JOHNSON

When guerrillas hear "No," they know that "No" is not "No forever." "Is that a forever decision? Is that the only decision you'll ever make? Am I in the game down the road? If you could learn about a solution, would you implement it? No, until when?"

■ WHERE OBJECTIONS COME FROM

Until a salesperson speaks, the prospect has no objections, only concerns. It's when a salesperson says something to which the prospect objects that objections arise.

In the traditional method of selling, a salesperson would qualify the prospect, making sure that they needed what was sold, that they could afford it, and that they could make a decision. After that qualification step, the salesperson delivered a brilliant presentation and doing so, created objections. In that brilliant presentation, they accidentally said things that the prospect found objectionable.

Salespeople who present before they know the issues are the source of all objections. When you face an objection, it's because a salesperson has talked with your prospect before you did, cre-

171

ating objections, or you've accidentally said or done something that caused them concern.

➤ Words That Create Objections

Salespeople even create scenarios that predispose a prospect to object. The old-school sales pro would say, "If I can meet your needs, *will* you buy from me?" That's a question that most prospects would answer with, "Yes." Yet, guerrillas know that this question is a trap. Any time a prospect smells a trap, they are extra wary. The prospect now actively listens for reasons not to do business with that salesperson, to get out of the trap. They listen to the presentation wanting to find objections.

Instead, guerrillas ask, "If I can meet your needs, *can* you buy from me?" This simple word change converts the trap into a test. Is this the right time, the right place, and are you the right person for me to serve?

➤ Creating Objections That Work for You

When guerrillas can't make the sale because the situation isn't quite right, they will leave behind a time bomb. This is an idea that will cause the prospect to object when talking with competitive salespeople. The time bomb takes the form, "When you talk to our competitor, make sure you ask about ____."

Think of concerns that your customers have mentioned about the competition, and ask your prospect to consider those concerns. Guerrillas do this without mentioning the competition's name. "Before I let you go, I'd like to leave you with this one idea: our customers tell us that their greatest concern is reliability and rapid repair when things break. I suggest that you think about how you'll know that the company you choose has the best reliability and the best repair policy."

■ WHEN TO HANDLE OBJECTIONS

Most salespeople are taught to handle an objection when it arises. Yet, when a prospect raises an objection, they own it. They have to change their mind for the sale to proceed. Most salespeople have been trained to overcome objections with piles of information or clever twists, making the prospect's objection wrong. But prospects will defend their objection because they don't want to be made wrong.

The preemptive strike is the best way to eliminate objections. Let your prospect state concerns, and you can help eliminate those concerns, something that both you and your prospect are committed to.

Guerrillas refuse to discuss their solution until they know the prospect's concerns and then only discuss things that eliminate their concerns. The "37 Magic Questions" in Chapter 17 let you sound out the potential concerns. These questions are specifically created to help you eliminate all of the common objections. You'll know what your prospect's concerns are before you begin to present.

➤ Object First

If you find a concern that you can't eliminate, raise the objection first. "You said that you need delivery in two weeks. Unfortunately, because of demand, we can't get it to you for four weeks. What do you think we should do?" Now you and the prospect are cooperatively finding a solution to what could have been your problem.

➤ Universal Criteria

The exception to presenting before understanding concerns is discussing universal criteria. All prospects wish to *save time, save money,* and *eliminate headaches.* These are universal. You can discuss them anytime, anyplace, anywhere and not raise an objection. Your prospects may not find the arguments as compelling as you do, but they won't object to the discussion.

■ *NO* CAN BE CULTURAL

We wrote most of this book at a cabin on Lake Melissa, on Mark's family homestead in northwest Minnesota. One afternoon, we were musing about the peculiarities of Minnesota manners. For example, even though people are always offering you food, it is impolite to accept on the first, or even the second, attempt. Natives will hold out for hours.

"Would you like a bar?" (a cookie baked in a pan)
"Oh, . . . no I couldn't."
"Baked 'em fresh."
"Well, . . . I don't want to be a bother."

"Oh, it's no bother. I've cut one for you already."
"I'm tempted, . . . but I couldn't."
"It'll only take a second."
"Well, . . . alright."
"Would you like some coffee with that?"
"Oh, . . . no I couldn't."
"Brewed it fresh."
"Well, . . . I don't want to be a bother."
"Oh, it's no bother. I've poured some for you already."
"Well, . . . alright."
"Would you like some cream?"

Moral: when someone says "no," they may just be trying to be polite. People don't stop having wants, needs, and agendas, we just give up. Clients' needs are constantly changing. Guerrillas keep going back, and they will take "no" for an answer again and again.

■ THE ABOUT-FACE

Often, a prospect has a concern and yet can't quantify it. Guerrillas use the *about-face* to get more information about the unquantified concern.

"I'm concerned about your quality," objects the prospect.

"Quality. When you say quality, what exactly are your referring to?" inquires the guerrilla, using a flat tone of voice so as not to sound condescending.

Use the about-face anytime you hear, "Your delivery takes too long." "What exactly is too long?" Or, "You don't have what I want." "Want? What exactly is it that you want?"

■ GETTING UNSTUCK ON PRICE ISSUES

Price is always more important in the mind of the seller than in the mind of the buyer. The buyer has a problem to solve and is willing to part with hard-earned cash to solve it.

➤ Don't Discount

According to a 15-year study conducted by the sales-training firm VASS, 67 percent of salespeople will volunteer to cut their price, *without being asked*. When a prospect understands the value of what you offer, price is seldom the real issue. When a salesperson needlessly cuts price, they're liquidating the company for the benefit of the customer.

It's in the prospect's best interest for the seller to think that price is most important. Unless your prospect can make you think your price is too high, they won't stand a chance of getting a discount.

All things being equal, prospects will select the lower price. Guerrillas make sure that all things are never equal.

A majority of your prospects won't buy on price alone. In a survey by the Forum Corporation, only 15 percent of industrial buyers change vendors when they find a lower price. The American Retailers Association found that only 14 percent of consumers base purchases solely on price.

What keeps buyers awake at night is not that they've paid too much, but that what they've bought won't work, or that the product won't be there when they need it. In a survey of 64 industrial buying agents, of those with more than two years' buying experience, 70 percent selected the vendor with the best delivery record, and 30 percent selected the vendor with the best quality record.[1] Those who bought from the lowest-price vendor had less than two years experience; they hadn't yet been burned.

➤ Discount Requests

It's part of a buyer's job to ask for a discount. If they don't ask, they won't get a better price. They have nothing to lose and everything to gain by asking for a price concession. Any buyer that's been to a negotiating seminar has been taught to ask for price concessions at least twice before settling on the final price. You'll hear, "You're going to have to sharpen your pencil to do business with me," or, "That price is unacceptable," or "You're sure proud of your products," or other indications that they want a lower price.

Expect to be asked to lower your price, and have weapons at the ready to keep your price intact.

---

[1] Steinmetz, Lawrence L. *How to Sell at Prices Higher than Your Competitors*. Boulder, CO: Horizon Publications, 1994. p. 19.

➤ Higher Prices Imply

When a prospect says, "Your price is too high," the guerrilla will say, "Thank you!" A product priced higher than the competition often means better quality or value.

Try this response: "We have no argument with people who sell for less. They know best what their products are worth."

➤ What's Too Expensive?

When a prospect says, "Your price is too high," the guerrilla will find out what "too high" means with the about-face. "Too high? When you say 'too high,' what do you mean? 'Too high' compared with what?" Find out if you're two cents too high, two dollars too high, or two hundred dollars too high.

■ PRICE SHOPPING

You'll often get calls requesting price quotes. Questions about price are easy to ask. Even the least educated prospect can ask about price. If a person knows exactly what they want, they'll call around for the best price. You choose how you want to handle their request. Many retailers refuse to quote prices over the phone; they invite the prospect into the store to talk it over.

➤ "Call Me Last . . ."

When Mark was buying a piano, he knew exactly what brand and model he wanted, so he called around for the best price and delivery. One guerrilla dealer refused to give him a quote. "Call me last, and I'll see what I can do." Not only did that dealer match the best price, he threw in a piano bench and free delivery, locking down the deal.

➤ "We'll Be the Most Expensive . . ."

A housepainter was frequently asked to quote jobs. Although he put a lot of time into carefully creating quotes, few people agreed to his price. Now this guerrilla prequalifies prospects with, "I'll be glad to give you a quote on painting your home, but I want you to know in advance that it will probably be the most expensive proposal you'll get." Fifty percent of the people hang up on him. He chuckles, knowing that they would never have agreed to his quote, and he's creating a reputation for being the best painter in town. The people that stay on the line ask, "Why?" Now he has the opportunity to educate them on his top-of-the-line approach.

➤ "I'd Prefer Not to Quote Until . . ."

Guerrillas never give price quotations without finding out about the customer's problem. A guerrilla who sells copy machines often gets requests for price quotes. She asks, "Who else are you considering?"

"We've decided on the model, and our company policy is to get three price quotes," they'll reply.

The guerrilla responds, "I'm in business to help you get the best possible copy machine at the best possible price and offer you the best possible service. I'm not in business to help you get a better price from my competitor. I'd prefer not to give you a quotation. I'd prefer to see how I could best serve you. May I come by to review your decision?"

■ MANAGING OBJECTIONS

Guerrillas know that objections are actually buying signals. If the prospect wasn't interested, they'd just say so. If they have an objection, it means they're interested, but they're not confident enough to move forward with their purchase. Here are some tools for managing objections created by other salespeople or that might arise accidentally.

➤ Go for the Concern

Your prospect's objection is masking an unexpressed *concern.* Instead of overcoming the objection, guerrillas go for the underlying concern. You can think of the objection like the tip of an iceberg—the real issues are hidden out of view, below the waterline. Before responding to the surface objection, guerrillas probe to expose the deeper concern.

➤ "I Don't Know Your Company"

The prospect's concern is, "I don't know enough about your company to make an informed decision. I've been burned in the past by people I don't know, and that's not going to happen again."

Guerrillas respond with, "What would you need to know about us to feel comfortable doing business with us?" Or, "How do you decide who is a viable vendor?"

➤ "We Like Our Current Vendor"

The prospects are comfortable with their current vendor, or they're not uncomfortable enough to change.

Guerrillas respond with, "Great, I'm so glad to hear that you've found a company that does everything exactly the way you want! Tell me, what do you like best about them? What do they do that drives you crazy? Is there anything that they aren't doing for you that I might be able to do for you?"

The Spare Tire

You might try the "Spare Tire" response. The guerrilla asks, "Do you drive a car?"

"Yes."

"Do you carry a spare tire?"

"Of course."

"Why? You have four perfectly good tires. Have they ever failed you?"

The prospect responds with something like, "No, but what if I have a flat?"

"Of course, and it will always be at the most inopportune time and the most inconvenient place. Right? That's why it's just prudent to carry a spare. I'd like to be your spare supplier. No matter how good they are, one of these days they will let you down, and it will be under the worst possible circumstances. Here's my number. You can get me out of bed at 3:00 A.M. if you need to."

Now, sit back, and wait for the inevitable to happen.

➤ "We Have a Long-Standing Relationship with (Supplier)"

In this case, the concern is that they may break a long-standing relationship or that the newcomer will not understand their needs in as much detail. The fact is that if they're a long-time customer, the current supplier is probably taking this business for granted.

An effective counter to this common objection is the "How do you know . . . ?" response. Ask them, "How long have you been using this supplier?"

"Forever."

"Then how do you know that you're getting the best possible deal, or even the most current technology? You should be trying other vendors routinely, if for no other reason than to keep your primary suppliers on their toes. Give us 10 percent of your business, let us show you what we can do, and if we can't do better than the company you use now, fine. The worst that can happen is that you get a better deal from your primary vendor."

➤ **"I Don't Like Your Company"**

The prospect is concerned with having an unpleasant experience buying from your company. You will never do business with this prospect until you understand why they don't like you. Then you must introduce new information to help them view your firm in a new light. They may not like you because of past experience, or because their boss didn't like you, or because someone they respect was disparaging about your company.

The guerrilla responds with, "Well, that makes it difficult to serve you. What has been your experience that makes you say that? What would we have to do to earn your trust?"

"Will you forgive me?" is a powerful way to reopen a damaged relationship. If they refuse to forgive you, move on, and wait for a change in management.

➤ **"I'm Too Busy Right Now"**

The concern is, "I don't see value in spending time with you right now." This happens. Prospects can be up to their ears in alligators and won't have time to consider your offer.

Guerrillas look for some way, no matter how small, to serve this prospect. "In ten seconds, could you tell me your most pressing problem?" Most prospects will give you ten seconds.

They could respond with, "I'm understaffed and looking for good workers."

Guerrillas bring more than their products to prospects. "I talk to lots of people every day. Sometimes, I run across people who say, 'Do you know anyone who's looking for good people? I want to do something different.' If I think they would be appropriate for your company, may I ask them to call you?"

The guerrilla has offered a small solution to that prospect's problem. You've established a caring relationship that opens the door wider the next time you call.

➤ **Delivery**

"I need it sooner than that!" the prospect exclaims.

Guerrillas respond with, "Maybe there's something I could do. Tell me more about your schedule."

Then explore ways to provide loaner equipment, deliver partial shipments, buy product on the open market to tie them over until you can deliver, find a partner to serve them short-term, or delay their deadline on your delivery by accelerating other parts of their schedule.

➤ Functionality

"It doesn't do what I need it to do," objects the prospect.

Guerrillas respond with, "What are you trying to accomplish? How will you know when you've found what you need?" Because you're the expert, perhaps there are other ways to accomplish the task that your prospect isn't aware of. Guerrillas carefully educate the customer: "Have you considered . . . ," or "Have you thought of . . . ?"

➤ Content Reframe

Take your prospect's concern and reframe the concern. It's like having a camera focused on one part of the problem and then moving the camera to focus on an opportunity that outweighs the concern.

"I don't think it's worth the extra money."

The guerrilla responds with, "I understand your concern. It seems like it's a lot of money to spend. Yet, you said that you're concerned with the cost of your line being down. The price difference between buying this more reliable product and buying the cheaper model is the cost of your line being down for one hour. What would keeping your line up and running one more hour be worth?"

➤ Context Reframe

Take your prospect's concern, and change the value of the concern by putting the concern into a different context. It's like a camera that's zoomed in tight on the problem and then zooming out to show a bigger picture. "I complained that I had no shoes until I met a man who had no feet."

"I'm not sure. Getting the large computer monitor seems frivolous."

The guerrilla responds, "You're right. I understand your concern. Yet, you said that you spend most of your day with your computer. And the reason why my customers invest in larger screens is to decrease eyestrain, to view more information at once, and to increase their productivity. I've never considered increasing my productivity to be frivolous.

➤ It's Just Like . . .

Use an analogy. Compare this situation with an experience from your prospect's past that had a happy outcome. For a delivery issue, the guerrilla offers, "Can you think of a time when you waited longer than you really wanted to get something, and when you got it, you were glad you waited? You have? Well, it's just like that!"

➤ Feel, Felt, Found

The universal objection buster is *feel, felt,* and *found.* The guerrilla wants to move the prospect from their position of feeling that the solution won't work, to a position that it might work. The traditional approach has been, "Your price is too high."

"I understand how you *feel.* Other customers have *felt* the same way. And they've *found* we're the best value."

■ SALES SAVERS

Sometimes, the sale doesn't work out the way you expected. The ultimate guerrilla weapon is the truth. Tell your prospect that you've made a mistake, and they'll be inclined to trust you next time. Guerrillas learn from every missed sale and often save the relationship in the process.

➤ "Before I Hang Up . . ."

The guerrilla says, "Before I hang up, let me ask you one final question. It was the price, wasn't it?" Talk about the one concern you weren't able to care for. Most often, your prospect will tell you what blocked the sale. You can now decide how to handle that barrier.

➤ "I Misunderstood You . . ."

If you do your presentation prematurely and accidentally create an objection, you can recover with something like: "Oh! Stop! Reset! Rewind! I misunderstood you. My fault! I told you about the wrong thing. Let's start over again."

➤ "I'm New at This . . ."

"I'm new at this. You're obviously a savvy buyer. What advice would you give a newcomer to this business? I'd appreciate any wisdom you have for me."

➤ "If You Were in My Shoes . . ."

"If you were in my shoes, what would you do in a situation like this?"

➤ "Could You Help Me?"

"Could you help me? I want to serve my customers, and, obviously, I'm not able to serve you. I'd be grateful if you'd tell me what keeps me from serving you."

➤ "I Guess I Blew It . . ."

"Well, I guess I blew it. Do you believe that people should learn from their mistakes? Would you help me learn from this one?"

Serve to Sell Again

Karl Albrecht and Ron Zemke, in their book, *Service America,*[1] say it costs five times as much to sell to a new customer as it does to make the same sale to an existing customer. Guerrillas know that the real money is in the subsequent sale, and they will spend far more than might seem prudent at first glance to buy back a customer's good graces.

■ YOUR GUARANTEE

Guarantees are important to TeleSelling, because they remove the risk of doing business with someone the prospect can't see or touch. The best guarantees are 100 percent money back, no quibbles. Guerrillas will either pay the return shipping or let the customer keep the purchase.

An effective guarantee begins with letting the customer know what their recourse options are. Federal Express promises to deliver by 10:00 A.M. the next day or your money back, "When it absolutely, positively, has to get there overnight." The best ones are simple, like the mail-order giant Lands' End: "Guaranteed. Period."

When the publishers of *Quicken,* a low-cost, personal accounting software package, were just getting started, their ads encouraged you to "Try *Quicken* for a month. If you like it, send us your

---

[1]Albrecht, Karl, and Ron Zemke. *Service America: Doing Business in the New Economy.* New York: Warner Books, 1995.

check. If not, just *keep it,* and owe us nothing." The offer seems ludicrous, but it was costing them more than the purchase price just to repackage and restock the returns. The just-keep-it guarantee is a real confidence builder and a real sales builder as well.

We're seeing many firms go beyond the "Your money cheerfully refunded no questions asked for a year"–type guarantees, to "Your money back plus five dollars," or "Double your money back." Our favorite was painted boldly on the side of a large truck: "Sunshine Trash Service. Your satisfaction guaranteed or double your trash back!"

Guerrillas use their guarantee as a way to calm concerns and close sales. "I could send out demo disks, yet why don't I just send out the whole product. You can review it at your leisure. If you decide to keep it, I'll bill your credit card in 30 days. If you decide it's not for you, I'll send a courier to pick up the package at no cost to you. I urge you to call our technical support about any questions you have, to not only get your questions answered, but to also find out how well our technical support works. Let me give you the toll-free VIP support number. Are you ready to write this down?"

■ ENCOURAGE COMPLAINTS

Guerrillas encourage customers to complain, because it provides valuable feedback about how they measure up. Customers who complain are telling you what you need to do to keep them as a customer.

Most customers don't complain. They simply take their business elsewhere. Think about the last time you went to a mediocre restaurant. Did you complain to the manager? Ninety-six percent of customers don't complain. Is it any different for your business?

Another factor to consider is that upset customers are very reluctant to complain. For every customer that does, you have 26 others who simply leave and say nothing; for every problem they bring to your attention, there are 13 customers who have had the *same* problem.

If you did complain, will you return to that restaurant? Seventy-five percent of customers will return if the complaint is resolved, and 90 percent will return if the complaint is resolved quickly. This reconnaissance can give them the competitive edge.

Remember from Chapter 10 that guerrillas track both satisfiers (if you do these, the customer will be more satisfied) and dissatisfiers (if you do these, they will be less satisfied). Satisfiers and dissatisfiers are independent. That is, failing to provide a satisfier will not provoke a negative response, and providing more satisfiers does not necessarily compensate for a dissatisfier. For example, lower prices (satisfier) will not compensate for poor housekeeping (dissatisfier). By eliminating the dissatisfiers, guerrillas make more customers happy while maintaining reasonable margins.

■ LIFETIME VALUE OF A CUSTOMER

A good way to determine how far you can go and still stay in the black is to calculate the "lifetime value" of your customer.

According to the US Department of Agriculture, the average American spends $5,283 per year on groceries, or about $100 a week. Twenty percent of Americans move every year, so that means that we stay in the same neighborhood an average of five years. We'll spend $5 \times \$5,283 = \$26,415$ (give or take a few dollars) at our neighborhood grocery store during our customer lifetime. At an average margin of 3 percent of sales, our lifetime value to our local grocer comes to about $792. So when a customer complains that the roast beef is off, there's nothing to be gained by questioning or quibbling. Replacing the product is a lot less expensive than replacing the customer. You may win this argument but lose this customer's future business to your competitor.

Do the same calculations for one of your customers, and the figures will shock you. Keep in mind that when a customer complains, you can spend up to that figure to make it right and still break even!

Now multiply the lifetime value of the complainer times the constituency of 13 others that they speak for, and you begin to see the real economics of providing aggressive customer recourse.

➤ Whatever It Takes

Push the decision-making authority down to the lowest level possible. Nordstrom's instructs their salespeople to: "At all times, use your own good judgment." A bank in Dallas authorizes tellers to waive up to $100 in charges or to spend up to $100 to make things right with a customer on the spot. Disputed overdrafts, errors in calculating interest, or mysteriously missing deposits are dealt with swiftly with the stroke of a pen, without an argument, and without having to check with a vice president. In branches of Chicago-based Bank One, elaborate point-of-sale displays promise to do "whatever it takes."

When a customer does complain, listen carefully. Ask, "That sounds important. Do you mind if I take notes?" Express your concern, "Sounds like we have a real problem here that needs some attention." Do not volunteer a solution; rather, ask what it would take to set matters straight. More often than not, they will ask for a *smaller* adjustment than the one you were prepared to offer. Then, whatever adjustment they suggest, do it, and a little bit extra.

Be careful not to overadjust for the error, or you risk leaving the customer feeling guilty. Once, after buying a new set of tires, I complained that they had been mounted white sidewall out, even though I had failed to express my preference. The shop not only remounted all four wheels, but over my protests, waived their normal charges for mounting and balancing. I'd have been quite happy had they simply (and cheerfully) remounted the tires. Their adjustment was so unreasonably generous that it felt condescending, and I haven't had the courage to face them again.

Most importantly, act *now*. Immediate attention to a problem is a far more critical satisfier than delayed compensation, no matter how lavish.

Finally, express your sincere appreciation by saying, "Thank you for bringing this problem to our attention. No doubt others have had the same experience. We appreciate the opportunity to improve." A customer who has had their complaint satisfactorily resolved is five times as likely to buy from you again!

■ TWELVE WAYS TO DEAL WITH ANGRY CALLERS

You might have angry callers for a variety of reasons. Some people may have had a bad experience with your product, your service, or your company. Some people may object to what you sell based on their belief system. And there are a few people who are just in a foul mood because of something completely unrelated.

➤ *Listen carefully.* Immediately begin taking notes. Tell them, "What you're saying is important. I'm taking notes, would you please slow down?" Now move from your regular, 70-words-per-minute typing speed to hunt-and-peck mode. This gives them a chance to take a breath, and they'll begin to calm down. Taking notes demonstrates that you're willing to listen and that you're trying to resolve the problem, whether you actually can or not.

➤ *Assume nothing.* Behave as if you are completely ignorant of the situation. Sometimes, your knowledge and your caller's account of the same events will be different. Allow for that difference. Say, "I want to understand the problem from your viewpoint. Let's start at the beginning, and tell me what happened." Ask lots of questions to clarify points you don't understand.

➤ *Stay positive.* Don't respond negatively to emotional language. A caller's anger usually isn't personal. They probably don't even know you.

➤ *Empathize.* Do your best to understand your caller's feelings. What if you were in their situation? "Oh, I understand. That would make me unhappy, too."

➤ *Agree to agree.* Make a commitment to work toward an agreeable solution. Say, "I'm sure we can work something out here."

➤ *Ask for suggestions.* Ask, "What would you like for us to do?" This moves them to consider a resolution of the issue. Don't say, "What do you want *me* to do about it?" That sounds like you don't care.

➤ *Adopt their point of view.* Listen to what your caller says, and paraphrase their account back to them for verification and clarification, even though you might not agree with it. This isn't the time to get into an argument. Who's right or wrong isn't the point. Right now, you want to get them calmed down and thinking rationally again.

➤ *Never dextify.* Do not attempt to *de*fend, *ex*plain, or jus*tify* what has happened. People don't want to hear you defend yourself. They want to be heard and to have their feelings recognized and acknowledged, even if you think they are wrong and crazy.

➤ *Never say "I'm sorry."* Don't apologize until the caller is prepared to accept your apology. Instead, say, "I apologize." "I'm sorry" is what you say when you bump into someone.

➤ *Work toward solutions.* Focus on what you can do, rather than what you can't. If the caller asks for something impossible, instead of saying, "I can't do that," make a counteroffer: "I understand your request. What I *can* do is. . . ."

➤ *Call in higher authority.* If your caller continues to be abusive, transfer them. "I'm afraid that I can't help you any further. May I find someone who can?" Wait for their response, and reply with, "Thank you!" Brief your colleague before handing off the call, and introduce your colleague to the caller with a formal title. "Mr. Olson, this is Jane. I have my manager Mr. Stephens on the line. He'll be working with you now." The change in status often breaks their abuse pattern. This is especially effective if the handoff is to someone of the opposite gender. A customer who feels justified being abusive to another man will often turn into a gentleman when dealing with a woman.

➤ *Let go of your anger.* If you hang on to the smallest bit of anger, you'll immediately have an impact on the next call you make, possibly causing you to blow the sale. Most callers don't care what just happened to you, so don't pass along the bad experience.

Calm yourself after encountering an angry caller. Take four quick, deep breaths to flood your brain with oxygen. Next, inhale while you count slowly to 7, and then exhale while you continue the count to 15. Anger changes your breathing pattern, and this exercise resets it to normal breathing.

Part

III

Managing a TeleSelling Department

Chapter
22

Finding the Right People

■ RECRUITING AND HIRING SALES GUERRILLAS

The best predictor of future sales behavior is current sales behavior. This guerrilla approach to screening sales applicants gives you an opportunity to observe their sales skills before putting them on the telephone. By seeing how well they sell themselves to you, you can predict with remarkable accuracy how effective they will be when selling to others.

➤ Set Up Voice Mail

Arrange with the telephone company to set up a dedicated number for you that rings into a direct-dial extension (DDE) or direct inward dial (DID) equipped with voice mail. You will only use this number when you need to recruit telesalespeople.

Run your classified ad outlining the basic qualifications for the job, but do not mention the name of the company. You do not want people dropping in or mailing resumes. The last sentence of the ad closes with the language, "To schedule an interview call (phone number)."

Put an outbound recording on the voice mail that says, "Due to the overwhelming response to our ad, we have had to automate our screening process. At the tone, please leave the following information: your name, your daytime and evening phone numbers, a brief summary of your qualifications, and why you think you would be a good candidate for this job. If your background meets our requirements, you will be contacted for an interview." (BEEEEP.)

Let the ad run for a week or two, and every few days, check the voice mail. Keep in mind that the outbound recording was intended to discourage callers from taking the next step because of the "overwhelming response." Job hunters who give up so easily are not good candidates, so we eliminate the quitters right up front. Those who do leave a message are more likely to take initiative and to follow through with your customers.

First, listen to the voice. Is it warm? Is it friendly? Is it intelligent? Is this the voice of someone who you would feel comfortable representing your firm? If so, save the message; if not, delete it.

➤ Did They Follow Directions?

Once you have narrowed the field, listen to the messages a second time with a legal pad and pen in hand. How well did each candidate follow the specific directions they were given in the outbound recording? This will be an accurate predictor of how well they will follow your directions in the future. Did they state their name clearly? Did they spell it if the spelling would be in doubt? Did they then give you their contact phone numbers and volunteer a best time to call? Did they summarize their skills and experience (benefits) or just read you their resume (features)? Most important, did they close with some sort of call to action; are they asking for the order?

➤ Situational Interviewing

If they pass this litmus test, call them back and conduct your initial interview by phone. What you *hear* is what you'll get, so listen to this candidate from the perspective of one of your customers. Open with the question, "Tell me about yourself." Confirm that they have the requisite experience by asking questions along the lines of, "Tell me about a situation in which you . . ." (dealt with some particular challenge or situation they are likely to encounter in your employ). Watch for them to try to take control of the interview (any good salesperson will) and start asking *you* questions.

➤ Ask for a Resume

By now, you should be able to make a decision. Is this someone you think you would like to hire? If so, they must pass one more test—the fax test.

Ask them, "Could you please fax me a copy of your resume? Yes, right *now.*" You will get one of two answers: either they will stall and apologize and make excuses ("My resume isn't really current, and it's late, and I don't have access to a fax machine," etc.) or they will say, "Sure. I can do that!" That's the response I would expect my salespeople to offer a customer in need. Then check the time/date stamp on the fax, and calculate how long it took them to get it to you. More than a couple of hours is too long.

You can reasonably ignore the resume, except for the references. Call each reference and ask, "Tell me about your experience with Mr. Smith. . . ." If the references check out, call the applicant back, and invite them in for a face-to-face interview. By now, you should have already decided that you would like to hire this person, or don't bother with the interview.

➤ Sell the Position

During the face-to-face interview, your primary objective is to sell them the job and to get them excited about the possibility of working for your firm. Give them the tour. Give other key personnel in the office an opportunity to meet them. Finally, after meeting all the finalists, make an offer to your favorite candidate(s).

Each of these hurdles is designed to give your candidate an opportunity to sell themselves to you as a potential employee. It is this sales behavior, more than any other factor, that is the predictor of their success.

■ TRAINING

We have this argument with our clients all the time: "I can't afford to train all my people!"

"Why not?"

"Turnover's too high."

"What do you mean?"

"Well, what if I train them and they leave?"

"What if you don't train them and they stay?"

Our friend Dan Burrus, in his book *Technotrends,* says, "Your people are your most upgradable resource. Not your computers, your software, or your vehicles. Your people."[1]

---

[1]Burrus, Dan. *Technotrends.* New York: Harper Business, 1993. p. xix.

Train with scripts, coaching (see Chapter 10), and tape-recorded feedback. Study your star producers, and train everyone else to model them.

■ MONITORING QUALITY

Set up a system to monitor the quality of the calls covertly. Sometimes little things make a big difference. Even verbatim scripts tend to drift over time, and tellers who use guided discussion may wander wildly off track without supervision.

■ INTERVENE OFTEN

Give your tellers frequent feedback about their performance and their technique. This is essential, not only with praise, but also with criticism. Let's say that you have a caller who appears to become impatient with younger customers. How do you correct the problem?

➤ Look, Listen, and Level

The first step is to isolate the specific behaviors that are objectionable. It would be pointless to tell the employee that they're being brisk or rude with young customers, unless you can substantiate your point of view. Discreetly watch and listen carefully for a few days. Take notes about the context of the calls, including the exact time of day. Check the customers' names on the call list or order form. You might even make spot calls back to ask customers how they felt about the way they were treated.

Carefully document each instance in which you feel your employee has acted inappropriately—what the customer asked for, what was said, and exactly how your employee responded. If the employee behaves differently with other customers, note those transactions as well to establish the contrast. When a pattern has clearly emerged, share your findings with your employee. Be objective and specific. Customer service is a very subjective aspect of business and is open to interpretation. "I've noticed an interesting pattern in the way you deal with customers. You have been spending an average of one-third as much time with customers under age 20 as you do with customers who are over 40, regardless of the size of their purchases."

Then level with them. "I'm concerned because more than one-half of the younger customers contacted in my follow-up calls expressed dissatisfaction with how they were served." Offer a rationale for your concern. "This could become a problem, because young customers represent nearly one-quarter of our sales today and future sales tomorrow. It would be a shame if we were somehow alienating them."

Finally, ask for their point of view. "What do you think?"

Unless mind reading runs in your family, give them the benefit of the doubt. Your employee may be unaware of the pattern, reacting to some unconscious trigger. Perhaps the employee has had a disagreeable experience with a young customer, creating a prejudice that spills over into their attitude. The opposite may also be true. The employee may be overly solicitous with more senior customers out of respect.

Your employee may deny that there is a problem. In that case, cite specific examples backed up with names, dates, and details. Separate the behavior from the person, but your feedback should be undeniably accurate.

Awareness will usually solve the problem. Behaviors that are being measured will usually increase. Try to, as Kenneth Blanchard says in *The One Minute Manager*, "catch them doing something right." When they've given outstanding service to a younger customer, comment on the change to reinforce it. "You really handled that customer with patience and tact. Well done!"[2]

■ COMPENSATION STRATEGIES

Michael LeBoeuf, in his book, *The Greatest Management Principle in the World*, contends that any behavior that gets rewarded will tend to be repeated. He advocates paying close attention to how employees get rewarded for performing (or not performing) the various aspects of their jobs.[3]

Incentive, or performance-based compensation, is nothing new. Commission plans for salespeople are common because their productivity is so easy to document. However, small businesses tend to eschew these compensation plans, thinking that "we're mom and pop—we're different." In the competitive envi-

---

[2]Blanchard, D. Kenneth, and Spencer Johnson. *The One-Minute Manager.* New York: William Morrow and Co., 1981.

[3]LeBoeuf, Michael. *The Greatest Management Principle in the World.* New York: Berkley Books, 1985.

ronment we're faced with today, you have no choice; you *must* use every management tool available to maximize your marketing firepower.

Guerrillas are not only intolerant of nonperformers, but they lavishly *reward* their stars, setting a higher standard of excellence for the whole organization. The problem is how to reward your people appropriately, particularly if they're not directly responsible for easy-to-measure activities like sales revenue.

Some simple guidelines can put this powerful management tool to work for you. The foundation of an effective performance-based compensation plan is a set of clear and specific goals for your organization as a whole, for each functional department, and for each individual employee. These goals must be objective and quantifiable. For example, "Increase inbound inquiry calls by 10 percent or to 650 per month by the end of the year," or, "Achieve an average rating of 4.5 of 5 on monthly customer satisfaction surveys." Subjective factors like attitude or good work habits may be included in review criteria, but if you can't measure it statistically, you can't use it as a standard for performance-based compensation. Then devise methods for gathering data to measure progress (or lack of it) toward these goals. What you measure is what you get, so inspect what you expect.

The first level of your plan should be directed at the individual, by isolating the particular behaviors that would produce the desired outcome. For example, pay a $10 spiff every time an employee asks for and receives a referral from a customer. This behavior, in the long run, will result in more people becoming familiar with your organization and more people buying.

The second level of compensation is directed at the group or unit level. Staff in administrative positions can be set up to share a periodic bonus upon completion of particular benchmark objectives, like "reduce the error rate in the shipping department to less than 5 percent, and share a $500 bonus."

The third level of your plan is structured to reward the collective. Set aside a fund to pay an annual bonus to everyone if the business meets its overall annual goals. In this way, you reward collective effort, as well as individual initiative, and you foster an environment of cooperation and teamwork. Peer pressure becomes a powerful force in keeping everyone on their toes.

Gain-share incentives are often very effective for cutting costs. Challenge employees to keep their own work area clean, reducing the cost of the janitorial service. Put one-half of the savings back into their pay envelopes.

Consider nonmonetary rewards as well. Recognize employees publicly at every opportunity for creativity, leadership, or innovation. For many, a certificate, plaque, or small trophy is more motivating than cash. Encourage competition for these awards by posting individual and departmental performance statistics where everyone can see them. Heated rivalries often develop over the coveted "Employee of the Month" parking space. Even seeing the sales thermometer bar moving up each week can be a powerful incentive.

Reward mistakes as well. Create a rotating gag prize for the employee who makes the biggest mess, the most costly mistake, or the dumbest error. This award should be presented in an atmosphere of friendly fun, never to punish or embarrass. Laughing these things off serves two purposes: first, it encourages people to take risks by letting them know that it's OK to fail, and second, it allows them to pay their dues with co-workers, appease their conscience, and get on with their jobs.

Finally, never argue with results. If a team member goes about achieving their objective in an unconventional way, reward them anyway. What works for you may not work for them. Encourage your people to take responsibility for achieving their objectives, reward them progressively, and stand back. They will amaze you with their ingenuity!

■ INVEST IN YOUR STARS

Guerrilla managers also lavishly reward their stars. They set high standards and goals and are constantly on the lookout, trying to catch someone doing something right. They encourage independent thinking and innovation, and they never argue with results. They are ruthless enforcers of the new ethical standards, highly intolerant of nonperformers who would bring down the curve. They do not abide racist or sexist language in the office, on the shop floor, or even on the docks. If you have more than 15 people working for you right now, fire one of them. That's right. Fire someone. There's someone in your operation right now who is unhappy with their job, and you're unhappy with the job that they're doing, and you already know who they are. Do them a favor by giving them a new opportunity, somewhere else. Chances are they won't be missed, and the rest of your organization will breathe a sigh of relief at their exit.

The competition can't outspend you on things that don't cost money, and this new ethical high ground can give your organization the competitive edge you need to succeed. Plus, it costs you nothing! Fail to elevate your standards, and the competition will eat you alive.

Chapter

23

Measuring Your Success

■ WHY MEASURE?

The basic purpose of a test is to set up a structure that will make three things happen:

1. Permit you to make effective calls to decision makers.

2. Enable you to gather essential data on the efficiency and effectiveness of your TeleSelling operation. This information could include the number of dials per hour and per day; the number of busy signals and connects; how much time is spent waiting to speak to the right person and callbacks; the average call length required to make an appointment or a sale; the number of "yes," "no," "maybe," and "call me later" responses; the best times to call; the average dollar value per sale; the total daily sales, and so on. Such information should be automatically captured in your contact management system.

3. Help you to compile a relational database of valuable information about each customer and prospect.

■ POSTPERFORMANCE CHECKLIST

What worked well?
What didn't work?
What should be different next time?
How are your numbers?

■ MEASURE THE TELESELLING RESULTS

Review what you've accomplished, both for completion and for effectiveness. Did you get what you expected from this campaign? Did you get your target number of contacts, leads, and discussions done? How many new callers did you get to know? How many sales have you closed with your calls?

■ POSTCAMPAIGN SURVEY

After-campaign surveys can help you measure how well the list went for you and how well it reflected the buyers you wanted to reach. Sixty to ninety days after the campaign, select a cross section of prospects, and call until you've talked to 100 of them. Ask these questions:

"We spoke to you back in October about our newest product. Do you have a quick minute, so we can find out how your decision went? Have you bought yet?"

1. If *no,* "Are you still in the market?"

   A. If *yes,* "Would you like a salesperson to contact you?"

2. If *yes,* "From whom did you buy, and what did you buy?"

   A. If the prospect chose a competitor, "Because we want to serve our customers better, what was it that caused you to select them instead of us?"

Tabulate the results, and see how well you did and how well your competition is doing, too.

■ CONDUCT A MAIL SURVEY

1. Decide upon the goal of the survey. What outcome do you want? What do you want to improve? Do you want to improve your people's appeal and effectiveness? How will you know when this goal is achieved?

2. Determine your budget for this survey. Don't forget tabulation and possible phone follow-up expenses.

3. Based on your goal and budget, decide what you will do. We recommend a one-page, self-mailing return survey (with business reply postage-paid) that goes out in your company envelope with a message typed or stamped on the cover that says, "We really need your opinion." These are inexpensive to produce and easy for the respondent to complete and return.

4. Choose a premium to help boost returns. Premiums that work well are drawings for merchandise or discount certificates for what you sell. One of our clients enclosed a dollar bill and a note that said, "We recognize your time is valuable. Would you please take a minute to complete the enclosed questionnaire?" The response rate was nearly 100 percent.

5. Choose about five questions, depending on your goals. Reinforce that the questionnaire is confidential and that no numbers will be reported individually. Include an optional blank for name and address. Consider number coding the pieces for tracking. Questions could include:

   ➤ What did you find most exciting about our product?

   ➤ Did you plan to make a specific purchase decision?

   ➤ Did you make that decision yet?

   ➤ How do you go about making a purchase decision?

   ➤ What was your impression of our sales staff?

   ➤ What do you remember best about the call?

   ➤ What could we do differently to serve you better?

You can also ask respondents to rate your performance on a five-point scale ranging from "strongly disagree" to "strongly agree." Ask them to rate variables like:

➤ The sales staff was knowledgeable.

➤ I got the information that I was looking for.

➤ I want to do business with your company.

If response is poor two weeks after the mailing, do a telephone follow-up, and survey a sample by phone.

■ CUSTOMER SURVEYS

➤ Five Rules for Getting Customers to Respond to Your Surveys

We've all seen them. Stacked on hotel front desks, tucked into the folio with the guest check. Long forms, with endless, empty blank spaces: "Could we have your comments, please? PLEASE?" And as customers, we despise them. Follow these simple guerrilla tactics, and you'll get the feedback you need:

Limit One
Limit your survey to one side of one 8½-by-11-inch page.

Limit Ten
No more than ten questions or items on your survey.

No Fill-ins
Instead of asking customers to fill in the blanks, ask for a letter grade, a numeric rating (from one to ten), or give them a list of choices to check off. Make it easy.

Fax Back
Include your fax number at the bottom of the page, and encourage your customer to fax it back to you. It's cheaper than enclosing an SASE, and you'll get better responses.

Reward Them
Say "thank you" to customers who respond by acknowledging their reply, entering them in a drawing, or sending a small gift (like a credit toward their next purchase). The best way to reward respondents is to share the results of your survey. People are naturally curious about what others have said.

National Car Rental recently sent me a survey and included 500 frequent-flyer miles on the airline of my choice. I bit, and I'm a more loyal customer for telling them what a great job they've done.

Creating Your TelePresence

Creating a Guerrilla Marketing Calendar

Guerrillas use TelePresence in making their presence felt, even when they can't be there in person. We're not talking about your company's presence, but *your* presence. Here's how to show up when you can't be there in person.

■ YOUR TELESELLING CALENDAR

Your properly conducted TeleSelling program creates profits for your company, your owners, your shareholders, and income for you. You market to compel people who can buy from you to buy from you. You want them to think of you, and only you, at the instant they need what you sell. It's your job to keep prospects and customers constantly educated and reminded of what you offer. It's not their responsibility to remember you when they need you. Your buyers are most inclined to choose the person or company who's recently given them the most attention. Your marketing plan systematically lavishes business-building attention on your buyers.

Everything you do is marketing. It's the way the staff at the front desk answers the phone. It's the quality of the paper you use for your letterhead. It's the design of your brochures. It's the words you select for your advertising. It's the ability for you to deliver on time, exactly the way the customer was promised and exactly what they expected. It's the cleanliness of your store, your E-mail address, the location of your factory, the quality of the pen that you use to write up a customer's order. It's all marketing. Every activity must move you to further profits, or you're wasting your time, your energy, and your career.

So do everything on purpose to create the profits your company deserves and to keep your competitive edge. One surefire way to do this is to plan to continually upgrade your marketing.

➤ Marketing Is a Process, Not an Event

TelePresence is not placing a single ad or any one campaign; it's an ongoing process of reaching out to your prospects' and customers' ever changing desires and fickle decision-making processes. A formula for failure is to create events in a vacuum, without thought to related events or coordination with other marketing partners. There are too many things that can go wrong, go over budget, or go to the competition. The secret is a long-term plan with a TelePresence calendar.

Your TelePresence calendar is a daily and weekly plan that lets you maximize your marketing investment. You'll be able to consolidate print runs and mailing jobs, look for synergistic events, and guarantee that your event timing is perfect. You can publish your calendar to your boss and colleagues, so they know what you're doing. You can use your calendar to ensure you meet critical deadlines that can mean the difference between an expensive failure or a high-profit success.

➤ How to Design Your Marketing Calendar

Select a planning method that works best for you, whether that's a sheet of paper for each week of the year (52 pages for your plan), a word processor document, or a project management program, such as Microsoft Project. You'll need enough room to brainstorm, and you'll want a system that makes it easy to send out regular updates to your team.

Round up all the events to which you're already committed. Look at industry trade shows, annual trade magazine roundups, directory deadlines, product releases and introductions, seasonal sales and offers, and other traditional marketing events.

Break each of these into weekly activities and deadlines, and put them on your marketing calendar. Include budget costs, time requirements, and people resources. Factor in approval cycle times and some padding for Murphy's Law. Estimate expected results, and the return on your investment.

You may wish to create a timeline estimate on the profitability of your campaign. When will you break even? When will you be profitable? If you don't know for sure, make an educated guess. A thought-out guess of the outcome is a better planning tool than a foggy notion.

➤ How to Make Your Marketing Calendar Pay Big

Review your entire calendar for the year. How can you combine events and weeks to maximize sales impact and minimize costs? For example, if you're going to print brochures, can you combine your trade show flyer on the same print run? When you're paying big bucks to an art director and package designer, can you recycle the graphics for other marketing events? If you're recording a radio ad, can you include a few more minutes of voice work for your audiocassette program? Can you include your latest media release with the brochure you're sending to prospects? Are you including a product catalog with your annual report? Your shareholders are on your marketing mailing list, aren't they?

Compare your event timing with other events that you don't have control over. Timing can make the difference between success and failure. For example, educational seminars are best attended on Tuesdays and Thursdays, yet these same seminars will suffer if Zig Ziglar's motivational stadium event is in town that day. Never advertise on radio and TV competing with Super Bowl Sunday or the World Series. The April 15th tax deadline has an impact on consumers' buying attitudes. July and August are the lowest-response months for business-to-business, direct-mail offers. Schedule marketing events to arrive when your buyers make decisions or when there are natural life transitions, such as New Year's or back to school. Consider the impact and opportunities of all the holidays, whether you observe them personally or not.

Look for synergistic opportunities, combining marketing events with normal maintenance activities. For example, when you reprint your letterhead and business cards, include your Web address. Put your WWW address on every envelope mailed. People will keep the envelope and refer to the Web address the next time they're Net surfing. Consider inviting your entire staff when planning training events. Invite your support staff to your sales-training event.

➤ Testing, Tracking, and Reporting

Invest 15 minutes a week to review your entire annual plan. Look for new marketing opportunities and synergistic events. Review the results of the completed events. What's working, what's not? Are you getting the return you expected? Why? What could you change now—on the fly—to get better results? What projects have slipped that change the marketing calendar timing? Has anything changed in the approval process? This 15 minutes is the most profitable meeting you'll attend.

Then take five minutes more, and write a paragraph or two on the status and results of your critical marketing events. E-mail that to your colleagues and bosses. (If you have to print out, copy, and distribute a memo, one of your first marketing goals is to get your company on E-mail. According to an *Inc.* magazine survey, 91 percent of small businesses have and use E-mail.) Keep an archive of these reports for your salary and performance review and to impress and update new bosses.

Invest 15 minutes a day to review your weekly and daily marketing plan. On a scale of one to ten, rank the progress and outcome of your events. You can then decide quickly which programs need more time and resources and which ones to cut, minimizing your losses. Do this and you'll have much better control of your marketing events and budget.

➤ Patience!

Successful marketing is a combination of planning, patience, and persistence. Your marketing calendar helps you with each of these key success factors. Start your calendar today, and watch your profits and your career skyrocket.

➤ Brainstorm Your TelePresence Events

Here's a list of ideas to get you brainstorming on the Tele-Presence events that will increase your profits. Here's the secret: find out how your customers get important information, and formulate your offers to reach them that way. If they read magazines, place PR or write articles for the magazines they read. If they commute by car, create an audiotape that they can listen to on the way to work. If you can reach them by telephone, create a TeleSelling blitz.

TelePresence Events

PR and media releases when it's about you.

Telephone effectiveness training of you and your staff.

Telemarketing blitz, touching as many customers as possible.

Educational event at industry trade shows to share your message with many at the same time.

Attend your customer's industry trade show to find more customers just like them.

World Wide Web page for 24-hour accessibility. Update it regularly to keep them coming back.

On-line news group participation. The secret here is that you can include a small "signature line" at the bottom of your posting. Netiquette dictates no more than three lines of commercial message.

Articles placed in newspapers, newsletters, and trade magazines to establish your expertise.

Article reprints that customers find valuable.

Advertising specialties, such as gifts or special offers, to remind them of you everytime they use it.

Software and screen savers that are in their face.

Public educational seminars. The invitations and the seminar materials keep your TelePresence active.

Educational booklets and pamphlets, especially when they pertain to doing the job better or more easily.

E-mail newsletters.

Faxed flash bulletins.

Printed newsletters.

Audiocassette programs.

Videotape brochures.

Newspaper and magazine columns.

Billing inserts.

Postcard decks.

Yellow pages ads.

Small gifts to customers at random intervals.

Radio talk shows.

On-line chat sessions.

Radio and TV advertising.

Postcard reminders and offers.

Free samples.

Frequent-buyer club.

Product-of-the-month club.

Customer service training.

Inviting vendors to your company picnic.

Sales training.

Referral program.

Refurbishing your store and office.

Customer feedback program.

Competitive analysis.

Rewrite your sales letters.

Chapter **25**

Staying in Front of the Customer

■ FORK OVER NEW CUSTOMERS

One of our clients, Computers America—a distributor of PCs, peripherals, and supplies in San Rafael, California—enclosed a fork with a batch of sales letters, a rep's business card speared on the tines. The attached note said, "We're hungry for your business. I'd like to buy you lunch. Call and we'll schedule it at your convenience. Bring the fork, and I'll pick up the tab." They had an overwhelming 85-percent response.

■ USING ADVERTISING SPECIALTIES

Guerrillas use advertising specialties imprinted with their company name, logo, and phone number to keep their names unobtrusively visible for months, even years. Any advertising specialty item should reflect the quality of your product and the good reputation of your firm. You don't want your logo on a cheap pen that doesn't write.

Your giveaway should be something that your customer will not throw away. There is a subconscious discounting of who you are when they throw away something you've given them. It should be something genuinely useful, and it should be kept in a place where the prospect will refer to it when they need your product.[1] A good example is the Domino's Pizza refrigerator

---

[1] For a free database search of over 400,000 ad specialty items that may work for your business, call Corporate Pride Promotional Products at 888-333-2291.

magnet. You come home, find nothing in the fridge, and call Domino's delivery. If you can't position your giveaway effectively, don't use it.

The best premiums are those that help your customer get their job done faster or better. They have a high perceived value and cost you very little to reproduce. Information premiums have the highest perceived value and the lowest relative cost. Examples are reprints of articles, special reports, audio- and videotapes, computer software, and books. Such premiums self-select your prime prospects, because they are of little use to the general public.

An effective guerrilla premium is a laminated wallet card covered with valuable reference information that your customers use regularly. For example, a Century 21 office in Denver gives out a threefold city street guide that doubles as their business card. Spectranetics, a company that builds lasers for clearing arterial blockages, created a plastic wallet card summarizing the recommended treatment options for various patient conditions. The cardiologist can discreetly review the technical details of the procedure before scrubbing up. A welding equipment distributor gives out wallet cards with recommended amperage settings for welding a variety of alloys.

The best premium is:

➤ Something that a customer wants

➤ Something that helps them do a better job

➤ Something that they wouldn't necessarily buy for themselves

➤ Something their organization wouldn't buy for them

➤ Something that is specialized enough to self-qualify them as a potential buyer

Specialized tools make excellent premiums. For example, a dive table card for scuba enthusiasts or a plastic slide rule for landscapers, used to calculate application rates for fertilizer. Another example is a wine selection book for a meeting planner or a keyboard-mounted calculator for a computer programmer.

You can also use a controlled giveaway to attract and pre-qualify inbound calls. Some of the most desirable giveaways are apparel items, such as T-shirts, hats, and sunglasses. Ask the prospect to complete a survey, or ask them to listen to a presentation to qualify for the prize.

Send prospects imprinted office essentials. Your TelePresence is felt everytime your prospect uses the item.

An overwhelming 98.3 percent of respondents ranked *usefulness* over quality (71.8 percent), attractiveness (61.5 percent), tastefulness (59.8 percent), convenience (45.5 percent), and uniqueness (43.7 percent),[2] as most desirable.

Guerrillas know that gifts need not be expensive to have a big impact. They'll use:

➤ A list with major cities and their area codes on one side and a list of area codes with the corresponding cities on the other side

➤ A pocket currency converter

➤ Business card or Rolodex® card files

➤ Customized sales tax tables

➤ Luggage tags

➤ Memo boards

➤ Multiyear calendars

➤ Organizing accessories

➤ Page markers for their day planner, technical or sales manuals

➤ Rulers

➤ Time zone calculators

➤ Tip charts.

■ CANDY JAR

James Alexander, a sales representative for CompuCentre in Montreal, uses jelly beans as his secret selling weapon. He gives his corporate computer customers a covered-glass jelly bean jar, imprinted with his store's blue logo.

---

[2]The survey published in *Target Marketing* magazine was sponsored by Promotional Products Association International, in conjunction with Southern Methodist University and Louisiana State University. It surveyed 1,500 small business owners, marketing executives, and purchase agents.

The jar sits on the receptionist's desk, advertising Compu-Centre to every visitor who enters. Now, he has a regular excuse to call—he has to resupply the jelly bean jar. While he's there, he makes a list of each employee's preferred flavors, so he can keep their favorites in stock.

He also checks the status of the computer equipment, visiting with each of the operators and clerical staff. This way, he is able to find out about technical problems, software bugs, and future needs well before the competition has been invited in to bid.

■ WHAT TIME IS IT?

A person looks at a timepiece at least 75 times a day. That's 27,000 times a year. Give your customers a clock or a watch to embed your company logo into their subconscious.[3]

■ BUY THEM A SNACK

One guerrilla sends his marketing materials in a box along with a drink and a healthy snack. The note inside says, "Take a break on me! All you'll need is five minutes to see how we can help your staff feel better and be more productive!"

A speaker colleague of ours includes a bag of microwave popcorn with her demo video.

■ POSTCARDS WHILE ON VACATION

People love to get picture postcards from interesting places. Take your customer and prospect list with you, and on the first day of vacation, send key people a postcard. When you get home, you'll find your customers have thumbtacked your post-card to their bulletin board. You get lots of TelePresence.

■ NOTEPADS

Our colleague, Bob Berg,[4] suggests printing up notepads with your picture, address, and phone number in the upper right

---

[3]For more information, call Top-USA Corporation, Worthington, OH, 800-843-3381.

[4]Berg, Bob. *Endless Referrals.* New York: McGraw-Hill, 1994. p. 33.

corner of the page and sending one to your customers and prospects every month. Practically everyone uses notepads, and when people constantly see your picture, you become familiar to them. You want them to think of you, and only you, whenever anything concerning your business comes up.

■ SEND A SERIES

On Monday, the prospect found on his desk a plain, white envelope with his name written on the outside in neat script. It contained an ordinary playing card—the ten of hearts. Tuesday, another envelope appeared on his desk, this time containing a jack of hearts. Wednesday, another envelope and the ace of hearts, and on Thursday, the king.

Friday morning, the receptionist calls. "Excuse me, sir, there is a woman here to see you. She identifies herself only as the 'queen of hearts.'"

"Send her in."

■ BILL STUFFERS

Guerrillas view sending invoices as a golden opportunity to stay in touch with their best prospects—people who have already bought from them.

If you send out a one-page invoice, you have room in the envelope for three more pages. Add a newsletter, or a page of your favorite jokes. It eases the bite of the bill. Insert a coupon along with the invoice. Invite them to trade in or trade up.

Make Your Sales Letters Sizzle

Powerful, new word processors and database management software make it easy to generate mass mailings. Here are some simple rules for keeping your next sales letter out of the round file (Figure 26.1).

Ⓐ Keep sentences short and easy to read, nine to eleven words. Use clear, simple vocabulary, not because readers are simple, but because they're lazy.

Ⓑ Keep paragraphs short as well, three or four sentences. Cut out everything extra. Make every word work like a galley slave. Keep it all on one page.

Ⓒ Open with a "thank you," an example, or a statement with which everyone can agree. The tone should be light, friendly, and informal.

Ⓓ Put your second most important idea in the first paragraph. Put the least important idea in the second paragraph. Close with the most important idea.

Ⓔ For emphasis, use **bold**, or *italics*, or <u>underline</u>, but never <u>***combine***</u> them.

Ⓕ Concentrate on benefits, not features, and don't try to tell the whole story. Just generate a response.

Ⓖ The most powerful four-letter word you can use.

Ⓗ Use the merge function to include a personalizing comment or item. A geographical reference using the city field accomplishes this easily.

(Continued)

THE GUERRILLA GROUP inc

Unconventional Weapons and Tactics for Your Business.

[date]

[first] [last]
[title]
[company]
[address1]
[address2]
[city], [st] [zip]

Dear [first],

(A) **(C)** **(D)** Getting into business is easy. Staying profitable is tough, especially in these tough times. Your members need all the help they can get. They depend on you to bring creative, quality programming to [city].

(H)

(B) That's why we created "The Guerrilla Selling Seminar." It will show your members how to use *unconventional weapons* **(E)** *and tactics* to increase your sales. It's based on the best-selling book, presented by the author, and customized for your audience.

(I) For a convention keynote, half-day work session, or full-day special event, this program is a sure hit. Its ideas and techniques will help your members **(F)** survive and succeed. The Wichita Chamber of Commerce just raised over $10,000 with "The Guerrilla Selling Seminar." Our proven marketing program reduces your risk. Let us show you how. **(I)**Call 1-800-247-9145 **(M)** for a free information packet, and put the recession in retreat. **(G)**

Sincerely,

(J)

Orvel Ray Wilson

(K)

P.S. Respond before September 1, and take advantage of **(L)** reduced speaker fees, available only to nonprofit organizations.

Figure 26.1 Sample sales letter.

❶ Close by asking for some direct action: call, write, or expect to hear from us soon.

❿ Indent paragraphs, and tab the closing to the right.

Ⓚ Even though the P.S. is at the bottom, it's the FIRST thing people read. Put your hook or premium offer here in a single sentence.

Ⓛ Include a deadline, or offer a reward for prompt action.

Ⓜ People are seven times as likely to respond if the call is toll-free.

■ YOUR SALES LETTER

Have your troops poised for a quick after-call attack by having literature packages preassembled and sales letters prewritten, preferably by a professional direct-mail copywriter.[1] Because your letter is the next sales contact you'll make, it needs to work hard, motivating your prospective customer to make the next step. You'll be better off when you pay your copywriter and printer more than you pay the post office. Take a close look at your investment in the sales collateral. It's key to completing the sales process you started with your call. You'll probably spend thousands on literature, printing, postage, and assembly, so invest in help from a specialist. Ideally, your after-call letter should be personalized, at least with the person's name, and better yet, a reminder of what the prospect was interested in and why.

There are four types of letters you can send to your prospect: a form letter, a personalized letter, a customized letter, and an individually written letter.

Form letters open with "Dear Friend" or some such bland and impersonal greeting. Most of the time, they are printed on company letterhead, although sometimes we see photocopies on cheap paper.

Personalized letters have the recipient's name in the greeting. This is the minimum acceptable letter that we recommend for guerrillas. Personalization is well worth the extra expense, and it gives an image that your company is one with the personal touch. You can do a mail merge with a laser printer, creating personalized letters very inexpensively.

---

[1]David Garfinkel, Overnight Marketing, 415-564-4475.

If you have the database to handle it, customize the letters. Customized letters are assembled from prewritten sentences and paragraphs that are selected depending on the information you gathered on the phone. This is a very effective way to have high impact, but it requires a well-designed database and a skilled writer.

Individually written letters should go to the hottest prospects and VIPs. Take the time to write or dictate a letter to these people. The letter should remind them of what you discussed and the commitments they made on the phone.

■ SPECIAL REPORTS

"Say a computer store wants to sell software, hardware, and Internet hookups," says Dan Kennedy. "Why not target people with kids, offering a free report entitled, 'How to Get Your Kid into the College of His and Your Choice'? Let's say 18 of the 101 tips involve the use of the computer. At the end of the report, put in another offer: 'Come to our education fair from March 22 to 24. All of tips 50 to 68 will be on display, with free Internet access and instructors available.' Have a discount offer that day for software or hardware, and give away a demo of 'The Five Greatest Educational Tools for Your Computer.' These are measures that offer value, cost little, and generate goodwill and sales."

Chapter 27

Just the Fax

A fax machine is important to your TelePresence, because you get real-time delivery. Your prospect gets the information the instant you send it. Your sales materials are in the hands of the decision maker while you are still on their mind, not a few days later after other things have become more important.

■ WHAT TO FAX

Many companies use a faxable brochure to make sure there is a match before proceeding with an expensive literature package or proposal.

Companies now offer instant information about their services and products with fax-on-demand. You dial up their computer (often with a toll-free number), follow the voice prompts, select what information you want, and instantly receive the information on your fax machine. This concept and technology can be extended to provide valuable information charged to a credit card or billed with a 900-number.

Some companies now offer faxed information bulletins. Usually on a subscription basis, these services range from daily investing tips, to industry-specific news, to late-breaking events, to monthly newsletters. As postal rates increase and faster delivery time is needed, faxed communication is becoming a widespread distribution method. It costs less to send one or two sheets with a fax than to mail them through the post office. A fax of up to 117 pages actually costs less than overnight delivery (based on phone charges of $0.17 per minute, average 45 seconds per page versus a $15.00 overnight service fee). By faxing documents at night and on weekends when phone rates are lowest, you can save even more.

➤ Design Considerations

When designing your letterhead, logo, or faxable brochure, keep in mind that a major portion of your communication with clients will be via a fax. Here are a few things you should consider.

Use type sizes larger than nine points. In the 200-by-200-dpi world of faxes, this is the legible minimum.

Select fonts that have a large "X-height"—that is, the size of the lower case "x." This will keep your faxes as legible as possible. The font Lucida Fax, available from Microsoft and Adobe, is tailored specifically for clear faxing.

Line drawings work best when faxing. If you must include a photograph, create a halftone with a screen density that will reproduce well on a fax. Have your printer make a fairly coarse halftone screen of 85 dots per inch. Because a normal fax transmits at 98 dots per inch, an 85-dot-per-inch photograph will send with a minimum of problems. Halftone photos take extra time to send over a fax.

Send your faxes in the fine mode. This doubles the dot density and creates an output that is better than many dot matrix printers. It takes from 20 to 50 percent longer to transmit the fax, but because the fax is your image, it is worth the extra time and expense.

Borders and other black space take extra time to send. To minimize phone costs, avoid using screens or shading, as this takes the longest of any graphic to transmit.

Test before you finalize your design. Send your pieces in both fine and standard modes, and make sure you are satisfied with the results. It's your quality image!

■ UNSOLICITED FAX (DON'T DO IT)

The Telephone Consumer Fraud Protection Act[1] specifically bans the transmission of unsolicited advertisements to tele-

---

[1]Copies of the complete Telephone Consumer Protection Act and the FCC's Report and Order in CC Docket No. 92-90, released on 16 October 1992, are available from American Telephone Association, 4605 Lankershim Boulevard, Suite 824, North Hollywood, CA 91602-1891. Phone: 818-766-5324 or 800-441-3335. Fax: 818-766-8168.

phone facsimile machines. If, however, the caller has an established business relationship with the intended recipient, then prior consent is assumed until a "do not fax" request is received.

By law, each fax transmission must have either a header or footer that clearly states the caller's name, telephone number, and the date and time of transmission. All fax machines manufactured after 20 December 1992 must have the capacity to print this information on either the first page or, preferably, every page of the transmission. Again, the company or person on whose behalf the fax has been sent is ultimately responsible for compliance.

■ BROADCAST FAX

Computer software, like WinFax Pro and ACT!, allows you to transmit the same document to hundreds or even thousands of recipients, right from your own computer modem. Internet providers, including Compuserve, offer services that do the same thing. You upload your document and your list, and they do the rest.

➤ Fax-on-Request

Always include in your sales literature a number that customers can call to request information by fax. Add a tag to your voice mail, explaining that, "If you leave us your fax number, the information you need will be faxed to you as soon as possible."

➤ Fax-on-Demand

Software is available that allows you to configure an old computer to function as a fax-on-demand terminal. Equipped with a hard disk and modem/fax board, the system answers the phone and an outbound recording explains the directions to the user. The caller can request documents from a list by pressing the buttons on their touch-tone phone. When they hang up, the computer dials their fax number and delivers the requested documents, all automatically.

Many direct-mail and catalog companies are saving money by including a spoiler on the corner of the catalog page that says, "For more information about this product, dial our fax-on-demand and request number 243."

Chapter

Creating Effective Newsletters

Guerrillas use newsletters to stay in contact with their prospects and customers. They use them to position themselves as a professional colleague, as an important resource, and to generate increased sales. Guerrillas also use them to enhance their professional image within a particular industry by serving readers with "How to . . ." articles tailored for that industry.

■ DEVELOP YOUR OWN STYLE

For a newsletter with impact, create a unique editorial and layout, and stick with it. The year-to-year consistency of your newsletter builds credibility with prospects and customers. Also, it is convenient when readers know what to expect.

➤ Advertising

If you accept advertising in your newsletter, keep it minimal. Guerrillas know the impact is greatest when the letter is full of news your customers can use. The exception is when guerrillas run an ad at no cost for their best customers' products and services. The best way to say "thank you for your business" is to give customers more business.

Three-quarters of the newsletter should feature "How to . . ." articles or information about the industry that is important to your readers, or better yet, articles about your customers. The remaining 25 percent of the content should focus on your business, new product introductions, meetings, events, and company success stories.

Newsletter articles can often be written by talking with your customers. Just say, "I'd love to feature you in our newsletter. Do you think you could write 300 words about how you've been successful using our products? Oh, and by the way, if you have a photo, we can use that, too." Reward them by creating a tear sheet of the article that they can use for their own PR.

Build a file of articles you can use. Do book reviews on new titles that would be interesting and useful for your customers. Amazon.com, the world's largest on-line bookstore, provides a free service called Eyes that will let you build a list of key words; any time a new book is published containing those words, you will automatically be sent a notification by E-mail.[1]

➤ Photos

Spice up the newsletter with photographs and artwork. Limit the grip-and-grin photos of people shaking hands or receiving awards. Most customers don't care. Save those for your internal newsletter. Guerrillas use clip art carefully. Choose clip art that's unique and that reflects the quality and identity of your company. You can find artists at your local college who will draw custom cartoons for you for a few dollars. Customers love checklists and directories of resources.

➤ Convenience

Position important information where it's convenient for your reader. Always include phone numbers, Web site, and E-mail addresses. Include a distribution checklist so your customers can route the newsletter to others. Three-hole-punch the newsletter to encourage them to file it after reading, or save money by simply printing black dots where the holes normally go, and your customers will punch it themselves.

➤ Layout

When it comes to layout, guerrillas often do it themselves. Templates included in programs like Microsoft Publisher®, Microsoft Word®, PageMaker®, AmiPro®, or WordPerfect® can give you a quick start. Have your authors write to a word count specification, often 900 words per typeset page, and use the type-tracking adjustment to get articles to fill the pages neatly.

---

[1]http://www.amazon.com.

Have at least three people proofread your work, but don't let your proofreaders rewrite the text! Ask them to check for grammar, spelling, and the correct listing of people's names and professional designations. Double-check dates and times. Ensure accuracy by calling all phone numbers listed.

■ PRINTING

Save money on color printing by creating a one-color shell with your masthead and standing information. Then print enough to last for the year, and drop in the monthly news items with black ink. If you have limited numbers, you can use a quick-copy shop, such as Kinko's.

When using copier technology to print your newsletter, screen photos to 85 lines. This density will give you the best resolution possible on a copier. You can do this with your laser printer for scanned photos using Adobe PhotoShop, or a print shop can do it for you.

Some of the more sophisticated electronic printing systems, like Docutec, can even print the addresses on your newsletter as they are being run. This saves you time and money when running small batches of newsletters.

■ HOW SHOULD YOU MAIL?

Guerrillas often choose to send their newsletter as a self-mailer, folded over to $8\frac{1}{2}'' \times 5\frac{1}{2}''$ and sealed closed with a small sticker or bit of tape. Although an envelope provides some protection, it also adds weight and expense. A self-mailing newsletter arrives ready to read. Keep in mind that international mailings must be placed inside an envelope.

Even though it's more expensive, guerrillas mail first-class for surest delivery. You want to let your customers know that they're first-class. Some companies just toss bulk mail at the mailroom. Wherever possible, use real stamps to get noticed. On larger mailings, you may opt for indicia (like those you see on most bulk-rate mail). You can use indicia for first-class, too, to save all that licking and sticking. The one benefit of indicia is that your newsletter won't go through the canceling equipment, so it may arrive in better shape.

■ WHO TO MAIL TO?

Send your newsletter to customers, prospects, and important people who you want to know about your company, products, and services, such as your local, state, and national government representatives, as well as editors of trade journals in your industry.

■ HOW OFTEN?

Produce your newsletter at least quarterly. Anything less than that and you will lose continuity. You want to establish your newsletter as a routine part of your customers' lives.[2]

---

[2]For a complimentary copy of "War Stories—The Guerrilla Selling Newsletter," call 800-247-9145, or send an E-mail to postmaster@guerrillagroup.com.

Chapter 29

Become an Author and an Authority

Become a recognized expert in your business world. By becoming an author, you're automatically recognized as an authority. Whether you're a banker, salesperson, contractor, retailer, doctor, lawyer, or masseuse, being recognized as an expert in your field creates an identity and TelePresence that you cannot buy with advertising, billboards, radio, or TV commercials.

When you're the recognized expert, the press calls on you when they need information and opinions—and prints your ideas. When you're the recognized expert, publishing companies want to print your book. When you're the recognized expert, people are willing to pay for your advice, knowledge, goods, and services. And it really doesn't matter what you charge for them.

So, how do you become viewed as the recognized expert? If you're an expert in your field already, it's a matter of letting your market know about your expertise. One of the fastest ways to be proclaimed an expert is to make it easy for the media to call you an expert. Consider listing yourself in one of the Who's Who directories, such as the *Yearbook of Experts, Authorities, and Spokespersons.*[1]

■ WRITE FOR TRADE MAGAZINES

Getting published in a trade journal is one of the most powerful ways to create a TelePresence. You position yourself as an expert

---

[1]Published by Broadcast Interview Source. http://www.yearbook.com or 800-YEARBOOK.

and establish credibility that will be tough for your competition to match. Your name and ideas get distributed to thousands of potential clients and customers. Authorship establishes you as an authority in your field, and it builds name recognition in the minds of your prospects.

➤ On Assignment

Next time you call a customer, ask them, "What's your favorite trade journal?" Get a copy from the library, look up the number on the masthead, and call the managing editor. This is the person responsible for getting the magazine out on time. Tell them, "I'm writing a roundup article on the future of our industry." (A roundup article consists of interviews of key industry leaders with their thoughts presented in a contrast-and-comparison format. Guerrillas write about the future, because it's always news.) "Would you be interested in publishing it?" They'll readily agree, because they're always dying for good material. Now you have an assignment.

Call top officers that you want to get to know. Say, "I'm writing an article on assignment for (trade journal) on the future of our industry. When may I have five or ten minutes to ask you a few questions?" They almost always grant an interview, because they always want the free PR.

Ask permission to tape-record the conversation for transcription. Ask questions like, "What do you think is the biggest challenge to the future success of our industry? What should the industry be doing now to eliminate those barriers? What do you think the industry will be like in ten years?" Cut and paste together the interviews, writing introductory and closing phrases and transitions. This takes only a couple of hours. Ask the subject of your interview to send you a black-and-white glossy photo of them for inclusion, if possible.

Include your photo and a small caption with the byline, "For more information, call to receive a free copy of our recommended list for . . . ," and include a toll-free number and an E-mail address.

Oh, yes, it will be published. You interviewed the people whom the editors want quoted in their journal. Send a copy of the final printed article to the people you interviewed with their words highlighted. Better still, frame it. Enclose a note thanking them for making your article so powerful.

When working with editors, always insist on a written agreement that spells out what rights you are granting, even if you are not being paid for the article. Most publications automatically take all rights, so unless you spell out what rights you're granting, you lose control of your intellectual property. Grant only the rights necessary for the publication to run the article, but it is essential that you reserve all other rights. If the article is appearing for the first time, you can grant the publisher *first rights*. If the material has been published previously, you are granting *reprint rights only, one-time use*. You may want to publish the material again in another journal, magazine, booklet, or even include it in a book. You may also want to develop audio- or videotapes, CD-ROM, DVD, or other materials that would involve *electronic* rights. You may want to publish in other languages. A client of ours in Romania ran several articles in a Romanian magazine, so we granted "Romanian language reprint rights only, one-time use." In any case, if you have inadvertently given up your rights to the material, it will create complications later on.

Send copies of the article to prospects and customers to create an impressive TelePresence.

■ WRITE A BOOKLET

Newspaper, magazine, and newsletter publishers have to fill the pages of every issue with material that serves their readers. All you have to do is make it easy for them to do their job, and they'll gladly call you an expert. The easiest way to help them is to publish an informational booklet that they can draw on for material.

During your most creative time of the day, grab a cup of coffee, and sit down with a piece of paper and a pencil. Brainstorm ideas in your field of expertise that people need to know. Jot down the simple and the sublime, the obvious and the esoteric. Use reverses—do this, don't do that. Apply ideas from other disciplines to your area of expertise. Write things down that people haven't thought of, as well as the stuff that everybody knows. Write down at least 50 ideas; 100 ideas would be even better.

Next day, review your list, and put a check mark by 20 to 50 of these ideas that no one else is really talking about or that are critical to the success of your profession or your customers. Then, every day, two or three times a day, write just two paragraphs on each of these topics. Don't cover them in depth, say just enough to get things going. If you have short examples, use them.

After two or three weeks, you'll accumulate several paragraphs on lots of topics that editors can use for fillers, and readers will pay to read. You'll have a short publication that is a wealth of information. Add this copyright notice to the title page: "Copyright (current year) your name. All rights reserved. Permission to reprint quotes and excerpts is given and encouraged. Please include the following credit line: Reprinted from *Your Title,* your name, your toll-free telephone number." Take this to a printer, typeset, create a cover, and price it at $9.95. Print 1,000.

Look for newspapers, customer newsletters, trade journals, and other publications to send it to. Don't limit your list to your current markets. You'll be surprised at the industries that need what you have to offer. Look at the magazines that cross your desk. Look at *Newsletters in Print,* found in the reference section of your public library. This guide includes contact information for small newsletters listed by interest. Look at other publication directories, such as the *Standard Rate and Data Service* (SRDS) *Directory.* Review the *Gale Encyclopedia of Associations* for trade and association newsletters.

Mail your publication to the managing editors, along with a cover letter that points out how this information is important to their readers, that they can reprint it with the credit line, and offer to write a custom article for their readers. Consider including a testimonial letter from a satisfied client. Consistently mail to publications, sending out a few each day.

Expect the phone to ring with orders from readers wanting to order the booklet, and expect checks to arrive in the mail for your publication. Send out your publication promptly with an offer for other products and services. These orders will lead to future business.

Expect editors to contact you to write more. Now you're on your way to becoming an industry expert. Then clients will call you to buy what you sell.

Electronic Brochures

The average home in America contains three TVs, and over 90 percent of homes have at least one VCR. Cassette players are pervasive in cars and on the belts of Sunday joggers. Putting your message in electronic form makes it easier for you to market to a mass audience.

■ AUDIO BROCHURES

If your customers drive to work or exercise regularly, odds are good that they're listening to a cassette tape or compact disc. Guerrillas create audio brochures that sell for them 24 hours a day, whenever the prospect wishes to listen. Tell your customers how to use the tape. Hand them your audio program and say, "Just slip in this program while working around the house, exercising, or driving on your next errand and you can learn how to. . . ."

➤ Why Create Audio Brochures?

Guerrillas create audio brochures to tell their compelling story so prospects will buy. Audio brochures never have a bad day; they deliver a well-rehearsed, high-quality sales presentation everytime. Use audio brochures to educate your customers on how to buy and use what you sell. Guerrillas know that the most dangerous thing to their competitors is an educated customer.

Create short audio business cards that introduce you and your company. Use them for product updates or as an easy-to-use audio newsletter. Some companies find that audio users' manuals work well for them.

You can also use audio to bring other people and their message to your customers. Record testimonials over the telephone or when a customer comes into your location. Or you can read excerpts from fan mail. Interview other experts, bringing their advice and insight to your prospects and customers.[1]

Create audio bonus products to give your customers more value. Include tips and tactics for using what you sell. Create a recording of the history of the company or the story of the development of your unique technology.

What Should They Be Like?

The most common format is audiocassette. You can duplicate 45-minute cassette tapes in low quantities for less than two dollars each. Prices drop to one-quarter of that in runs of thousands.

Compact disc players are installed in over one-half of the new cars sold. When you make your master tape, ask the engineer to ensure that the tape is CD-ready. CDs can be made for about ten dollars each in small quantities, one-tenth that in thousands. The biggest issue with CDs and spoken-voice recording is restart cueing. With a cassette, when you resume your listening, the tape picks up right where you left off. Not so with a CD. The CD starts at the beginning every time. Some CD players have a resume cueing feature that solves this problem.

A Nightingale-Conant survey found that the average drive time in America was 22 minutes, so they started the now-common practice of making training tapes 22 minutes in length on each side. Use whatever length makes sense for your message, but always make side two slightly shorter than side one.

Select a title that promises ideas and information that your customers want, such as a banker who offers, "Increase Your Cash Flow in One Week," or a chiropractor who features, "Relieve Your Back Pain Now!," or the apartment-leasing company that offers, "Tips and Ideas for Living Well."

➤ How to Write and Record Them

Here are five ways you can get your audio brochure recorded.

---

[1]We love to do this. Call us at 800-247-9145 to schedule an interview.

Radio Talk Show

The fastest and easiest way to create an audio program is in a radio-talk-show format. With this format, you can have your first audiotape program in just 60 minutes. Stage a radio show using a colleague as the host and you or another expert as the guest. Or you can play the host and interview special guests. If a radio station interviews you, take along a blank, high-quality cassette to the studio, and ask them to record the broadcast. Use C-90 cassettes (45 minutes per side), and flip them on the half hour during the station break (leaving ample margin for error). Have your duplicator edit out the commercials.

Write your own list of interview questions ahead of time. This will make the show go more smoothly and help you deliver value. Think, "If someone were paying me $1,000 an hour to pick my brain, what questions should they ask?" Plan on three minutes per question. So if you want a one-hour program, come up with a list of 20 questions.

Be clear about your own agenda for the interview, because some hosts will not ask the questions you've provided. Sidestep these sidetracks with a transition, and get back to the main points you want to make. You can record these types of programs at a local radio station for a small fee.

If you'd like to interview experts who aren't available locally, you might do a phone interview. Most radio stations are equipped with a phone bridge, which automatically matches the levels of the inbound telephone line to the microphones in the studio.

To achieve the highest possible quality, create a virtual studio. Each party simultaneously records their own side of the telephone conversation, and later, the two tapes can be cut together by an engineer to create the illusion of both parties being in the same studio. This works best if both parties record on digital audiotape (DAT) or digital mini-disk.

Live Seminar

Record your performance at the next live seminar you present on DAT. You can also create a high-quality recording using a hi-fi VCR. Use a handheld microphone or attach a lavaliere microphone. Have the tape transcribed to produce an editing script. The audio engineer will use this script to make the edits to remove the "uhs," "ums," and missed words. Find audio editors by looking in the yellow pages under recording studios. Ask them about their experience working with words-on-tape editing.

Read the Script

Excellent results can be achieved by editing a live-performance transcript into a studio script. You can read from the script later in the studio. This approach captures your natural speaking style, while giving you control over the recording environment.

Plan on 125 words of script per finished, recorded minute. For best results, use a producer who understands spoken-word production.[2] Guerrillas always use a script, so their thoughts are well organized and they communicate clearly. You'll get the best results when you record your scripts in a professional recording studio.

Audio Play

The most complex audio project is to create a teleplay script for multiple voices and characters, with music and sound effects. Do this right by hiring an experienced producer and director.

License Them from Others

Another easy way to get audio programs is to license existing programs from others. With minor recording and editing, you can add an introduction, close, and your own special message.

Add Music

Copyright laws prohibit using music without permission. Yet, if you really want to use the latest movie theme, you can obtain a mechanical license and pay a few cents' royalty for every copy you duplicate.[3] Or use copyright-paid music, sometimes referred to as needle-drop music. One fee, and you can use it all you wish.[4]

The Intro

The opening words of the tape must sell your customer on why they should listen to the rest of it. Promise what you'll deliver in

---

[2]If you want to do this yourself, read Judy Byers's book, *Words on Tape,* Denver, CO: AudioCP Publishing, 1997. 800-582-9392.

[3]For information on obtaining a mechanical license for a particular piece of music, call the Harry Fox Agency, Inc., 212-370-5330.

[4]We like The Music Bakery, 800-229-0313.

the program. Structure the program so that the first side is a little bit longer than the second side, so your listener can conveniently flip over the tape to continue listening. The flip-the-tape message resells why your customer should go on to the next side. Start the second side with a little bit of music to let the listener know they're in the right place. When the voice starts immediately, some listeners may think that they have missed something and rewind the tape. At the close of the tape, sell the next step with a call to action: what do you want them to do? Instead of repeating your phone number on the tape, refer your listener to the cassette label for your contact information. If your location or phone numbers change, it's easy to reprint the labels, but it's very expensive to remaster the recording.

➤ How to Duplicate Them

If you have limited production requirements, you can buy a dual-cassette deck and duplicate them one at a time. For numbers in the low hundreds, take them to an audio duplication house. Your recording studio can help with potential duplication vendors.

➤ How to Package Them

You can obtain laser printer–ready, die-cut cassette labels (Avery #5587) at your office supply store and print them yourself. On the tape label, include contact information, such as your toll-free phone number, Web address, and E-mail address. Protect your recording with a copyright notice: ℗, © (or Copyright) the current year, your name, all rights reserved. The ℗ protects the performance of the program; the © protects the packaging.

Black lettering on a white label on a white cassette shell creates a generic look that guerrillas will want to avoid. Low-cost options are transparent cassette shells; colored cassette shells; solid-color, die-cut label stock; or send plain cassette labels to your instant printer to add a color background. In short runs, it may be practical to print the labels on a computer color printer.

For the outside packaging, there are many options, including black-and-white or color J-cards, printed cardboard sleeves, and cardboard or plastic clamshell boxes. Check with your tape duplication vendor for suggestions. For the greatest impact, coordinate your audio program packaging with your other marketing materials.

■ VIDEOTAPES

"One of my client companies sells seals for industrial pumps," says Dan Kennedy.[5] "The ordinary seal has to be replaced every 30,000 pumps, taking four hours of downtime; however, this company's seal lasts 300,000 pumps and takes only two hours to replace. How would you sell it? The conventional approach is to send out a representative to each factory with a bag of seals under one arm and a box of doughnuts under the other. He'll wait around for an hour, waiting to see someone. That uses up time, and it's also bad positioning."

Kennedy says that you're in better position to close a sale if you manage to get the customers who might need your product to come to you. This is where the direct-response methods come in. "Suppose you send every prospect a brochure that offers him a free video showing how to cut his downtime in half when he's servicing his pump. It's closely related to your business, but it's not about your company or product."

"Once the guy responds and says, 'I want to see the video,' he doesn't view you as a pump parts salesperson anymore. His defenses come down, because he feels as if he's in charge when he says, 'I think you're the guy who can help me. Tell me how this works.' Now you're in a good position to tell him about your longer-lasting seal. If you cold-marketed the same prospect, your results would not be as good."

With its free-video offer, the client company more than doubled its closing ratio per 100 prospects—from 3 to 7. That opens the possibility of hiring more representatives, who sell more and make more money.

Most people will pop in a short videotape for a quick look. Here are the secrets to making a video brochure that works hard for you.

➤ Professional Production

Hire a professional to write, script, and produce your tape. Because your viewer will be comparing your tape with the last TV show they saw, budget as much as you can for a solid production. You can create a high-quality videotape for about the

---

[5]From an article in *Success* magazine about Dan Kennedy and his Magnetic Marketing Strategies. For his catalog, fax 602-269-3113 or www.innercircle.com.

same price as it costs to design and prepress a large brochure or catalog.

Instead of spending money on high-priced special effects that only impress once, guerrillas pay for great writing. Go for a program delivering an information-packed, powerful message that customers will want to watch over and over.

➤ Length

Make the tape as long as necessary to tell your story, but never let it get boring. The best time length is in eight-minute blocks. This is the typical length of most TV show segments, and viewers get restless after eight minutes.

➤ Call the Number on the Label

Instead of reading your phone number in the voice-over, making them scramble for a pencil, just say, "Call the number on the tape label." If your phone number changes, you don't have to reedit the videotape.

Savvy guerrillas print reference charts and graphs on the tape face and tape box for extra value.

➤ Make a Few Copies

With traditional print media, you have to print tens of thousands of copies to get a good price. With video, you can run just a handful of copies (like ten) and still get a reasonable price.

Chapter 31

Marketing Yourself On-Line

The Internet is a very powerful way to maintain your TelePresence with customers. It is one of the fastest-growing arenas of electronic commerce. On-line services, like America Online and CompuServe, serve millions of members, and enrollments are rapidly increasing. If you haven't joined the on-line community, you're missing a tremendous opportunity.

A common misconception is that you can place a few free classified ads in Web sites and sit back while droves of people worldwide respond to your offer. Another is that you can put up a Web site anywhere in cyberspace and do nothing else while 60,000,000 Internet surfers eagerly line up and buy from you.

Generating customers on the Internet is all about creating exposure for your business. The more exposure the better, because recognition leads to sales. The Internet is just one more weapon in the guerrilla marketer's arsenal. On the Internet, the cost of creating this exposure is far less than traditional marketing vectors, like paid advertising or direct mailings.

Users of the Internet are supplied with a set of marketing tools for doing business, including E-mail, Web sites, Newsgroups, FTP, Web classifieds, and so on. But they are just that—tools! You must use them to generate business.

Succeeding on the Internet requires a commitment and a guerrilla marketing plan revolving around as many of these tools as possible. The more of these you use, the more exposure you will create for your business.

■ NETIQUETTE

The secret to using E-mail for on-line marketing is to understand and abide by the unwritten rules of *netiquette*.

Keep your messages short and to the point. Internet users do not want to sit around scrolling through pages and pages of lengthy sales letters. They want to open and read short messages so they can get through more of them per hour.

Your ad or E-mail message should fill one screen, 10 or 12 lines at most. You want to arouse their interest, then redirect them to get more information. "If you want (. . . this or . . . that) . . . , visit our Web site at: (URL address). If you have questions, E-mail me at: (E-mail address)." If they want more information about your offer, they will contact you. If they want to visit your Web site, they will.

Keep your subject lines or "RE:" lines simple and believable. NEVER SET THEM IN ALL CAPITALS, and !!!!!!!!Go Easy On The Exclamation Marks!!!!!!!! These flags mean *delete me unread*. The guerrilla tactic is to keep your headline simple and intriguing. An effective subject line might read, "Three things you should know," or "How You Can Get a Free Web Page," or "Free Report: '18 Ways to Obtain Free Advertising.'" People often do open and read these messages, and they do respond.

Change the headline or subject line every time you E-mail. Readers may delete your message if they think they've seen it before. Every time you send an E-mail or post a new message, use a different first line or headline.

When you offer something free—a free report, a free booklet, or a free gift—make it a no-strings, unconditional offer. Make your prospects grateful and curious enough to want to request more information. It might make them come back and say "Thank you" and "What else do you do?" or "How many reports do you actually have?"

Try to be a helper or advisor. Offer to inform and assist. People will remember you if you help. They'll be grateful, and maybe they'll give you a chance to tell them more. When you post messages to newsgroups, make your message useful and helpful. If you see a subject line from someone who is seeking help or has a question, open, read, and respond to their message. Let them know you're there to help. Give them the information they need, or direct them to someone who can. Their gratitude might show up later as an order.

A student had posted a message that said something like, "Answer 30 questions." I opened it, and I found she was working on a paper on newsgroups. She listed her 30 questions and asked if I would take the time to answer them and return them to her. I did, and it was fun. I E-mailed her my 30 answers. She E-mailed me back and said they were the best answers she had received. She thanked me for them and said that she showed them to her husband who needed advice. I E-mailed him some free information, one of my articles, with a list of other products, and he sent me an order.

➤ Bulk E-Mail Headers That Get Read

Begin by saying: "Sorry for Intruding, . . ." (then your 10- or 12-line message). Add a "Thanks for reading this" note and a "Forgive me, if this has reached you in error. (And) if you wish to receive no more mailings, just hit the reply button and say 'remove!' " Be friendly, be courteous, and do what others ask of you. If they wish to be removed from your list, remove them.

One of our E-mailings' subject lines had "Forgive me, but . . . ," and another had "Here's Three Things . . . ," and another had "I'm sorry. . . ." They got a lot of responses back. They made the reader curious enough to open the message and read "the three things . . . ," or to find out why we were sorry, or why they should forgive us.

We gave them two or three short paragraphs, offered a free report if they had not yet seen it, and closed with a big "Thank You." Another thing we do is put "Re:" in front of our subject line, because it makes people notice the message, and it makes them think we're responding to their message. It often works, because most people answer an E-mail, then they delete it. We tend to forget whom we've E-mailed recently. In some of the messages we send out, the subject line reads, "Re: Forgot to mention . . . ," or "Re: In case you didn't know. . . ." But, be careful. It can backfire on you and make some people mad.

➤ Attach a File

You can also send a piggyback attachment with your E-mail. The attached file could be a document, like a contract or technical report; it could be a spreadsheet, containing ROI calculations or price comparisons; it could even be a picture, sound, or Power-Point slide show, complete with narration, that presents your product. Many of the new generation of digital cameras allow you to shoot a photograph and instantly upload it to the Internet.

In most E-mail systems, attaching a file is as easy as clicking on the "Attach File" button before sending off your message.

Understand that people on the Net want information quickly. They want as much as they can get, and they want it all free. So, give them free stuff: offer a free sample report, a free subscription to your newsletter, free Web site locations, the names of the best newsgroups, how to list with search engines and a list of the best ones, or where to post as many ads as you wish, free. (Those are all articles that we have available. Any one of them is free for the asking.)[1] Offer some kind of free help or a free sample, and a lot of people will respond. Then, once you have their name, hang on to it, work it for all you're worth, and don't let them go, even if they never send you an order.

■ THREE STEPS TO GENERATING BUSINESS ON THE INTERNET

Any business (large or small) that wants to successfully gener-ate customers and sales on the Internet must find solutions to the following three success ingredients to succeed long-term.

➤ An Internet Plan

Develop a specific guerrilla marketing plan that outlines how you will design your Web site to optimize sales and how you will promote your site to bring in visitors again and again.

More specifically, you must provide solutions to the follow-ing questions:

➤ How will you design your Web site so customers will order from you on-line once they visit?

➤ How will you attract visitors to your site?

➤ How will you get visitors to become repeat visitors, turn-ing them into a residual income stream?

➤ Will you offer on-line credit card orders, and if so, where and how will you get this technology onto your Web site?

---

[1]E-mail your request to postmaster@guerrillagroup.com.

➤ Are you capable of writing motivating sales copy for potential Internet customers? If not, will you hire a copywriter to write your sales copy?

➤ How will you determine that your site is meeting expectations, and if not, what can you do to improve its performance?

➤ Succeeding On-Line

If you have a storefront, you establish credibility while easily providing valuable information to visitors at no cost. Your Web site is your storefront in cyberspace. Customers need a place to browse, where they can get the information they need to make an informed decision.

You must determine where to place your site to maximize your exposure for the least cost, and you must decide who will create and host your Web pages. Assign a designated Web Guerrilla who specializes in this field.

➤ On-Line Lead Generation

There are special places on the Internet, such as newsgroups, Web sites, and forums (many of which are free), that allow you to post ads, press releases, and other useful information about your business. Visit as many of these sites as possible (at least once or twice per month for several hours), and post classified ads, links to your Web site, and press releases about your business, products, and services.

With newsgroups, you should post daily, but you must be careful not to violate the rules of the group. One acceptable way is to answer others' questions or make comments on someone's post, followed by your signature at the end of your message. Your signature identifies who you are and how people can contact you (such as E-mail address, Web site, etc.), should they have an interest in your business.

Another strategy is to get free links from related, noncompetitive Web sites in exchange for a link on your site. Find them by doing searches at Yahoo!, Infoseek, and the other large search directories. E-mail the Webmaster, and ask if they would be interested in reciprocal links.

By implementing these tactics, you will establish a guerrilla lead-generation machine that continually feeds new customers and sales to your business worldwide.

➤ Internet Resources

A common misconception is that if you put your company on the Internet you will be guaranteed success. The reality is you have to promote your Web site. The following list of resources has places you must know about if you want to keep up with the latest on-line marketing issues and survive the virtual jungle of competition on the Internet.

Discussion Groups and Mailing Lists
I-Sales: Internet-Sales HelpDesk Moderated Discussion
http://www.mmgco.com/isales.html
Formed in November 1995, the Internet Sales Moderated Discussion List provides a forum for helpful discussion of on-line sales issues by those engaged in the sale of products and services on-line.

➤ Published once a day, Monday through Friday (9,000 subscribers).

➤ To subscribe, send an E-mail to: I-sales_helpdesk@gs2 .revnet.com with the subject header blank and the word "subscribe" in the body of the message.

LinkExchange Digest Moderated Discussion
http://www.le-digest.com
The LE Digest is a moderated discussion for those wishing to build traffic to their Web sites. Some of the topics discussed include advertising opportunities on the Internet and WWW, banner design issues, testing banners for effectiveness, and other useful ways of promoting Web sites.

➤ Published once a day, Monday through Friday (50,000 subscribers).

➤ To subscribe, send an E-mail to: subscribe-digest@le-digest .com with the subject header blank and the body of the message blank.

WebPromote Weekly Newsletter Mailing List
http://www.WebPromote.com
This newsletter is packed full of useful on-line promotional tips to help make your on-line investment pay off. Newsletters pro-

vide tips on search engine relevancy techniques, strategic linking, and site announcement, to keep you informed of the best ways to build sustained traffic to your Web site.

➤ Published once a week (100,000 subscribers)

➤ To subscribe, visit their Web site and click on the "Free Newsletter" link

Clearly Internet Marketing Tip of the Day Mailing List
http://www.clearlyinternet.com/mtotd.html
The Marketing Tip of the Day (MTOTD) is a mailing list that sends out a specific action item per day that you can use to market your business on the Internet, including necessary steps with specific instructions for carrying out the action.

➤ Published once a day, Monday through Friday (1,650 subscribers).

➤ To subscribe, send an E-mail to: majordomo@databack .com with the subject header blank and the words "SUBSCRIBE MTOTD" in the body of the message.

The E-Marketing Digest by Webbers Communications
http://www.webbers.com/emark/
The E-Marketing Digest is a moderated discussion about electronic marketing techniques. The list provides subscribers an interactive forum where beginner and expert marketers trade information, war stories, resources, opinions, and advice on online marketing strategies.

➤ Published once a day, Monday through Friday (1,200 subscribers).

➤ To subscribe, send an E-mail to: majordomo@buck.ncia .net with the subject header blank and the words "SUBSCRIBE E-MARK" in the body of the message.

Web Sites
WebPosition by FirstPlace Software
http://www.webposition.com/userguide/
    TipsonImprovingYourSearchRankings_.htm
WebPosition gives you the critical reports you need to monitor, manage, and then improve your search positions. There's no

magic way to automatically put your page in the top ten positions. However, there are many proven techniques that can be used to move into the top ten, and even the number one slot, for your chosen keywords and phrases.

Graphic, Visualization, & Usability Center's (GVU) 8th WWW User Survey
http://www.gvu.gatech.edu/user_surveys/survey-1997-10/
The eighth survey was run from October 10 through November 16, 1997, and was endorsed by the World Wide Web Consortium, which exists to develop common standards for the evolution of the Web. Over 10,000 Web users participated in the survey. Questions were asked in the following areas: Electronic Commerce, General Demographics, Technology, Demographics, Data Privacy, Web and Internet Usage, Internet Shopping, Information Gathering and Purchasing, and Opinions on Internet Commerce. Results are available in a variety of mediums.

WebPromote—META Tag Builder
http://METAtag.WebPromote.com/
Achieving prominent listings within the search engines often depends heavily on just a few simple lines of HTML text that go into the header of your site. Fortunately, you don't have to be an HTML guru to install these tags, because WebPromote has developed a program that will create them for you. Enter your keywords and descriptions, and they'll send you the META tags to insert directly into your own Web pages.

THE GUERRILLA GROUP Sales Training Headquarters
http://www.guerrillagroup.com
Your Internet marketing endeavors can not be effective unless you know how to sell. Learn how to become a successful sales guerrilla from the experts who wrote the best-selling *Guerrilla Marketing* and *Guerrilla Selling* business book series. This site features a free-articles archive, a bookstore, information on customized on-site training, and the Guerrilla Selling Tip of the Week.

Chapter 32

Videoconferencing and Other Modern Miracles

Information is the new currency of the twenty-first century. Consider this: your competition is increasing the quality of their information while your information's quality is deteriorating. The likely outcome is a downward spiral; they'll increasingly control your market. You'll have a smaller marketing budget next year. So today's savvy marketer asks, "How do I get the best-quality information?" To stay ahead, your marketing kit has to be chock-full of information-gathering tools. And the best tool is face-to-face, one-on-one conversation.

A recent Carnegie Mellon study reported that face-to-face meetings transfer information four times more quickly than any other mix of information exchange. You may have found that face-to-face meetings with a stranger transfer more information than a phone call to a friend.

According to a survey done by Specific Diagnostic Studies, adults process information three ways: 37 percent through feelings and actions, 34 percent through what they hear, and 29 percent through what they see. Any sales professional admits to selling the most when the prospect touches and handles the merchandise. They'll tell you the next best way to sell is with a presentation, and the least effective way to sell is with a brochure (visual only). Face-to-face meetings are incredibly powerful, because they capitalize on all three information-processing modes.

The reality today is that there are fewer people to do the work. Plus, travel is getting more expensive and more anxiety producing than ever. Face-to-face meetings become more infrequent and less lucrative. It's increasingly difficult to get face-to-face meetings with the growing market of home-based entrepreneurs. And if you sell to consumers, door-to-door canvassing doesn't work, because no one's home during the day, and no one wants to be bothered during their personal time.

You can use videoconferencing technology to create face-to-face contact without being there in person. AT&T introduced videophone communication at the 1964 New York World's Fair. At the tender age of five, Mark recalls talking to his grandfather via picture phone in the AT&T exhibit. With Grandpa just around the corner, he "dialed" the number with push buttons. Grandpa answered in a funny voice (grandfathers do that), but Mark knew it was him on the little black-and-white TV screen. They shook their heads in wonder as they considered what their lives would be like in the future. Mark's grandfather never saw a home-installed picture phone in his lifetime.

More than three decades later, private video communication is still not widespread. The big barrier has been the available bandwidth of transmission lines. That little picture phone needed the equivalent of 1,500 phone lines just to make the connection.

Nevertheless, we stand at the threshold of a new era in videoconferencing. Through clever compression schemes, we can now send reasonable video transmission over one standard phone line. Our kids will grow up with picture phones.

The desktop videoconferencing industry has learned much from corporate videoconferencing suites. You may have participated in a videoconference during a corporate meeting or experienced one of Kinko's public videoconferencing suites at one of their copy center stores. Remote data sharing is available in Microsoft's Windows®. The industry leaders predict that desktop videoconferencing will one day be as common as the fax machine.

➤ Fax of the Future?

It's likely that the PC on your desk is only $200 away from becoming a videoconference system. With a $100 camera and $100 worth of software, your investment to see who's calling is less than the cost of a cheap fax machine.

Some PC manufacturers already ship selected models with cameras installed. Every off-the-shelf PC shipped today has the high-speed video display and the high-speed modem required for videoconferencing. Therefore, telephone-based desktop videoconferencing will initially dominate the market. With high-speed LANs and WANs, a virtual face-to-face video meeting is now easier than ever. You might even videoconference with colleagues in the same building, just to save time.

And you'll take a videophone with you. A major telecommunications company already supports wireless videoconferencing using off-the-shelf cellular technology.

Hundreds of thousands have downloaded and played with the CU-SeeMe Web-based video technology,[1] and VDONet Corp's VDOPhone.[2] You can experience live video on the Web at hundreds of sites.

Vendors of desktop videoconferencing software and hardware include Apple Computer, AT&T, EyeTel, DataBeam, FutureLabs, IBM, InSoft, Intel, PictureTel, and Xerox. At this writing, these solutions do not yet offer full-screen, full-motion video, but what they do offer is a start. Desktop videoconferencing may not replace the corporate videoconference suite, but you'll have a choice between the convenience of sitting at your desk or looking at a large, high-quality video image.

To assure that Macs and Suns and IBMs are all talking the same language, the International Telecommunication Union has settled on image compression and protocol standards for desktop videoconferencing. Expect current systems to interconnect without a hitch.

➤ You'll Know You're Understood

With voice-only communication, it's difficult to know when your message is clearly understood. People commonly check for understanding by asking, "Are you following me?" The answer is usually "yes," whether they really do or not.

When you talk face-to-face, you have your product in hand, pointing out key features. If a user has difficulty understanding, you can immediately sense the problem and can troubleshoot to the answer. And now, through a video image, you'll immediately know if they have some confusion.

---

[1] http://www.wpine.com.

[2] http://www.vdo.net.

With desktop videoconferencing, a furrowed brow or shift in body posture instinctively relays details about understanding. Just think how fun live video poker will be!

Imagine your service technician beaming live images from a customer's site to your headquarters-based experts, or an EMT sending video to the emergency room staff for immediate diagnostics. The medium transmits more than just data: you get a new level of emotional and human detail that is currently masked by documents and voice-only communication.

As companies downsize and spread out geographically, experts no longer share the same physical locale. Bringing together brainpower and know-how for troubleshooting and brainstorming gets expensive and time-consuming. With videoconferencing, you can bring in the experts anytime and anyplace.

➤ But Will Customers Want It?

Once users get a taste of desktop video at work, it's a simple step to take it home. Every grandmother loves to see her grandkids more often, and the proud parents will find some business-based excuse to upgrade the family PC. With millions of Americans telecommuting at least two days per week, there's great incentive to stay at home with the PC and the camera. The downside is that you'll have to wear business dress when you work at home, at least from the waist up.

If you want to encourage your customers to use desktop videoconferencing, send them the software. Several software vendors make it easy for you to get your customers on the videophone. They license their software for unlimited receive-only distribution, because they know they'll get the upgrade for the two-way video version when your customer decides to add a camera. Now you can at least send images one way, TV-broadcast style. You'll hear their voice, while they'll see and hear you. You might initially feel uncomfortable knowing that they can see you and you can't see them, but imagine the impact on your prospects and customers. You'll get increased mind share and make a lasting impression with your willingness to use cutting-edge technology to stay in touch.

➤ How to Take It to Market

Besides basic face-to-face phone calls, you'll soon be distributing video-based sales brochures to your customer's PC. They can either visit your Web site or call into your server to receive video-on-demand. You can deliver customer and sales force training the same way. Your sales team will get new product training when and where it's most convenient for them. Your corporate newsletter will resemble *E!* programming, and your competitive analysis may take the form of *A Current Affair.* You'll conduct more informal focus groups and poll your prospects and customers via desktop videoconferencing. You'll grab interesting customer stories and quickly create application videos for your sales force and customers—all right on your PC. You'll do desktop video production along with the desktop publishing you're doing now.

So, we wonder, when will we need a video answering machine program for our PC? Imagine it now, "I can't come to the cam, so click now if you want to see our latest product lineup, . . . click now if you want to see my vacation photos, . . . or leave a video clip at the black burst, show me what you need, and I'll see you when I phone." We'll probably have to ask our kids to program it for us.

■ SATELLITE PAGING

A more down-to-earth technology that is readily available is satellite-direct paging. Companies like SkyTel and Southwest Bell offer pagers that communicate with a satellite via a ground station. A caller can touch-tone in a number for you to call, and you will get the message instantly, in over 2,000 cities around the world.

These systems also include desktop software that lets your office (or your customer or your five-year-old) compose a text message on the computer, then transmit it to your pager via modem. The same platform usually integrates voice mail and pager notification. You can even receive stock market updates and sports scores several times a day.

■ CELLULAR, PDC, AND EMERGING TECHNOLOGIES

The days of the clumsy, noisy, expensive cellular phone are numbered. Soon, the new digital standards (PCS) will be replaced by Personal Digital Communication (PDC). The cordless phone you use with a base station at home slips into your briefcase, becoming a portable on the road. When you arrive at the office, you drop it back into a base station, and it becomes a land line again. Or pick it up and roam around the warehouse while you check on an order. The advantage is that only one number follows you everywhere.

■ SAVE ON CELL PHONE CHARGES

If you have voice mail connected to your cell phone, feel free to give your customers the number, and encourage them to call. Then, don't answer. Instead, let the calls roll to voice mail, where your outbound recording encourages them to leave a detailed message, and it explains that you will return the call just as soon as you're available.

This keeps the call short, and because many cellular providers do not charge for airtime used to retrieve voice mail messages (check with your provider), you save a bundle. If the call is truly urgent, by all means, return it on the run; otherwise, wait until you can get to a land line before calling back.

Also, investigate new digital and PCS phone services that include short-text messaging, in which your caller's comments appear right on the phone's display screen, just like a pager. The one we use (from Nextel) will automatically dial any number embedded in the text message simply by displaying the message and pressing the "send" key.

An additional tip: if your business routinely takes you on the road, call your cellular provider with a list of cities, and try to negotiate a "no-roaming" agreement. Many of the larger companies will give you same-as-home-area rates in selected markets if you ask them to.

■ TOLL-FREE NUMBERS

A customer has a question or problem. A reporter wants information about your company for a story. Someone wants an estimate right away. Guerrillas make it easy for them to call.

A potent high-tech weapon in the Guerrilla Selling arsenal is the toll-free number. People are seven times as likely to phone if the call is toll-free, and you don't have to be a big-budget company to make it pay. New services like AT&T's *ReadyLine* and Sprint's *Phoneline 800* bring the firepower of a toll-free number within reach of even the smallest company.

Measured, inbound toll-free service is surprisingly inexpensive, but it does pay to shop around. Expect a base charge of around five dollars per month, plus 10 to 15 cents per minute or less for the calls you receive. Rates may be lower in some states, and some are time-of-day and distance-sensitive. Custom calling plans and volume discounts may cut costs even further.

The number can be programmed to ring right into any existing telephone in the U.S. It can be rerouted just as easily, so as your business grows, your toll-free number can move with you.

➤ Don't Spell It Out

Unless you can get a vanity number that is a complete acronym, like 1-800-FLOWERS, stay away from clever combinations like 234-1234. People think they will remember them and then forget. It would be better to have a number that they have to write down.

Print your new toll-free number on everything, and use graphics and type to make it **stand out.** Give people a reason to call. ("For a free brochure on cutting costs, call toll-free, 1-800-XXX-XXXX.") Also, consider a toll-free number for your fax machine. You'll improve service, speed, quality, and convenience by encouraging a written response.

Advanced features can make your toll-free service even more practical. Area code routing allows incoming calls to be routed, based on the area code from which the inbound call was placed. This could be used to route calls directly to a field office or service center or to a specific salesperson at headquarters. Exchange code routing allows you to route calls by the local exchange as well, giving you even finer control over your territories. Single-number service allows multiple, toll-free lines in multiple locations to be accessed by a single, toll-free number. This simplifies advertising, reduces customer confusion, and enhances your market identity. Courtesy response automatically provides a prerecorded message to callers when the office is closed. Better still, couple a toll-free line with voice messaging, and never miss a call again. Using voice mail, salespeople working on several different accounts can keep in touch with the management team to coordinate plans and activities, to make important decisions, and to expedite shipping of samples or literature, all through a single toll-free line.

■ TOLL-FREE VERSUS 900 NUMBERS

Guerrillas avoid the much-hyped 900 numbers. There are a number of problems using 900 numbers to deliver goods and services. The number one problem is the psychological barrier in the minds of most prospects against dialing a 900 number. Because 900 services have been widely used for sex chat lines and gambling tip lines, few consumers have ever dialed a 900 number. Although there are a few valuable 900 number lines, such as stock quotation services, most other 900 services, such as psychic hot lines and celebrity chat lines, are viewed as trivial and a waste of money.

Because of this, most prospects will feel reluctant to dial their first 900 number and will worry about what their spouse will say when the phone bill comes.

Because of the publicity that 900 numbers have received, the FCC and FTC limit to whom you can advertise the service.

Although marketers have felt that the 900 number is the "credit card of the masses," this simply isn't true. These numbers are restricted to businesses in which you can substantially deliver the information and service over the telephone line, and they cannot be used to take orders for products and services delivered at a later time. You can't order a videotape that's delivered to your home via a 900 number. In general, the public doesn't believe that they can get information over the phone that's actually worth the $2.99 they pay.

There is also a relatively high level of "charge backs" in the 900 business. This is where customers refuse to pay the 900 section of their phone bill, claiming they didn't get what they expected. Some 900 lines have charge backs in the 10- to 15-percent level, and 5 to 8 percent are typical.

The most straightforward and universally accepted method of buying and paying for goods and services by phone is where the customer calls a toll-free number and pays with a credit card. Many Americans have a credit card and have used it to successfully place a telephone order for goods and services.

An alternative to taking credit cards is to accept checks by phone. With this payment method, the person ordering reads the numbers off the bottom of their check, and the check is cashed electronically by the merchant. This method has been available for several years and has recently been used success-fully by Olin Mills photographers in a nationwide telesales campaign as an alternative to credit cards.

Accepting credit cards permits up-selling and cross-selling services and merchandise, increasing the size of the order and substantially increasing profits.

Charge backs can be held to a minimum using standard confirmation and antifraud approaches. Expect about a 1- to 2-percent refund request rate when using credit cards.

A bonus to toll-free number ordering is the opportunity to preview the service. A person can call in and listen to a sample of the service or to testimonials from happy customers before being connected to a live operator for ordering instructions. This is an opportunity for people who are uncertain to experi-ence, at no risk to them, what you're offering.

Appendix

■ WEB ADDRESSES

The Anti-Telemarketer Source
http://www.izzy.net/~vnestico/t-market.html

Direct Marketing Association (DMA)
http://www.the-dma.org

Established in 1917, the DMA is the oldest and largest national trade association serving the direct marketing field. Members of the DMA market goods and services directly to consumers using such media as telephone, direct mail, catalogs, magazine and newspaper ads, and TV and radio advertising. The DMA is not the source of calling lists, and it does not sell calling lists to other companies.

Many people enjoy receiving information about products or services in their homes over the telephone. Many consumers find telephone shopping to be a convenient way to shop. However, some consumers would like to receive fewer telephone marketing calls at home. The Telephone Preference Service (TPS), a do-not-call service, is a free service to assist those consumers in decreasing the number of national commercial calls received at home. You may register with this do-not-call file by sending your name(s), home address, and home telephone number (including area code) to:

Telephone Preference Service
Direct Marketing Association
P.O. Box 9014
Farmingdale, NY 11735-9014

You must register with the TPS directly; second-party requests cannot be processed.

When you register with the TPS, your name, address, and telephone number are placed on a do-not-call file. This "delete file" is updated four times a year—January, April, July, and October—and made available to telephone marketing companies who choose to use it. Your name remains on file for five years. Typically, you will see the number of calls you receive begin to decrease approximately two months after your name is entered onto the quarterly file.

Although registration with the TPS will help reduce the number of telemarketing calls you receive, it will not stop all telemarketing calls. You may continue to receive calls from local merchants, religious and charitable organizations, professional and alumni associations, and political candidates and officeholders.

Calls of a business-to-business nature received at your place of employment are also not affected through registration with the TPS. Business names, addresses, and telephone numbers are not accepted on the TPS, and companies that market to other companies do not use this consumer-oriented do-not-call file.

Registration with the TPS will not affect sequentially dialed, automated, recorded-message (computerized) calls. If you receive a computerized call from a company you do not wish to hear from again, listen to the automated message to obtain the telemarketer's name and address or phone number. Then, contact the company directly, and ask to be placed on the company's do-not-call list.

JunkBusters (how to really get rid of junk phone calls, junk mail, etc.)
http://www.junkbusters.com

The Federal Trade Commission Telemarketer Guidelines
http://www.ftc.gov/bcp/telemark/out.htm

Minnesota Telemarketing Association
http://www.m-t-a.org

Business Communications Review
http://www.bcr.com

Call Center Magazine
http://www.teleconnect.com

Computer Telephony
http://www.computertelephony.com

Teleconnect Magazine
http://www.teleconnect.com

Bibliography

■ BOOKS

Albrecht, Karl, and Ron Zemke. *Service America!* Homewood, IL: Dow Jones–Irwin, 1985.

Alessandra, Tony. *Charisma*. New York: Warner Books, 1998.

Alessandra, Tony, and Rick Barrerra. *Collaborative Selling*. New York: John Wiley & Sons, 1993.

Alessandra, Tony, Rick Barrerra, and Phil Wexler. *Non-Manipulative Selling*. New York: Simon & Schuster/Fireside, 1987.

Alessandra, Tony, Gregg Brown, and Jim Cathcart. *The Sales Professional's Idea-A-Day Guide*. Chicago: Dartnell, 1996.

Alessandra, Tony, Jim Cathcart, and John Monoky. *Be Your Own Sales Manager*. New York: Simon & Schuster/Fireside, 1990.

Alessandra, Tony, and Phil Hunsaker. *Communicating at Work*. New York: Simon & Schuster/Fireside, 1993.

Alessandra, Tony, and John Monoky. *The Sales Manager's Idea-A-Day Guide*. Chicago: Dartnell, 1996.

Alessandra, Tony, and Michael O'Conner. *People Smarts*. San Francisco: Pfeiffer/Jossey-Bass, 1994.

Alessandra, Tony, and Michael O'Conner. *The Platinum Rule*. New York: Warner Books, 1996.

Aronson, Sam. *Everyone's Guide to Opening Doors by Telephone*. Marina Del Rey, CA: S. Aronson Publishing, 1981.

Bandler, Richard, and John Grinder. *Reframing*. Boulder, CO: Real People Press, 1979.

Basye, Anne. *Opportunities in Telemarketing Careers (VGM Opportunities)*. Lincolnwood, IL: VGM Career Horizons, 1994.

Belasco, James A. *Teaching the Elephant to Dance*. New York: Crown, 1990.

Bencin, Richard L. *Strategic Telemarketing: How to Fit This New Medium into Your Marketing Plans.* Philadelphia, PA: Swansea Press, 1987.

Bencin, Richard L., and Donald J. Jonovic. *Encyclopedia of Telemarketing.* Englewood Cliffs, NJ: Prentice-Hall, 1989.

Berne, Eric. *Games People Play.* New York: Ballantine, 1964.

Bettger, Frank. *How I Raised Myself From Failure To Success In Selling.* Englewood Cliffs, NJ: Prentice-Hall, 1975.

Blimes, Michaeal E., and Ron Sproat. *More Dialing, More Dollars: 12 Steps to Successful Telemarketing.* New York: American Council for the Arts, 1986.

Bly, Robert. *Recession-Proof Strategies: 14 Winning Methods to Sell Any Product or Service in a Down Economy* (Booklet). New Milford, NJ, 201-559-2277.

Bly, Robert W. *Secrets of Successful Telephone Selling: How to Generate More Leads, Sales, Repeat Business, and Referrals by Phone.* New York: Henry Holt, 1997.

Boyan, Lee. *Successful Cold Call Selling: Over 100 New Ideas, Scripts, and Examples, from the Nation's Foremost Sales Trainer.* New York: American Management Association, 1989.

Brown, M. T. *Making Money with the Telephone.* Hollywood, CA: Future Shop, 1982.

Callaghan, Ed, and Peter W. Nauert. *Technoselling: How to Use Today's Technology to Increase Your Sales.* Highland Village, TX: LoneStar Publishing, 1995.

Cates, Bill. *Unlimited Referrals.* Wheaton, MD: Thunder Hill Press, 1996.

Cathcart, Jim. *Relationship Selling.* New York: Perigee Books, 1990.

Covey, Stephen R. *The Seven Habits of Highly Effective People.* New York: Simon & Schuster, 1989.

Davidow, William H., and Buro Uttal. *Total Customer Service: The Ultimate Weapon.* New York: Harper & Row, 1989.

Davis, Lou Ellen. *The Insurance Agent's Guide to Telephone Prospecting: Money-Making Power Strategies from a Top Teleprospector.* Naperville, IL: Financial Sourcebooks, 1992.

Fisher, Peg. *Successful Telemarketing: A Step-By-Step Guide for Increased Sales at Lower Cost.* Chicago: Dartnell Group, 1985.

Freestone, Julie, and Janet Brusse. *Telemarketing Basics: A Practical Guide for Professional Results.* Los Altos, CA: Crisp Publications, 1989.

Gerber, Michael E. *The E Myth.* Cambridge, MA: Ballinger, 1986.

Gilles, Jerry. *MoneyLove.* New York: Warner Books, 1978.

Girard, Joe, and Stanley H. Brown. *How to Sell Anything to Anybody.* New York: Warner, 1977.

Gitomer, Jeffrey. *The Sales Bible.* New York: William Morrow, 1994.

Godin, Seth. *Emarketing.* New York: Berkely Publishing, 1995.

Goldner, Paul S. *Red-Hot Cold Call Selling: Prospecting Techniques That Pay Off.* New York: American Marketing Association, 1995.

Good, Bill. *Prospecting Your Way to Sales Success: How to Find New Business by Phone, Fax, Internet and Other New Media.* New York: Scribner, 1997.

Goodman, Gary S. *You Can Sell Anything by Telephone!* Englewood Cliffs, NJ: Prentice Hall, 1984.

Guiducci, Joan. *Joan Guiducci's Power Calling: A Fresh Approach to Cold Calls & Prospecting.* Mill Valley, CA: Tonino/Power Calling, 1993.

Harlan, Ray, and Walter M. Woolfson, Jr. *Interactive Telemarketing: How to Beat the Boiler Room with a Quality Approach.* Bradenton, FL: McGuinn & McGuire, 1995.

Hoge, Cecil C. *The Electronic Marketing Manual/Integrating Electronic Media into Your Marketing Campaign.* New York: McGraw-Hill, 1993.

Jamison, Brian, et al. *Electronic Selling: Twenty-Three Steps to E-Selling Profits.* New York: McGraw-Hill, 1997.

Johnson, Deborah, and Steve Kennedy. *How to Farm Successfully—By Phone.* Carson City, NV: Argyle Press, 1995.

Jutkins, Ray. *Direct Marketing: How You Can Really Do it Right.* Costa Mesa, CA: HDL, 1989.

Katz, Bernard. *How to Win More Business by Phone.* New York: Unwin Hyman, 1985.

Komando, Kim. *Cyberbuck$: Making Money Online.* Forest City, CA: ICG Books Worldwide, 1996.

Laborde, Gene Z. *Influencing with Integrity.* New York: Sintony, Inc., 1984.

LeBoeuf, Michael. *The Greatest Management Principle in the World.* New York: Berkley Books, 1985.

Levinson, Jay Conrad. *Guerrilla Marketing Attack: New Strategies, Tactics & Weapons for Winning Big Profits from Your Small Business.* Boston: Houghton Mifflin, 1987.

———. *Guerrilla Marketing Weapons: 100 Affordable Marketing Methods for Maximizing Profits from Your Small Business.* New York: Plume, 1990.

———. *Guerrilla Marketing Excellence: 50 Golden Rules for Small Business Success.* Boston: Houghton Mifflin, 1993.

———. *Guerrilla Marketing Revised for the '90's.* Boston: Houghton Mifflin, 1993.

———. *Guerrilla Advertising: Cost-Effective Tactics for Small-Business Success.* Boston: Houghton Mifflin, 1994.

———. *Guerrilla Marketing for the Home Based Business.* Boston: Houghton Mifflin, 1996.

———. *Guerrilla Marketing With Technology.* New York: Addison-Wesley Publishing Company, 1997.

——. *The Way of the Guerrilla: Achieving Success and Balance as an Entrepreneur in the 21st Century.* Boston: Houghton Mifflin, 1997.

Levinson, Jay Conrad, and Seth Godin. *Guerrilla Marketing Handbook.* Boston: Houghton Mifflin, 1994.

——. *Get What You Deserve! How to Guerrilla Market Yourself.* New York: Avon Books, 1997.

Levinson, Jay Conrad, and Charles Rubin. *Guerrilla Marketing Online.* Boston: Houghton Mifflin, 1995.

——. *Guerrilla Marketing Online Weapons: 100 Low-Cost, High-Impact Weapons for Online Profits and Prosperity.* Boston: Houghton Mifflin, 1996.

Levinson, Jay Conrad, Bill Gallagher, and Orvel Ray Wilson. *Guerrilla Selling—Unconventional Weapons and Tactics for Increasing Your Sales.* Boston: Houghton Mifflin, 1992.

Levinson, Jay Conrad, Mark S. A. Smith, and Orvel Ray Wilson. *Guerrilla Trade Show Selling: New Unconventional Weapons and Tactics to Meet More People, Get More Leads, and Close More Sales.* New York: John Wiley & Sons, 1997.

Mackay, Harvey. *Beware the Naked Man Who Offers You His Shirt.* New York: Ivy Books, 1990.

——. *Swim With The Sharks Without Being Eaten Alive.* New York: Ivy Books, 1988.

Mahfood, Philip E. *T E L E Selling: High Performance Business-To-Business Phone Selling Techniques.* Chicago, IL: Probus, 1990.

Maltz, Maxwell. *Psychocybernetics.* New York: Pocket Books, 1960.

Maslow, Abraham. *Motivation and Personality.* New York: Harper and Row, 1954.

Masser, Barry Z. *Power Selling by Telephone.* Englewood Cliffs, NJ: Prentice-Hall, 1983.

——. *Complete Handbook of All Purpose Telemarketing Scripts.* Englewood Cliffs, NJ: Prentice-Hall, 1990.

McCafferty, Thomas A. *In-House Telemarketing: The Masterplan for Starting and Managing a Profitable Telemarketing Program.* Chicago, IL: Probus Publishing, 1994.

McHatton, Robert J. *Total Telemarketing.* New York: John Wiley & Sons, 1988.

Mercer, Laurie J., and Jennifer Singer. *Opportunity Knocks: Using PR.* Radnor, PA: Chilton Book Company, 1989.

Naisbet, John, and Patricia Aburdene. *Megatrends 2000.* New York: William Morrow and Co., 1990.

Parinello, Anthony. *Selling to VITO the Very Important Top Officer.* Hollbrook, MA: Bob Adams, Inc., 1994.

Pekas, Mary D. *Basic Telemarketing: Skills for Sales and Service Productivity.* Eden Prairie, MN: Paradigm, 1990.

Penoyer, Flyn L. *Teleselling Techniques That Close the Sale.* New York: American Management Association, 1997.

Peoples, David. *Presentations Plus: David Peoples' Proven Techniques.* New York, NY: John Wiley & Sons, 1988.

Peters, Tom, and Robert Waterman. *In Search of Excellence.* New York: Warner, 1982.

Porterfield, James D. *Teleselling: A Self-Teaching Guide (Wiley Self-Teaching Guides).* New York: John Wiley & Sons, 1996.

Rackham, Neil. *Spin Selling.* New York: McGraw Hill, 1988.

Ramacitti, David F. *Do-It Yourself Publicity.* New York: American Management Association, 1990.

Richardson, Linda. *Selling by Phone: How to Reach and Sell to Customers.* New York: McGraw-Hill, 1994.

Rinke, Wolf J. *The 6 Success Strategies for Winning at Life, Love and Business.* Deerfield, FL: Health Communications, 1996.

Riso, Don Richard. *Personality Types.* Boston: Houghton Mifflin, 1987.

Schiffman, Stephan. *Cold Calling Techniques (That Really Work!).* Boston: Bob Adams, 1991.

———. *Stephan Schiffman's Telemarketing.* Boston: Bob Adams, 1992.

Schoonmaker, Alan N. *Negotiate to Win: Gaining the Psychological Edge.* Englewood Cliffs, NJ: Prentice-Hall, 1989.

Schwartz, David. *The Magic of Thinking Big.* New York: Prentice-Hall, 1965.

Schwartz, Evan I. *Webonomics: Nine Essential Principles for Growing Your Business on the World Wide Web.* New York: Broadway Books, 1997.

Shafiroff, Martin D., and Robert L. Shook. *Successful Telephone Selling in the '90s.* New York: Perennial Library, 1990.

Shook, Robert L., and Eric Yaverbaum (Editors). *I'll Get Back to You: 156 Ways to Get People to Return Your Phone Calls.* Boston: Harvard Business School Press, 1996.

Sisk, Kathy. *Successful Telemarketing: The Complete Handbook on Managing a Profitable Telemarketing Call Center.* New York: McGraw-Hill, 1995.

Sloane, Valerie. *Telephone Sales Management and Motivation Made Easy.* Omaha, NE: Business By Phone, 1996.

Slutsky, Jeff. *Streetfighting.* Englewood Cliffs, NJ: Prentice-Hall, 1984.

———. *How to Get Clients.* New York: Warner Books, 1992.

Sobczak, Art. *Telephone Tips That Sell: 501 How-To Ideas and Affirmations to Help You Get More Business by Phone.* Omaha, NE: Business By Phone, 1996.

Stevens, Michael. *Telemarketing in Action: A Handbook of Marketing and Sales Applications* (McGraw-Hill Marketing for Professionals Series). New York: McGraw-Hill, 1995.

Stevenson, Robert Joseph. *The Boiler Room and Other Telephone Sales Scams.* Champaign-Urbana, IL: University of Illinois Press, 1998.

Stone, Bob, and John Wyman. *Successful Telemarketing: Opportunities and Techniques for Increasing Sales and Profits.* Lincolnwood, IL: NTC Business Books, 1986.

Stone, Merlin, et al. *Telemanage Your Customers: A System for Telephone Account Management.* Brookfield, VT: Gower, 1990.

Strauss, Lawrence. *Electronic Marketing: Emerging TV and Computer Channels for Interactive Home Shopping.* White Plains, NY: Knowledge Industry, 1983.

Toffler, Alvin. *Future Shock.* New York: Random House, 1970.

———. *Powershift.* New York: Bantam, 1990.

Trisler, Hank. *No Bull Selling.* New York: Frederick Fell, 1983.

———. *No Bull Sales Management.* New York: Bantam, 1985.

Walther, George R. *Phone Power: How to Make the Telephone Your Most Profitable Business Tool.* New York: Putnam, 1986.

Walther, George. *Power Talking, 50 Ways to Say What You Mean and Get What You Want.* New York: Berkley, 1992.

Warfield, Allen, and Al Brooks. *Effective Telemarketing: How to Sell over the Telephone.* Humor Books, 1993.

Weiss, Alan. *Million Dollar Consulting.* New York: McGraw-Hill, 1992.

Willingham, Ron. *Integrity Selling.* New York: Doubleday, 1987.

Zajas, Jay J. R., and Olive D. Church. *Applying Telecommunications and Technology from a Global Business Perspective.* New York: Haworth Press, 1997.

Zigler, Zig. *Secrets of Closing the Sale.* New York: Berkley Books, 1984.

Zinsser, William. *On Writing Well.* New York: Harper & Row, 1988.

Zunin, Leonard. *Contact: The First Four Minutes.* New York: Ballantine, 1988.

■ AUDIOTAPES[1]

Battles, Brian. *How to Listen Powerfully.* Boulder, CO: CareerTrack Publications, 1988.

Bliss, Edwin. *Getting Things Done.* Boulder, CO: CareerTrack Publications, 1985.

Brinkman, Rick, and Rick Kirschner. *How to Deal With Difficult People.* Boulder, CO: CareerTrack Publications, 1987.

Canfield, Jack. *Self-Esteem and Peak Performance.* Boulder, CO: CareerTrack Publications, 1987.

---

[1]To order audio and video materials, call CareerTrack Publications (800-334-1018), or in Colorado (303-447-2323), or Nightingale-Conant Corporation (800-323-5552).

Cathcart, Jim, and Anthony Alessandra. *Relationship Strategies.* Chicago, IL: Nightingale-Conant, 1985.

Dolan, John Patrick. *Negotiate Like the Pros.* Boulder, CO: CareerTrack Publications, 1990.

Garfield, Charles. *Peak Performers.* Chicago, IL: Nightingale-Conant Corporation, 1986.

Merrill, Douglas. *The New Time Management.* Chicago, IL: Nightingale-Conant Corporation, 1983.

Moidel, Steve. *Memory Power.* Boulder, CO: CareerTrack Publications, 1989.

Parinello, Anthony. *Selling to VITO: The Very Important Top Officer* (6-hour audiocassette series). San Diego, CA.

Peters, Tom. *The New Masters of Excellence.* Chicago, IL: Nightingale-Conant Corporation, 1988.

——. *Thriving on Chaos.* Chicago, IL: Nightingale-Conant Corporation, 1988.

Robbins, Anthony. *Unlimited Power.* Chicago, IL: Nightingale-Conant Corporation, 1989.

Smith, Debra. *Telephone Skills.* Boulder, CO: CareerTrack Publications, 1987.

Sommer, Bobbe. *How to Set and Achieve Goals.* Boulder, CO: Career-Track Publications, 1987.

Tracy, Brian. *The Psychology of Achievement.* Chicago, IL: Nightingale-Conant, 1988.

Wilson, Orvel Ray. *Sell Like The Pros.* Boulder, CO: CareerTrack Publications, 1990.

——. *Guerrilla Selling—Live!* Boulder, CO: The Guerrilla Group, Inc., 1996.

■ VIDEO TRAINING MATERIALS

Cross, Thomas B. *Introduction to Call Centers,* 1996, VHS tape.

Sanborn, Mark. *Team Building—Volumes 1 and 2.* Boulder, CO: Career-Track Publications, 1989.

Smith, Mark S. A. *How to Get the Most Leads from Your Trade Show.* Boulder, CO: The Guerrilla Group, Inc., 1996.

Wilson, Orvel Ray. *Guerrilla Selling—Live!* Boulder, CO: The Guerrilla Group, Inc., 1996.

■ MAGAZINES AND JOURNALS

Direct Magazine, 11 River Bend Drive South, Stamford, CT 06907-0949. 203-358-9900.

Target Marketing® magazine, 401 North Broad Street, Philadelphia, PA 19108. 215-238-5300.

Telemarketing® & *Call Center Solutions* magazine, One Technology Plaza, Norwalk, CT 06854. 800-243-6002.

TeleProfessional magazine, 209 West Fifth Street, Suite N, Waterloo, IA 50701-5420. 888-835-3776.

Index

About-face strategy, 174
Acknowledgments, 74, 160, 169–170, 186, 202, 228
Acquisition cost, of customer, 25–26
ACT!, 92, 222
Active listening, 74
Administrative assistants, treatment of, 113
Advertisements, in newsletters, 223–224
Advertising specialties, 211–213
A-E-I-O-U exercise, 62
After hours calls, 130
Albrecht, Karl, 183
Alexander, James, 213–214
Amazon.com, 33, 224
American Retailers Association, 175
American Telemarketing Association, 104
Analogies, 181
Angry callers, 186–188
Annual Guide to Telemarketing, 24
Apologies, 187
Appointments:
    cancelled, 140
    organization of, 103–104
    with prospects, 140–141
    selling questions and, 145–146
    voice mail messages and, 125
Asking for order(s). *See* Closing process
Assignments, writing, 228
Associations, as information resource, 99
Assumptions, 187
Attention, control of, 18, 118–119
Attitude, importance of, 15–16, 196
Audio brochures:
    duplication of, 235
    format, 232
    packaging, 235–236
    purpose of, 231–232
    writing and recording guidelines, 232–235

Audio play, for audio brochure, 234
Audiotapes, for training, 49, 194
Authority, in proposal presentation, 149
Authorship, writing tips:
    booklets, 229–230
    trade magazines, 227–229
Awards, for sales staff, 197
Axelrod, Mitch, 168

Background noise, 19–20, 61, 118
Barrus, Dan, 193
Berg, Bob, 214
Binders, lead management system, 94
Blanchard, Kenneth, 195
Bock, Wally, 22
Bonuses, 196
Booklets, writing guidelines, 229–230
Books, in training resource center, 48
Breathy voice, 57
Broadcast faxes, 222
Brochures:
    audio (*see* Audio brochures)
    video-based, 249–250
Budget(s):
    customers', 144
    for mail survey, 200–201
Bulk E-mail, 240
Business-to-business call guidelines, 10
Buyers, 17 things that drive them nuts, 19–23
Buying calls, 112–113
Buying signals, 165

Call center staff, 26–27
Caller's satisfaction:
    communication gap between men and women, 79
    Contact Evaluation form, 70–72
    customer control and, 76–77

Caller's satisfaction *(Continued)*:
  political correctness, 77–79
  salespeople, evaluations of, 72–76
Call guide, 89–90
Call log, 11
Call-tickler reminders, 92
Cancelled appointments, 140
Canned pitch, 19
Cat and the Lion exercise, 61
Cellular phones, 104, 250–251
Change resistance, 143
Charge backs, 253–254
Cialdini, Robert, 147
Classified ads, recruitment process, 191–192
Clerical skills, sales staff evaluations, 73,
  75–76
Clinic time, 52
Closing process:
  buying signals, 165
  closing on the phone, 166–167
  commitment, asking for, 165
  confirmation calls, 167
  5-4-3-2-1 referral system, 168–169
  fulfillment package, 167
  referrals, asking for, 168
  thank you notes, 169–170
  wrapping up the sale, 165–166
Closing sales, generally:
  celebration of, 38
  guarantees and, 184
  process overview (*see* Closing process)
Closing statements, 166
Coaching, 36, 194
Cold calls, 14, 37, 108–110
Commission, 195–196
Commitment:
  asking for, 165
  early, 139
  in successful programs, 41–42
Communication skills. *See* Speech/commu-
  nication skills
Communication styles:
  general *vs.* specific, 151
  most effective approaches for, 151–152,
    154–155
  options *vs.* procedural, 154
  types of, overview, 149–155
Compensation plan, management strategies,
  195–197
Competition/competitors:
  acknowledgments and, 169
  identification of, 143
  incentive programs and, 42
  as motivation strategy, 38, 144
  objections and, 172
  price shopping, 176–177
  pricing issues, 176
  training and, 49–50

Competitive intelligence, 50
Complaints:
  angry callers, 187–188
  encouragement of, 184–185
CompuServe, 222
Computer-based lead management systems,
  91–93
Computer software programs:
  faxes, 126, 222
  newsletters, layout and printing,
    224–225
  videoconferencing technology, 248
Concern:
  for customer needs, 177
  reframing, 180
Confirmation calls, 167
Consistency, in proposal presentation, 148
Consumer reports, 161
Contacting customers, 105
Context reframe, 180–181
Convenience, for customers, 29–30
Copyright, audio brochures, 235
Copywriter, for sales letter, 218
Cost justifications, 144
Coupons, 27
Credibility, importance of, 3, 17, 34, 228
Credit cards, 254
Cross-selling, 28, 254
Customer(s):
  acquisition cost, 25
  angry callers, 186–188
  complaints from, 184–185
  11 ways to get them to buy more from you,
    27–31
  lifetime value of, 185–186
  motivations for change, 143–144
  needs (*see* Customer needs)
  proposal retention, 163–164
  relationships with (*see* Customer relation-
    ships)
  videoconferencing and, 249–250
Customer loyalty, 43
Customer needs:
  identification of, 136–137, 142
  proposal presentation and, 160
Customer relationships:
  building strategies, 179
  objections and, 177–179
  proposal presentation and, 149
  with prospects, 141
  referrals and, 139, 148
  trust development, 179
  truth in, 16–17, 181–182
Customer service, quality of, 194–195. *See
  also* Caller's satisfaction
Customer's lifetime value (LTV):
  calculation of, 25–26
  importance of, 185–186

Customer surveys, 202
Customized sales letters, 219

Daily debriefs, 103
Daily planners, 93
Database management system, of prospects:
  quality and testing lists, 100
  as resource, 99–100
Deception, 16
Decision maker:
  identification of, 115–116, 145
  role of, 97
Decision-making, players in:
  decision maker, 97
  decision-making team, 98
  economic buyer, 97
  gatekeeper, 95–96
  influencer, 96
  selling questions for, 145
  spy, 97
  user, 97
Decision-making team, role of, 98
Delivery:
  records, importance of, 175
  scheduling tactics, 179–180
Demographics, 36
Demonstrations, 18, 160–163
Denasal voice, 58
Desktop videoconferencing, 247–250
Dextify, defined, 187
Diction, 20
Diet, effects of, 55, 60
Direct Marketing Association, 12
Direct response, 236
Discounts, 27, 43, 174–175, 219
Discourteous behavior, 20–21
Discussion groups, on Internet, 243–244
Dissatisfied customers:
  complaints from, 184–185
  impact of, 22
  reasons for, 72–73
Distractions, dealing with, 118–119
Do-not-call list, legal requirements, 11–12
Down pitch voice, 58
Duplication:
  audio brochures, 235
  videotapes, 237
Dynamic range, in voice, 59

Early calls, 105, 114
Economic buyer, role of, 97
Electronic equipment needs, 2–3, 15
Electronic mail. See E-mail
E-mail:
  file attachments, 240–241
  headers for, 240
  netiquette, 239–240
Emotional appeal, 162

Empathy, 187
Employees:
  incentive programs for, 42. See also Compensation plan
  management-staff relationship, 195–196
  recruitment and hiring process, 191–193
  staffing needs, 26–27
Encyclopedia of Associations (Gail), 99
Ending calls, timing of, 20
Entrepreneur, 49
Environmental influences, in workspace, 47–48
Etiquette:
  office staff and, 113
  on-line (*see* Netiquette)
  telephone, 22, 67, 74
Exercise(s):
  stress reduction strategy, 54, 188
  warm up, 62
Existing customers, service strategies, 16–17, 183–186
Expectations:
  of sales management, 103
  of salespeople, 36
Expertise:
  development of (*see* Authorship, tips for)
  reward for, 42
Extra calls, 104–105

Face-to-face meetings, power of, 246–247
Failure:
  common causes of, 32–35
  of incentive programs, 39
Fair-care-share, 15
Faxes:
  broadcast, 222
  cost of, 220–221
  design of, 221
  unsolicited, 221–222
  voice mail messages and, 126
  what to fax, 220–221
Fax-on-demand, 220, 222
Fax-on-request, 222
Federal Trade Commission, 10
Feedback:
  customer surveys, 202
  mail surveys, 200–201
  from management, 194–195
Feel, felt, and found strategy, 181
Financial matters, approaches to, 139, 144
First contact, guidelines for, 110–112
First rights, to publications, 229
Fishman, Arnold L., 24
5-4-3-2-1 referral system, 168–169
Flat voice, 58–59
Follow-up calls, importance of, 14, 38, 116–118, 162, 164
Form sales letters, 218

Frame of reference, for motivation:
    external, 156–157
    internal, 155–156
Free products, 22, 86
Frequently Asked Questions (FAQs), 19
Frontal voice, 58
Fulfillment package, 167–168
Functionality, of product, 180
Furniture in workspace:
    desk, 46
    ergonomic chair, 47
    mirror, 47
Fusion-marketing, 28

Gabrielsen, Ron, 134
Gatekeeper:
    dealing with, 113–115
    in decision-making process, 95–96
General communication style:
    elements of, 149–151
    most effective approach with, 151–152
    specific style vs., 151
Giveaways, marketing strategy:
    bill stuffers, 215
    candy jar, 213–214
    notecards, 214–215
    postcards, 214
    series, 215
    snacks, 214
    timepieces, 214
    types of, generally, 211–213
Glides, 63
Goal-setting:
    acquisition cost of customer, 25–26
    call center staff, 26–27
    customer needs and, 142
    11 telephone sales strategies, 24–25
    11 ways to get your customers to buy more
        from you, 27–31
    teleselling, 25
    written goals, 37
Golden selling hour, 105
Greatest Management Principle in the World,
    The (LeBoeuf), 195
Guaranteed products, 88, 183–184
Guerrilla, characteristics of, 14–15
Guerrilla Marketing Newsletter, 49
Guerrilla Selling–Unconventional Weapons and
    Tactics for Increasing Your Sales, 48
Guerrilla teleselling, generally:
    guerrilla, characteristics of, 14–15
    reasons for, 12–13
    sales skills, 18
    samples of, 1–2
    17 things that drive buyers nuts and how to
        avoid them, 19–23
    traditional sales vs., 15–17
    unique environment, 17–18

Handoffs, 21, 67
Hawthorn Effect, 72
Haynes, Shawn, 33
Headline, for follow-up calls, 116
Health tips:
    diet, 55, 60
    exercise, 54, 62, 188
    smoking, 61
    stress reduction strategies, 54–55
    voice problems, 61
    water consumption, 48, 54, 60
High-pressure tactics, 13
High prices, implications of, 176
Hiring process, 191–193
Hoffman, Donald, 24
Hold button, telephone etiquette, 22, 67, 74
Hot lists, 98
Humor:
    international calls and, 68
    stress reduction strategy, 55

Inbound calls, greeting, 65–68
Incentives programs:
    compensation plans, 195–196
    creation of, 40–41
    for customers, 27, 43–44
    failure of, 39
    kickoff parties, 44
    as positive reinforcement, 39–40
    pricing strategies, 161
    sales letters and, 219
    for sales staff, management strategies,
        195–196
    successful, elements of, 41–42
    types of, overview, 39–44
Index cards, lead management system,
    93–94
Individually written sales letters, 219
Industrial sales, cost of sales calls, 2
Influence: The Psychology of Persuasion (Cial-
    dini), 147
Influencer, in decision-making process, 96
Informal speech, 64
Infoseek, 242
Initiative, level of:
    proactive style, 158–159
    reactive style, 159
Insincerity, 110
International callers, inbound calls, 67–68
Internet, on-line marketing:
    marketing plan for, 241–242
    netiquette, generally, 239–241
    newsgroups, 241
    resources, 243–245
    service providers, 222
    web addresses and sites (see Web addresses;
        Web sites)
Interruption log, 52

Interruptions:
  control strategies, 51–53
  telephone etiquette, 19
Interviews:
  on audio brochures, 233
  hiring process, 192–193
  writing assignments, 228
Introduction(s):
  on audio brochure, 234–235
  initial appointment, 141
  opening lines, 109–110, 163
  in script, 81

Japanese management, American management distinguished from, 17
Jargon, 72

Kennedy, Dan, 219, 236
Kickoff parties, 44
Killer words/hidden messages, 82–83
Kordahl, Eugene B., 24

Language. *See* Word choice
  evocative, 89
  jargon, 72
  mispronounced words, 63
  political correctness, 77–79
  pronunciation, 20
  racist, 197
  sexist, 197
  slang, 64
Laptop computers, benefits of, 92
Late calls, 105–106, 114
Lawsuits, 11
Lead management systems:
  binders, 94
  computer-based, 91–92
  daily planner, 93
  dual systems, 92–93
  index cards, 93–94
  on-line marketing, 242
LeBoeuf, Michael, 195
Legal issues:
  copyright, 235
  fraud, 10
  for publications, 229
  solicitations, 11
License, for audio brochure, 234
Lighting, in workspace, 47–48
List brokers, 98–99
Listening skills, 74, 119
Long-distance calls, 111

Magazines, in training resource center, 48–49
Magic selling questions, 142–146
Mailing lists, on Internet, 243–244
Mail survey, 200–201
Management. *See* Sales management

Management-staff relationship, 195–196
Marketing, generally:
  defined, 205–206
  fusion, 28
  newsletters and, 215
  on-line, 238–245
  strategies for (*see* Marketing strategies)
Marketing calendar, 206–207
Marketing strategies:
  brainstorming, 208–210
  teleselling calendar and, 206–207
  testing, tracking, and reporting, 208
Massage, stress reduction strategy, 55
McIntosh, Mac, 167
Meditation, stress reduction strategy, 55
Meetings:
  face-to-face, 246
  morning, standard, 51
  precall sales, 103
  scheduling (*see* Appointments)
Microsoft, 148, 206
Mistakes:
  correction strategies, 181–182, 185–186
  mispronounced words, 63
  reward strategies, 197
Morning meetings, 51
Motivation strategies:
  for customer, 89, 143
  external frame of reference, 156–157
  incentive programs and, 40
  internal frame of reference, 155–156
  management of, 157–158
  positive reinforcement, 39–40
  for salespeople, 35–39
Motorboat exercise, 62
Muffled voice, 58
Music:
  on audio brochure, 234
  stress reduction strategy, 54

Nasal voice, 58
Netiquette, 239–241
New customers. *See* Prospects
  acquisition cost, 25–26
  marketing strategies, 211–214
  reward for, 43–44
Newsletters:
  advertising in, 223
  articles, types of, 223–224
  convenience items, 224
  distribution list, 224, 226
  frequency of, 226
  layout, 224
  mailing considerations, 225–226
  marketing strategy, 215
  photos, 224
  printing, 225
900 numbers, 253–254

"No," interpretations of, 21, 173–174
Note-taking, 117, 120–121, 163, 186–187

Objection(s):
 about-face strategy, 174
 busters, 90
 customer needs and, 173–174
 management of, 177–181
 price issues, 174–176
 price shopping and, 176–177
 prospects and, 139
 sales savers, 181–182
 sources of, 171–172
 when to handle, 172–173
Objectives. See Goal-setting
Office staff, treatment of, 113
One Minute Manager, The (Blanchard), 195
On-line marketing:
 impact of, 238
 internet, generating business on, 241–245
 netiquette, 239–241
 on-line lead generation, 242
 success factors, 242
"Only," use of, 161
Open-door policies, 52
Opening lines:
 ones to avoid, 109–110
 suggestions for, 163
Opening moves:
 appointments, organization of, 103–104
 attention, control of, 118–119
 best time to reach prospects, by industry,
  106–107
 buying calls, 112–113
 cold calls, 108–110
 contacting customers, 105
 daily debriefs, 103
 decision maker, identification of, 115–116
 early calls, 105, 114
 extra calls, 104–105
 first contact, 110–112
 follow-up calls, 116–118
 gatekeepers, dealing with, 113–115
 golden selling hour, 105
 late calls, 105–106, 114
 listening skills and, 119
 note-taking, 120–121
 precall sales meeting, 103
 rapport, maintaining, 118
 sensitive subjects, handling, 121–122
 snappy answers to stupid questions,
  107–108
 unlisted addresses, 108
Options communication style:
 elements of, 153
 most effective approaches with, 154
 procedural style vs., 154
Organization chart, 115–116

Orotund voice, 58
Outside consultants, training from, 49

Packaging:
 audio brochures, 235–236
 customer needs and, 30
 videotapes, 237
Pagers, 250
Partnerships, fusion-marketing, 28
Pauses, in speech, 59
Pekas, Mary, 100
Performance evaluation, management strate-
  gies:
 compensation plans, 195–197
 feedback, 194–195
Performance measurement:
 customer surveys, 202
 mail survey, 200–201
 postcampaign survey, 200
 postperformance checklist, 199
 purpose of, 199
 of results, generally, 200
Persistence, 132–133
Personal digital assistant (PDA), 92–93
Personalized sales letters, 218
Personal Selling Power, 48
Phone Power/Telemarketing Professional, 24
Phone tag, 125
Plosives, 63
Polarity response, 168
Political correctness, 77–79
Positioning, 25, 28, 161
Positive reinforcement, in staff-management
  relationship, 195
Postcampaign survey, 200
Postperformance checklist, 199
Potentials in Marketing, 49
Power talking rules, 83–86
Precall letters, 100
Precall sales meeting, 103
Premiums, marketing strategy, 212
Presentations. See Demonstrations; Proposal
  presentations
Price, generally:
 incentives, 161
 objections and, 174–176
 quotes, 176–177
Primacy, in proposal presentation, 163
Principles, in proposal presentation, 164
Privacy Journal, 10–11
Proactive prospects, 158–159
Problem-solving skills, 16, 33, 74, 142
Procedural communication style:
 elements of, 153
 most effective approaches with, 154–155
 options style vs., 154
Product knowledge, 19, 32–33
Professional associations. See Associations

Profitability, incentive programs and, 41–42
Promotions:
  incentive programs, 41
  legal requirements, 11
Pronunciation, 20
Proof statements, 161–162
Proposal presentation:
  communication styles, 149
  customer retention, sales strategies, 163–164
  demonstrations, 160–163
  follow-up to, 162, 164
  influencing prospects and customers, 147–149
  information needs, 149–152
  initiative level, 158–159
  irresistible strategies, 161–162
  motivation, locus of, 155–158
  questions, 164
  rate of response, 147
  styles, types of, 160
  tangibles/intangibles in, 160–161
  tasks, organization of, 152–155
Prospecting, information sources for, 109
Prospects:
  appointments, contact strategies, 140–141
  diagnostic questions for, 137
  incentives for, 43–44
  qualification of, 138–140
  relationship-building, 141, 179
  response rate, 139–140
  sources for, 98–100
Publications, in trade magazines, 228–229

Quality management, 194
Questions:
  diagnostic, 137
  5-4-3-2-1 referral system, 169
  in mail survey, 200–201
  open-ended, 117
  postcampaign survey, 200
  in power talking, 84
  in proposal presentation, 164
  in script, 81–82
  sensitive, 121
  snappy answers to stupid questions, 107–108
  37 magic selling, 142–146, 173
  on voice mail, 128–129

Radio-talk-show format, audio brochures, 233
Rapport, maintaining, 118
Razor reading, 48
Reactive prospects, 159
Recency, in proposal presentation, 163
Reciprocation, in proposal presentation, 148
Reciprocity, 114
Recruitment process, 191–193
Reeves, Sarah, 134
References, in hiring process, 193

Referrals, 139, 148, 168–169
Relationship Manager, 92
Reliability, projection of, 161
Repeat business, 30
Reprint rights only, one-time use, defined, 229
Resistance, dealing with, 116
Restricted telephone numbers, 12
Resumes, hiring process, 192–193
Return appointment, 28–29
Return on investment (ROI), calculation of, 26
Reward system, management strategies, 197–198
Roundup articles, 228
Rule of 72, 164

Sales & Marketing Management, 48
Sales letter(s):
  precall, 100
  sample of, 217
  special reports, 219
  types of, 218–219
  writing guidelines, 216, 218
Sales manager, responsibilities of:
  compensation strategies, 195–197
  feedback to sales personnel, 194–195
  quality management, 194
  recruitment and hiring process, 191–193
  reward system, 197–198
  training process, 193–194
Salespeople, generally:
  guerrilla, characteristics of, 14–15
  motivation strategies, generally, 35–39
  weaknesses of, 32–33
Sampson, Elliott, 42
Satellite paging, 250
Scarcity, impact of, 149
Script:
  for audio brochure, 234
  development of, generally (*see* Script development)
  for voice mail, 128–129
Script development:
  call guide, 89–90
  customer motivation strategies, 89
  evocative language, 89
  introduction, 81
  killer words and hidden messages, 82–83
  objection busters, 90
  parts of script, 81
  power talking rules, 83–86
  superlatives, avoidance of, 88
  ten magic words, 86–88
  testing, 82
  training process and, 194
  word choice, 80–82
Secretaries, treatment of, 113
Secrets, 87
Securities and Exchange Commission, 12

Seminar format, audio brochures, 233–234
Sensitive subjects, handling, 121–122
Service America (Albrecht/Zemke), 183
Service Intelligence, 19
Slutsky, Jeff, 133
Social proof, in proposal presentation, 148, 161
Sole suppliers, 28
Spare Tire response, 178
Special list, 139
Special offers, 29
Special reports, 37, 219
Specific communication style:
    elements of, 150–151
    general style *vs.*, 151
    most effective approaches with, 152
Specifics, in proposal presentation, 163–164
Speech/communication skills:
    contractions, 63–64
    dynamic range, 59–60
    glides, 63
    importance of, 20
    mispronounced words, 63
    pauses, 59
    plosives, 63
    political correctness, 77–79
    rate of speech, 59, 110
    slang, 64
    vocal energy, 59
    voice (*see* Voice, teleselling)
Speed of response, importance of, 139–140,
    158, 167
SportGems, 86
Spy, in decision-making process, 97
Staffing needs, calculation of, 26–27
Standards, setting, 15
Stress management strategies, 54–55
Subassembly, 29
Subscriptions, to information bulletins, 220
Success, 49
Success:
    assessment of, 199–202
    elements of, 41–42
    obstacles to, 33–35
    sample stories, 162
Superlatives, avoidance of, 88
Supporting documentation, 152, 161
Support staff, treatment of, 113
Surveys:
    customer, 202
    mail, 200–201
    postcampaign, 200
Sweepstakes, legal requirements, 11
Swett, Melissa, 35

Tag team telephone, 37–38
Tai Chi, 62
Tape-recording calls, as training, 37

Team buying, 18
Technotrends (Barrus), 193
Telegraphs, in script development, 83
Telemagic, 92
Telemarketing, traditional, 12. *See also* Traditional sales
Telephone Consumer Fraud Protection Act,
    221–222
Telephone equipment:
    cell phones (*see* Cellular phones)
    extra-long cord on headset, 47
    headset phones, 45–47
Telephone etiquette:
    guidelines for, 19–23
    inbound calls, greeting strategies, 65–68
Telephone sales strategies, generally, 24–25
Telephone solicitations, lawsuits and, 11
TelePresence:
    brochures, electronic, 231–237
    cellular phones, 250–251
    creation of, 2–4
    events, generally, 209–210
    experts, 227–230
    faxes, 220–222
    newsletters, 223–226
    900 numbers, 253–254
    on-line marketing, 238–245
    Personal Digital Communication (PDC), 250
    sales letters, 216–219
    satellite paging, 250
    script development and, 82
    staying in front of the customer, strategies
        for, 211–215
    teleselling calendar, 205–210
    toll-free numbers, 251–254
    videoconferencing, 246–250
Teleselling. *See* Guerrilla teleselling
    benefits of, 13
    calendar (*see* Teleselling calendar)
    consumer backlash and, 9–10
    future directions, 2–3
    legal issues, 10–12
    setting goals and objectives, 25
Teleselling calendar:
    design of, 206–207
    purpose of, 205–206
Teleselling Consumer Fraud Protection Act
    (TCFPA), 10
Ten-second commercial, 112
Testimonials, 161, 230, 254
Thank you cards/notes, 160, 169–170
Thin voice, 59
37 magic selling questions:
    objections and, 173
    overview, 142–147
Three-minute commercial, 128
Throat clearing, 20, 60

Throaty voice, 58
Tight voice, 57
Time-frame questions, 145
Timing of call, 21, 105, 110–111, 114
Toll-free numbers:
    benefits of, 251–252
    900 numbers *vs.*, 253–254
Tone:
    inbound calls, 66–67
    of voice, 110
Total quality management (TQM), 17
Trade magazines, writing for, 227–229
Traditional sales:
    guerrilla teleselling distinguished from,
        15–17
    objections, management of, 171–172
Training:
    management strategies, 193–194
    resources for, 48–49
Travel costs, 2
Trust development, 179. *See also* Customer
    relationships
Truth, importance of, 16–17, 111, 181

Uniqueness, in proposal presentation, 163
Universal criteria, 173
Unlisted addresses, 108
Unsolicited faxes, 221–222
Up pitch voice, 58
Up-selling, 254
User, in decision-making process, 97

Value-added products, 43, 109
Vanderport, Rich, 168
Videoconferencing, 246–247
Videotapes:
    presentations on, 236–237
    for training, 49
Video technology, videoteleconferencing,
    246–248
Visual aids, 162
Vocabulary, power talking rules, 84–86
Vocal energy, 59
Voice, teleselling:
    background noise and, 61
    diaphragm breathing and, 61
    illness and, 60–61
    pauses, 59
    range, 57, 59–60
    rate of speech, 59
    screaming, 60–61
    smoking and, 61
    throat clearing, 60
    tone of, 110
    types of, 57–60
    vocal energy, 59
    volume, 60

warmup exercises, 61–62
water and, 60
Voice mail:
    after-hours messages, 130
    alternate access, 130
    effective messages, strategies for, 123–128
    getting calls returned, strategies for,
        130–135
    menu system, 21, 129
    in recruitment and hiring process, 191–192
    response time, 129–130
    use as sales tool, 128–130
    screening cycle, 130
    toll-free numbers, 252

Web addresses, 129, 243–245, 255–257
Web site(s):
    as information resource, 115–116
    on-line marketing resources, 244–245
Who's Who directories, 227
WinFax Pro, 222
Winget, Larry, 132
Winning strategies, elements of, 15–17
Word choice:
    communication gap between men and
        women and, 79
    demotivators/motivators, 89
    evocative language, 89
    importance of, 80–82
    objections and, 172
    "only," impact of, 161
    political correctness, 77–79
    power talking rules, 84–86
    superlatives, 88
    ten magic words, 86–88
Workspace:
    biological factors, 47–48
    elements of, 45–47
    training resource center, 48–50
Writing assignment, for trade journals, 228
Writing guidelines:
    audio brochures, 232–235
    booklets, 229–230
    newsletters, 223–224
    sales letters, 216, 218
Written communications, with
        customers/prospects:
    faxes, 220–222
    newsletters, 223–226
    sales letters, 216–219

Xerox, 30

Yahoo!, 242
Yeack, Bill, 3

Zemke, Ron, 183

About the Authors

■ JAY CONRAD LEVINSON

As an author, speaker, workshop leader, and owner of a successful marketing firm, Jay personifies the true entrepreneur. Before embarking on his life of writing and public speaking, he was a vice president and creative director at one of the largest advertising agencies in the world. With an award-winning career in advertising and a nationally syndicated column, Jay has authored 25 books, including the best-selling marketing book ever, *Guerrilla Marketing* (Boston: Houghton Mifflin, 1984) with over 800,000 copies sold. His work has been translated into 37 languages. He is also coauthor of *Guerrilla Selling: Unconventional Weapons and Tactics for Making the Sale* (with Bill Gallagher, Ph.D., and Orvel Ray Wilson, Houghton Mifflin) and *Guerrilla Trade Show Selling* (with Orvel Ray Wilson and Mark S. A. Smith, John Wiley & Sons, Inc.). The books have led to a rapidly growing newsletter, *The Guerrilla Marketing Newsletter,* two successful audiotapes, a videotape, columns on marketing in 12 national publications, and presentations at major conventions throughout the world.

He served as senior VP and creative director for the world's largest advertising agency, J. Walter Thompson, and sat on the board of directors at Leo Burnett Advertising in the United States and Europe. His work has won major awards worldwide, in virtually every marketing media, including direct mail, television, radio, and magazines. Current clients include Fortune 500 companies, and start-ups that want to be.

Levinson's small business expertise has also been demonstrated in his *Earning Money Without A Job, 555 Ways To Earn Extra Money* (Holt, Rinehart & Winston, 1979 and 1982), and *Quit Your Job!* (Dodd, Mead, 1987).

■ MARK S. A. SMITH

An internationally renowned speaker and writer on trade show selling, Mark has been producing and delivering seminars on sales topics since 1982. He has published over 300 articles on various marketing topics. He is a contributing editor to *Potentials in Marketing* and is regularly featured in *Cintermex*, a Latin American trade show journal. Mark has self-published two books (*How to Be Your Best at Trade Show Selling*, and *49 Ways to Be Your Best at Trade Show Selling*, with 10,000 now in print), two videocassettes (*How to Get the Most Leads from Your Trade Show* and *The Ten Things Most Companies Do at Trade Shows That Don't Work, and How You Can Fix Them*), and three audiocassette programs on the subject of trade show selling, including one targeted at volunteer and nonprofit organizations. He is coauthor of *Guerrilla Trade Show Selling* (with Orvel Ray Wilson and Jay Levinson, John Wiley & Sons, 1997).

Although he graduated with a degree in electrical engineering, he went straight into sales support for Hewlett-Packard. Based in Amsterdam for three years, he was European product manager. Later, he was international sales manager for a high-tech software company, growing sales by 600 percent over four years, primarily with TeleSelling efforts and trade shows.

Mark has served as the president of the Colorado Speakers Association and has served on the adjunct faculty at Front Range Community College of Denver for their Applied International Management program.

■ ORVEL RAY WILSON, CSP

An internationally acclaimed author and standing-ovation speaker on sales, marketing, and management, Wilson's speaking career, launched in 1980, has taken him to over 1,000 cities in the U.S., Australia, Canada, England, Germany, and the Soviet Union. His content-packed programs are entertaining, motivating, and memorable. He is the coauthor of the run-away, best-selling books, *Guerrilla Selling: Unconventional Weapons and Tactics for Increasing Your Sales*, with Bill Gallagher and Jay Conrad Levinson (Houghton-Mifflin, 1992) and *Guerrilla Trade*

Show Selling: Unconventional Weapons and Tactics to Meet More People, Get More Leads, and Close More Sales, with Mark S. A. Smith (John Wiley & Sons, 1997).

Already in its ninth printing, *Guerrilla Selling* has since been published in German, Korean, and Romanian. It was featured as "one of the 10 most important business books of the decade" in the July 1994 issue of *Sell!ng* magazine. His articles appear regularly in dozens of industry and trade magazines. He also edits *War Stories—The Guerrilla Selling Newsletter,* published quarterly.

He started his career early, selling garden seeds door-to-door when he was 12 years old, and he founded his first company at 19. Over 25 years of real-world sales experience spans the range from encyclopedias to advertising, from automobiles to computers. He's taught closing techniques to Xerox field reps and job search skills to Indochinese refugees.

In 1980, he founded the Boulder Sales Training Institute, and his client list has since grown to include industry leaders like Apple Computer, Century 21, and CellularOne. He has taught in the management development programs for the University of Colorado and the University of Denver, and he has created innovative business courses for Harbridge House, the University of Toledo, the Spring Institute for International Studies, and Australia's Canberra College of Advanced Education. He has even pioneered workshops on capitalism for the Tyumen School of Management in the Russian Republic.

Recognized as a leader by his peers as well, Orvel Ray has served as president of the Colorado Chapter of the National Speakers Association in 1986 and served two additional terms on their board of directors. In 1997, the National Speakers Association bestowed upon him the highest earned award in the speaking profession, the Certified Speaking Professional, an honor held by fewer than 1 percent of all professional speakers.

He's led hundreds of large-audience seminars and on-site workshops, including "How to Give Exceptional Customer Service," "Managing Multiple Demands," "Taking Control of Your Workday," "Effective Collection Strategies," "Power Presentation Skills," and "Dealing with Difficult People." He has also collaborated with best-selling authors to develop seminar versions of *Guerrilla Marketing* by Jay Conrad Levinson, *The Time Trap* by Alec McKenzie, and *Don't Do, Delegate!* by Jack Kelly and John

Jenks. He is the author of four audiotape albums and several videos, including *The Art of Persuasion—A Win/Win Approach, Selling Smart* (CareerTrack Publications, 1988), *Guerrilla Selling—Live!,* and *Guerrilla Selling in Action.* All enjoy international distribution.

Orvel Ray is the president of The Guerrilla Group, Inc., an international training and consulting firm serving clients worldwide.

Continue Being a Guerrilla

Call **THE GUERRILLA GROUP** toll-free at 800-247-9145 for free information about:

- ➤ Guerrilla Selling
- ➤ Guerrilla TeleSelling
- ➤ Guerrilla Trade Show Selling
- ➤ Guerrilla Marketing
- ➤ Guerrilla Negotiating

Sales and marketing consulting for groups and individuals. Customized on-site seminars and training programs in formats ranging from a 30-minute keynote to a multiday bootcamp. We also offer books, audiotapes, videotapes, newsletters, seminars, lectures, workshops, and other professional services.

THE GUERRILLA GROUPinc
800-247-9145
WEB: http://www.guerrillagroup.com
E-mail: postmaster@guerrillagroup.com